Southern
Savory

Southern
Savory

by Bernice Kelly Harris

THE UNIVERSITY OF NORTH CAROLINA PRESS
CHAPEL HILL

Printed by the Seeman Printery, Durham, North Carolina

Manufactured in the United States of America

To William Olive—

In memory

Preface

The minty herb *satureia hortensis,* often called summer savory, is much used as a seasoning in cooking. Savory, used in the title of the following impressions and reminiscences, is meant to suggest that people in whatever time or region are the seasoning that imparts flavor and spice to the human experience.

B. K. H.

Contents

Southern
Savory

· 1 ·

The Picture

IT WAS a sultry July morning, 1892.

A stranger made his way along our little road of sand and ruts. He crossed the bridge beyond the wild cherry tree and reined his horse straight toward Papa's tobacco barn.

The colored hands paused over their sticks of tobacco, wary of the strange man heading their way. They began to speculate about the odd traption in the foot of the stranger's buggy. It looked like a quare varmint to some of them.

Aunt Cherry stared fearfully at the three-legged traption, with its head shrouded in black like a widow's veil. She mentioned graveyards and trickeration.

Uncle Dick agreed it might be a thing to trick folks. Though nearly thirty years away from slavery, they still were not free from conjuration. Just last spring some grudgeman threw under his doorsteps a packet of graveyard dust, Uncle Dick recalled. And the dust, wrapped all in black cloth like that in the stranger's buggy, had put such a fix on him he nearly coughed himself to death.

Aunt Cherry tensed for flight. For she had coughed, too, till that black packet of graveyard dust had been located and disposed of.

The younger hands stared and idled, ready to run at a suspicious movement from the buggy man.

It might be a weepon to shoot at folks, Uncle Nat quavered. And that buggy man might be the Yankees again.

"Whoopee! Look out!" Papa teasingly broke into the speculation, tickled at the scared crowd. But when they took to their heels, overturning sticks of tobacco and wooden horses, he called them back reassuringly. "The dog's foot! It's just the picture man," he hastened to tell them. He had not himself forgotten his childhood awe of weapons in the hands of Yankee soldiers swarming over the place some twenty-eight years before. "And that's a picture-taker under the black cover, a camera on a tripod. Not a varmint."

It was some time before the crowd could be persuaded to pose for a picture. Papa was so proud of his pretty tobacco that he was willing to spare the cash for a picture of it, and he wanted all hands in it. Picture men were about as strange as varmints along this road. It branched off from the county highway near the railroad crossing and wound through sand and ruts to the Johnston County line only a quarter mile from our farm. Tramps often turned at the crossing and came this way to beg for food, and peddlers came to sell their wares. But picture men kept to the county road.

Uncle Dick and Aunt Cherry never did get in the picture. They peeped out from behind the log barn, and only Aunt Cherry's white head rag and Uncle Dick's ragged felt hat showed.

I did not show either.

As soon as Mama realized the family's picture was to be made against a background of barn and field hands at work, she tried to get Papa to change into his Sunday clothes. In the picture, though, he is wearing his work clothes and a wide-brimmed straw hat.

Mama hurried to the house just down the road from the barn, changed the two little girls into crisp ginghams and pretty sunbonnets, and then put on her wedding dress. It was brown broadcloth with a silk front, and narrow pleated ruffles edged the basque and outlined the draped overskirt.

So Mama sat among the field hands in fine attire. For all that it was hot weather and her wedding dress was wool and long-sleeved and overly snug at the time, for all that she had cooked breakfast and dinner and hung out a line of clothes before helping string tobacco that morning, she looked out at the stranger in serene unflustered dignity.

Rachel Floyd and Pearl pulled down their sunbonnets over their little faces, timid before the awful responsibility of having their first picture taken.

I always felt there with the group, though I did not join them until some months later.

From the time I first noticed the picture I was puzzled by one thing. Where was I at the time? I was not altogether satisfied by Aunt Cherry's story that I had been found the following October in an old stump at Rocky Branch. Yet I always seemed to have a sense of nativity about this little stream and went there often, as though in response to a need to touch home base.

By the time the youngest child was born the old stump story had changed. Aunt Cherry said Dr. Robertson had brought William Olive to us in his doctor's satchel.

Of Grandfathers and the Earthquake

I NEVER saw that picture man's camera on a tripod. But there were little pictures in my mind, extending beyond what my eyes saw. Mama in her wedding gown at the tobacco barn was a likeness of the way she was, always wanting things to be nice for her and her family. Papa in his work clothes was how he was, too, always indifferent to outside.

Other differences in persons, before shading off into the neighborhood pattern, were likenesses more clear than color of eyes or hair, than size or shape. Smallpox scars and sad ballads and red bonnets were who certain kinfolks were and others were not. They were like spicy herbs Mama used in cooking, they seasoned life.

Out of the pictures in my mind instinctive loyalties grew. Grandpa Poole had my loyalty because he had been a Confederate soldier. Grandpa Kelly had not been in the War. The grandfathers alike prided themselves on being plain people, we children were told, for whom nobility was in character rather than in exploits. All the same there was a difference in the likenesses.

One reality I had of Grandpa Kelly, who for the most part remained just a framed face on the parlor wall, unreal and remote. He came by the tobacco barn one March morning when I was toddling there after my sisters. From the doorway he saw that I was being left out of things, that the little sisters were not pleased to have the baby following them around in their play. Catching my eye, he motioned me out of the barn. Then he shut the door on the other little girls. From the darkness inside they began screaming.

Standing with Grandpa Kelly outside the closed door, I was at first a bit pert over the prank we were sharing. Then as the cries of distress grew louder, I started screaming too. I knew we were not on the same side. Grandpa seemed to know how I felt. Without delay he opened the door and tried to explain he had only meant to teach little girls to play together. He started to console us. We rebuffed him and ran home to Mama, the daughter and the sister of Confederate soldiers. From the safety of our porch we glanced back at the old man. The March wind had blown his hat off and tousled his thin gray hair. He was looking after us, baffled and a little sad as though he knew he had somehow been rejected by the very little rebels who were his grandchildren.

Grandpa Poole did not ever look sad or baffled. He was serene in the pews at church as in his armchair at home. A saint, he was often called. We were as aware of him as of the sky. Yet our total conversation with him was contained in greetings. "How are you, Grandpa?" we would ask. Or, "Good evening, Grandpa." Or, "Are you well, Grandpa, are you feeling as well as common?" It ended there. Our prayers were longer than our greetings to Grandpa.

We thought of God and Grandpa together. Sometimes we dreaded to go in the presence of either. "Be sure to speak to your Grandpa the first thing," Mama always instructed us before we crossed the branch to the old Poole homestead. So it had to be got over with, like prayers, but we were shy about asking a saint if he was as well as common.

Grandpa was not austere in bearing. He had such a meekness about him that it made him seem more withdrawn from the workaday world where uncles plowed cotton and corn and hollered at mules. Usually he sat by the fireplace in an armchair upholstered in flowered carpeting, or on the front piazza with his Bible open on his lap. At church he talked to the Lord as though He were on the bench by him. His grace at the table made us feel we were about to take Sacrament.

Even before our day, when Grandpa's vigor was not affected by the afflictions of age, he was regarded as other-worldly, we were told. During the Charleston earthquake of 1886, which was felt terrifyingly in Wake County, neighbors turned toward Grandpa as to a city of refuge. On that dread evening houses shook, dishes rattled, pictures fell from walls. Women rose from sick beds. Mama, unmarried at the time and in bed with typhoid fever, was one of them. Neighbors armed themselves with guns, believing that powerful human beings or strange wild varmints or elephants escaped from cages were abroad to shake houses down on them. Some thought dynamiters were at large. Others wondered if the Yankees had come back.

Cousin John Kelly raised his voice in a fearful cry across the woods. "Murder!" he shouted, and the echoes carried his cry resoundingly. Cousin John later declared he had called, "Come here!" But across the hill at Grandpa Kelly's it sounded like "Murder!"

So Grandpa and his family headed toward the Calvin Poole place. Some of them were armed with muskets, which had hitherto served no more violent purpose than to kill squirrels and rabbits.

Grandpa Poole told his neighbors he thought there had been an earthquake. His musket, used against Yankees some twenty-five years before, was hanging undisturbed in its brackets over the door. His Bible was open on his lap.

The frightened neighbors put aside their guns. They waited in the living room close to Grandpa Poole until the tremors were over.

· 3 ·

Confederate Scout

GRANDPA POOLE's gun did not suggest violence to us, though it had been designed to shoot Yankees. Grandpa did not shoot birds or rabbits, and Yankees were remote from our world.

They were less remote from Papa's. He had met them face to face during the War. With a certain eager pride Papa often told the story of his brush with Yankee soldiers. From their camp nearby they were constantly foraging the countryside. Papa was a small child when they raided the Kelly place, taking away with them the corn and hay, the farm animals, the smoke-house meat.

"What's your name, sonny?" one soldier asked the little Kelly boy.

"William," Papa told him.

"You crawl under the house," the Yankee bade him, "and shoo all the chickens out from under there for us."

Papa crawled under the house as bidden. And there he stayed till the last soldier had left.

"I never shooed out a single chicken," Papa always concluded his story. "Not a single one!"

Grandpa Poole and his oldest son, Paschal, had been Confederate soldiers. So Mama's side of the family had a lot of war stories. Because of a disability, we were told, Grandpa Kelly had not been in the War. So Papa could not tell waiting children about any family exploits on his side. Except that he had been a rebel at five, had refused to shoo chickens out for the Yankees.

Old Mr. Penny enlivened our childhood with stories of the Civil War and of woods animals. He lived with Uncle Paschal, his son-in-law, and served unofficially as postman along our road. Before there was Rural Free Delivery, Mr. Penny walked three miles to the nearest post office and brought mail once or twice a week to the neighbors. Often he came to sit till bedtime with us.

We children were entranced by the way he looked as well as talked. He had a long yellow beard and sharp little eyes that sometimes were just twinkling slits in his ruddy face. He impersonated woods creatures so vividly that at times we almost forgot he was Old Mr. Penny.

During the War Mr. Penny had been a scout to report on the defections in his precinct. His zeal was not comparable with that of churches in eastern North Carolina which turned members out for "the sin of desertion." Over and over in the minutes of Mt. Carmel Baptist Church there are references to the withdrawal of fellowship from members for the sin of desertion. Old Mr. Penny was loyal to the Confederacy, but he took certain things into consideration before reporting neighbors' defections.

Certain Republicans in the neighborhood had not believed in the war against Lincoln. Having no slaves themselves, they had not believed in slavery. Habitually before his scouting missions Mr. Penny had sent warnings to those neighbors who were following the dictates of their consciences and refusing to go to war. "Lie low tomorrow, boys," he had cautioned them. "I'll be going on my rounds."

Sometimes these neighbors hid out in tobacco barns, sometimes in caves under smokehouse floors, sometimes in the swamps. A prominent farmer of the neighborhood made himself a pair of wooden shoes in order that the scout's dogs could not, so he believed, track him to the swamps. It was his habit to make the others go in a different direction from the one he took, since their trail would not be protected by wooden shoes. It was understood he would head east and the others west. Once in the swamps, both groups would bear south until they came to their secret hiding place. There they found comfort in one another's company.

But one day they did not part company quickly enough, or wooden shoes were not any protection after all. For the scout's dogs took after the man heading east, and he had to climb a tree in a hurry.

Mr. Penny pretended not to see the man behind his leafy screen. He just let the dogs bark on awhile before he called them off. All the time the neighbor in the wooden shoes perched there in the tree.

This ending to Mr. Penny's story made Zaccheus and his sycamore in the Sunday school lesson seem much less remote to us.

"A Thousand Years"

Mr. Perrin, who owned the wooden shoes, lived just below the sandbar from our cottage. His long white house with the columned porch and lacy wooden trim adjoined Uncle Paschal's big oak grove on the other side. Living near him was a lively experience for neighbors.

For Mr. Perrin lifted the monotony from that little road of sand and ruts. He had spells of falling out and making up with neighbors, mostly with Papa and Uncle Paschal since they were handiest to him. Grudges and one-sided feuds developed without any cause that people could fathom. Suddenly after refusing to speak to them for days, Mr. Perrin made some extravagant gesture of neighborliness as a token there were no longer hard feelings over whatever the hard feelings had been over. Gifts thrust upon them during the making-up spree sometimes troubled neighbors, for how could they know the gesture would not boomerang when the generous mood passed?

Once at church Mr. Perrin got so worked up over the pressures for money that he threw his pocketbook with all its contents into the collection basket when it was passed. The uncles sent the money right off to the orphans before Mr. Perrin had time to change his mind.

For all his moods, he had the regard and affection of

neighbors, who realized he had a keen mind and many fine traits. Little heed was paid him when he got up in the pictures, as one aunt described his moodiness. Bereaved, he was sympathized with. Lonely, he was visited. But he was expected to bear and forbear like everybody else. So when word got around that Mr. Perrin was wishing somebody would cut his throat and end it all for him, the women of the neighborhood were upset. But the men said, Humph! Mr. Perrin would run like a killdeer from death, never fear!

There was a sense of relief among neighbors when he married Miss Mary Jane, a spinster from Swinney Old Field. It turned out, though, that the lonely moods persisted in spite of this second marriage. Neighbors suspected that the domestic situation down the road was not altogether happy, but they did not mean to get involved in man and wife trouble.

Late one afternoon the farm bell down at Mr. Perrin's started ringing.

"Something's wrong down there," Mama said, staring uneasily across the sandbar.

Ringing farm bells in the morning for field hands to go to work and again at dinnertime was customary and commonplace, but otherwise it was considered an alarm.

Mama began to change her dress. Papa in his work clothes struck out across the rock hill toward the long white house. Uncle Paschal left his shady bench under the yard oak and crossed the grove to find out what the bell was ringing about.

Miss Mary Jane told them. Mr. Perrin had taken laudanum and was already drowsing when she found him. He was in an armchair in the north room. The empty tickler he had drunk the laudanum from was lying on the hearth. Would someone, Miss Mary Jane cried, get the doctor?

Neighbors gathered quickly. While waiting for the doctor they went in and looked at Mr. Perrin. They saw the pint-size tickler lying in the fireplace ashes. Men began to try to rouse Mr. Perrin. Women stood outside the room and whispered and cried with Miss Mary Jane.

Uncle Dick and Aunt Cherry joined the scared tenants at the back. Aunt Cherry started heating water. She was experienced in the needs of vigils and wakes.

The doctor came. He did this and that. He tried emetics, stimulants. He kept working on Mr. Perrin.

Finally he shook his head. It was too late. The poison had done its work. His final direction was that Mr. Perrin be kept awake. There was dim hope of that, of course, but it was something to try.

So the men took turns walking Mr. Perrin. One supported his limp form on either side. Down the hall, through the rooms, across the long porch they walked up and down, up and down through the night. When one team tired, another took its place. Little keen switches were cut by the handfuls from maples and elms and applied with gentle briskness upon the old man's legs.

But the kindly switchings of neighbors did not arouse Mr. Perrin. Once or twice at the beginning he remonstrated petulantly. "Let me alone, Billy," he murmured to Papa, "let me sleep." To Uncle Paschal he cried drowsily, "Leave me alone, Pas. Leave me be. I want to sleep a thousand years."

The men kept walking the old man. The women were around, helping where they could.

The petulant cries from the front porch became more and more unintelligible. "Let me alone, Pas. Let me alone," Mr. Perrin mumbled. "I want to sleep a thousand years."

After dark Mama went home to her children. She sat most of the night at the south window, looking out toward the long white house beyond the sandbar.

Finally down there the little switches were all thrown away. Mr. Perrin settled into his long sleep without further interruption from neighbors.

When we were old enough to understand about the laudanum, we children were terribly impressed by the little switches used on a grown old man. We wondered if they made Mr. Perrin during his last hours think he was a child again.

Sometimes we stood musing before Mr. Perrin's white headstone in the churchyard. "Must Jesus bear the cross alone, And all the world go free?" was inscribed there. "No, there's a cross for everyone, And there's a cross for me."

We wondered what Mr. Perrin's cross had been.

· 5 ·

Politics and Mud

IT WAS like an earthquake to our childhood world to find
Mama crying that day. Mamas cried at funerals when loved
ones viewed the corpse and at revivals when sinners went up to
the front. But they never cried at home, never over the butter
molds. We wondered if the neighbors who had just left our
house had brought bad news.

At sight of Mama's tears we children tuned up. This time
she did not say as usual, "If you don't hush I'll give you something to cry over!" Instead, when we asked tearfully what was
the matter, Mama blurted out, "Politics!"

We were scared. Politics meant Red Shirts and guns,
Populists and hard feelings. We had heard a relative tell how
he had assembled at the polls with other Johnston County Red
Shirts, all armed secretly with guns to keep ex-slaves from vot-
ing. We had heard how one family during Red Shirt days, after
hearing a mob was forming against white people in their
neighborhood, took to the woods at sundown for safety during
the night. According to the story, the colored people along
that same road, after hearing that white people were forming
a mob against them, likewise took to the woods for safety
during the night. It was funny to us, in the security of our

firesides, that the two races running away from each other were so close together among the big trees.

But politics was not funny. It meant hard feelings among neighbors about who would be sheriff. It meant men sometimes had to vote for the wrong party to get right prices or else vote for the right party and bring panic to the cotton market. Today Mama went on to explain more about it than we had already gathered from fireside talk. Politics was dirty, she said. It was men's business, and women might as well go wade in mud as to get mixed up in it. Neighbors had just brought word that Cousin Eldora had meddled in politics, all because her cousin was running for sheriff of Johnston County. She had been speaking slight of the dead and gone, had blabbed out all over Poole's Siding that our Grandpa Kelly had been a Republican. It was nothing against our Grandpa Kelly's character if he had been a Republican, Mama cried out furiously, he had been a Christian same as the sheriff of Johnston County!

Then Mama straightened her face and bade us hush about politics, which was men's business, and go outdoors and play.

We hurried to the mulberry orchard, which was our Poole's Siding. Every fence jamb there was a house where neighbors lived. The Poole kinfolks had their being as the people we saw in them, moving about under the mulberries as they seemed to move in life. Today I played Aunt Add. Elwood was Uncle Cana, who had established the Siding as a flourishing shipping point for watermelons and cantaloupes and as a flagstop for train passengers. As Aunt Add that day I moved in and out of fence jambs among kinfolks, trying to undo the slight done to Mister Calvin Kelly by Cousin Eldora. It was a sin to say he was a Republican, I told neighbors, for wasn't he dead and gone?

Aunt Addie nodded sadly in agreement. She had helped sing "Nearer My Home Today, Today" over him at the graveyard. Aunt Emmie struck a few sad chords on her guitar and sang about the ship that never returned, oh she never returned, her fate was yet unlearned—a song that was in the mood of the question if not a direct reply to it. Aunt Henrietta was more direct. She tossed her head and said tch-tch upon the whole business, upon Cousin Eldora and the sheriff of Johnston County to boot! Aunt Mary said politics was as dirty as our muddy bottom, and women might better go fishing instead of meddling in it. Whereupon she seized her reed pole and can of bait and went forth to fish every branch and creek in Wake County. I ended my visiting that day by telling Cousin Eldora to her face that the Bad Boy was going to get her for calling Mister Calvin Kelly a Republican.

But I returned dispirited to my own fence jamb to cook supper for Uncle Cana, who had shipped a dozen carloads of melons from Poole's Siding that day. For I was aware that it had not been as Aunt Add I had said Mister Calvin Kelly, that instinctively I was disclaiming kin. Why did Grandpa have to be a Republican?

Later we children dealt with the slight more directly. One afternoon Cousin Eldora and her little girl came calling. We beckoned Janet outside. At play we threw a stick out into the middle of the bottom, which was muddier than usual after recent heavy showers, and dared Janet to retrieve it. She plunged in and sank over her shoetops into the miry ground.

Her screams brought Cousin Eldora and Mama from the house. Cousin Eldora dashed into the bottom to rescue her child. Heavily built, she began at once to mire. But she kept struggling toward Janet, sinking deeper and deeper into the mud. She lifted her skirts above her knees. As she churned her feet up and down in the mire, her white stockings became so plastered with mud only the tops remained white. We were tickled at the spectacle and scared too. Would Cousin Eldora keep miring down all the way to China, from which faraway land no ship could ever return, no letter ever be sent so Poole's Siding could learn of her fate? Would she mire clear down to the Bad Boy? Would we be called to account for this mess?

We knew all about switchings. Maple trees grew limbs that added to our knowledge from time to time. If a child got a whipping at school, he had another as soon as he reached home. If he didn't mind parents, if he was disrespectful to grown folks, if he broke any of the Commandments that had to do with childhood it meant a maple limb for him. Other omissions and commissions were dealt with as they came up. The last time Papa had whipped us, we were remembering now at the muddy bottom, Elwood and Pearl and I had left home never to return. We had taken up residence in the pasture back of our mulberry orchard and had resolved to live on pussley and hogapples ever afterwards. We had held out till dinnertime.

Mama did not mention switchings today. She directed us to bring planks and stovewood to the bottom, and with her help Cousin Eldora and Janet finally got back to firm ground. They went home immediately, trailing mud.

Surprisingly Mama did not ask questions about the incident. She dismissed it by saying Cousin Eldora's children had always been venturesome.

· 6 ·

The Peddler

I was the first to see the peddler. From the mulberry orchard I spied the low squat figure waddling along past the bridge with his canvas packs slung over his shoulders.

"The peddler!" I shouted excitedly, dashing into the house to find Mama. "The peddler's coming!" I could just contain myself. "Please let him open his packs, Mama. Please let us look!"

"I'm out of money," Mama said, changing her apron to go to the door. "How can I buy peddlers' wares, do pray?"

I was not discouraged. Always there was a little butter and egg money, I knew, and besides it didn't cost anything to look at the wares.

Already the peddler, with his excitingly strange accent, was crying out his wares at the front. "Nee-dles, pins, t'read, buttons, hamburgs, colognes—"

I was fearful his recital would be cut off and Mama would send him on to the next house. Usually he opened his packs anyway while she was still remonstrating and advising him to try the next place, where they would be sure to buy something from him. "It won't cost anything to look," I ventured. "Just to look, Mama."

"Side combs, laces, hat pins, shoe buttons, han'cheefs, ribbins, hamburg trimmings, buckles—" the peddler continued, dropping his packs on the floor.

In spite of Mama's remonstrances, he began to undo the straps. His persuasiveness and slick politeness did not waver under free inspection or rejection either. He sold his goods whether anybody bought or not. And children of Poole's Siding bought whether any money was passed or not. Doubtless mamas did too.

It must have paid the peddler a little that his goods were so much enjoyed. At least he had a rest on front porches as he peddled through the country on foot, and there was always a drink of cold water for him even when the nickels were slow. Joe Sugar had lunch with us sometimes when he peddled along our road, and though there were no charges for the food he paid with tiny trinket mirrors for each child in the family. A lot of little mirrors accumulated.

Joe Sugar and the other peddlers served country people miles from town. And they served children. Always they were Aladdin with magic rings and wonderful lamps. Always there might be magical trinkets to hand out, not just little mirrors.

"Scissors, t'imbles, neckties, stick pins, breast pins, safety pins, sweet soap—" The peddler was displaying his wares, and Mama was letting him. I began to relax. And buy.

"T'read, nee-dles, fancy combs, celluloid collars, ribbins—" He glanced at my unruly curls and added, "Roach combs—!"

"Three spools of white thread," Mama said, "number sixty. One package of needles. Then I'll look at your laces."

As the bargaining got underway, the peddler laid aside his black derby hat, took an ivory-colored handkerchief from his pocket and mopped his swarthy face. Beads of perspiration had formed during his florid persuasiveness and rolled down his neck under the stand-up celluloid collar. He wore a brown suit and purple striped shirt and a flowery necktie. A big red set sparkled from the ring on his stubby little finger, and a stick pin flashed from his tie.

"Bring some cool water," Mama bade me. "And call the other children."

Already upon my return the others were gathering around the packs. Mama always wanted them to enjoy a look too. I thought I glimpsed a little packet in her apron pocket, though the peddler's wares immediately diverted me.

Impulsively I touched the pretty ribbons. I kept hoping I might at least own a red plaid sash, even though grown people seemed to consider red dresses unsuitable. I had often chased gorgeous butterflies, meaning to bite off their heads. In this way, according to Aunt Cherry, I would own a frock the color of their wings. But I had never yet been able to follow through to the end. So I had never worn red Aunt Cherry's way either. Was it Red Shirts, I sometimes wondered, was it blood that made red an unfavored color?

The clean smell of new thread and cotton lace, hot from sunshine upon the wares, of cologne and sweet soap and warm brass and spicy dyes rose in a wave from the packs.

"Ribbins for the little girl," the peddler suggested, looking my way. "Or breastpin. See? Pearl doves wit' ruby eyes—"

If only he would snip off a length of red ribbon, I thought, and hand it to me as Joe Sugar handed out little trinket mirrors. If only he would!

Mama waved the doves aside and shook her head firmly over the red ribbon. She bought blue hair ribbon, thread, three yards of hamburg lace and a blue dotted Windsor tie. (There is a record of these purchases, for in a school picture made some time afterwards little William Olive is wearing a Peter Pan collar trimmed in the peddler's hamburg, and Darwin wears the dotted tie.) So Mama had compensated the peddler for opening his packs. I was instinctively aware that she had spent her butter and egg money to let us enjoy looking at the wares.

The peddler reached down under his goods and handed me a trinket, as though he owed something too. Then he closed his packs, shouldered them and trudged off down the road. I looked after him wistfully. I sighed with satisfaction. Nothing particular had been bought for me. But I owned. I owned the clean smell of new cotton goods and cologne and sweet soap.

I had touched red ribbins and pearl doves wit' ruby eyes. I had felt the mystery of strange people and strange places. I owned them. And I held in my hands a little trinket that had been along strange roads.

Down the road through the sandbar the peddler trudged toward Uncle Paschal's. If only Uncle Paschal and Aunt Henrietta would come tonight, I mused watching the waddling figure out of sight, and tell us what they saw and what they bought. It would make the peddler last a little longer. I rushed into the front room and seized the big Bible. Often we opened the Bible on a wish. If, upon opening the Book at random, we found the words, "And it came to pass," we then waited in faith for our wish to be realized. It would come to pass, we had Bible for it.

Today my wish was that Uncle Paschal and Aunt Henrietta might come to sit till bedtime. If I should chance upon the magic words, all I had to do was wait for night to come and Uncle Paschal. He would come. I would have Bible for it.

I did not that day find "And it came to pass."

But I looked in the little mirror the peddler had left as a trinket and saw him there more than I saw myself.

7

The Pill Man

THE MAN with the brown beard turned his road cart into our yard and started to alight.

It was not a peddler, I knew, for peddlers traveled on foot. It might be the lightning-rod man or the fruit-tree agent who always made lively talk along our road. It might be the picture man. In great excitement I ran to call Mama.

She had just come to the kitchen to take some baking soda. For some time she had been suffering with indigestion. Today after a dinner of ham and cabbage, baked tomatoes and boiled huckleberry dumpling with creamy nutmeg sauce, she was more uncomfortable than usual. She had tried to work off her discomfort by chopping the garden rows. Finally for relief she had turned to the only remedy there was in the house.

After changing her apron, she went to the front door. I was at her heels. If the picture man had come, I wanted to be in the family group this time.

"I'm A. Parrish," the man with the brown beard stated. "Do you have indigestion, flatulency, gas on the stomach—?"

He named other ailments, but I heard only the first. It was like opening the Bible and finding, "And it came to pass." For the Native Herb pills Mr. A. Parrish was selling were guar-

anteed to cure indigestion and tone up the system. I wanted
Mama cured and toned up. I wanted to hear the pill man talk.

Mama read the directions on the yellow box Mr. Parrish
handed her. The medicine fitted her need exactly. She did not
have the money right then, she told the agent, and her husband
was at the lower field. Was there maybe a smaller-size box?

There was any amount desired, she was assured. So she
emptied her purse of the nickels and pennies and received in
exchange a dozen brown pills. Then Mr. A. Parrish suggested
that Mama represent Native Herbs in the neighborhood. As
sub-agent she would get a discount on the big boxes, and by
retailing the pills in dozens and half dozens there would be a
little money in it for her. Mama agreed to give him her answer
on his return trip, after she herself had tried the remedy.

The Native Herbs were effective. Mama was relieved of
indigestion. Papa agreed for her to sell the pills among
neighbors provided they would come to our house after them.
He wasn't going to have her peddling pills around.

A few days later around dusk-dark the pill man hitched his
horse to our fence and bounced up the walk with a supply of
Native Herbs in his arms.

"I'm A. Parrish," he told Papa who was on the porch
resting after a hard day in the fields.

I cringed. Papa was sure to make something of the funny
way the man called his name. He was likely to blurt out that
he didn't care if it was *a* Parrish or *the* Parrish. He might even
say "the dog's-foot" to the agent. It was his way to be short
with salesmen. Even if he aimed to buy fruit trees or lightning
rods or enlarged pictures, it seemed he had to make a point of
being rough on agents first.

Agents were our excitement. They knew faraway places.
Their faraway places did not extend to China in our geography
book or to Astolat in our teacher's stories of knights and ladies.
But through them glimmered the hope that one day some kind
of enchantment might come along our road, that some Sir
Knight might materialize at our very door.

So we didn't want agents to stop coming. And we were
afraid they would if word spread among them that they would
be treated roughly in our neighborhood. Even Uncle John, who

was usually so genial and kindly, seemed impatient with agents. One followed him up and down the furrow once, trying to catch up and introduce himself and his wares.

"My name's Gillam," the agent panted. "Gillam's my name."

"I can't help it," Uncle John snapped and kept plowing.

Another man put a sign on his gate, declaring agents were not allowed there. So many stopped by to inquire the reason for the sign that the man decided it would save time to go on being rough on agents rather than to make explanations to passers-by.

Today Papa was not rough on the pill man. After telling Mr. A. Parrish to alight he asked him in.

Mr. Parrish wanted to stay all night. To reach his headquarters it would mean late and tedious traveling, so he preferred to pay a night's lodging along the road. He was made welcome under our roof and at our table. There were no charges. He paid, though. He left an extra box of pills.

He paid otherwise. He was good company. He made music for us. According to custom when traveling, he had brought his fiddle along, and we were entranced by his lively tunes. With the fiddle tucked under his brown beard, he moved the bow with deftness and speed. We could identify some of the songs. "Turkey in the Straw" seemed a little rowdy the way he played it. Mama looked at Papa. Papa glanced around to see if any of the children were patting their feet.

Mr. A. Parrish patted his foot and played on. He was a blunt man, we discovered that night and on later visits when he came with new supplies of Native Herbs. One night at supper Mama served light bread, leavened with her own homemade yeast. For all its wonderful flavor this yeast sometimes tended to toughen loaves in the rising process.

Mr. Parrish bit into the luscious warm bread, which began to stretch like elastic in his hand.

Mama observed apologetically that her dough had stood too long before being made out into loaves and was a trifle tough.

"A trifle!" Mr. Parrish exploded. "It's tough as a goat's hide!"

That was not funny to Mama. She had strict ideas about manners. Papa was usually strict too. But this time he laughed until he was hoarse. Mr. Parrish's comment became a funny family saying.

The coming of the pill man became as important as that of the peddler. Our supplies were usually low when he checked by, for the neighborhood was completely sold on Native Herbs. Papa counted out as many as Mama. For those neighbors who had been coming to him for their annual doses of calomel, so exactly and deftly measured out with his knife blade, were now advised to take herb pills instead. "They cured Rosie," Papa was wont to add. For all the ailments of our childhood, from knee-ache to spring fever, he prescribed ever afterward, "Take a Native Herb."

But Mama had other prescriptions for many of our ails. Often she bent over us and rubbed our aching knees until we were asleep. She doctored our spring fever with tasty sassafras tea. When we woke frightened from some midnight dream, she whispered reassurances. She did not often say pet names, but she acted them in our little emergencies. She was there, in the needs of flesh and spirit.

I had reason to be thankful to the pill man for more than good company and lively fiddle music. The sales from Native Herbs launched the first literary venture of the little Kelly girl who, strangely and unaccountably, wanted some day to be a poet. The entrancing stories our teacher told us about knights and ladies and castles in Astolat stimulated these poetical promptings. Astolat radiated dreams and romance and poetry. It was the capital of my childhood world more than Raleigh, the objective of my Progress more than Pilgrim's city.

I rode toward Astolat on pine saplings at Rocky Branch. I rode toward Astolat even when I churned and sloshed butter-milk and dreamed.

Mama read in *Farm and Fireside* that a Chicago composer by the name of Carl Jacobsen wanted song poems to set to music. She sent my song poem, "My Home by the Sea," to Mr. Jacobsen in Chicago. Pills paid for the music.

8

The Tramp

"COME TO the house in a hurry!" Mama called to us one morning.

We were playing in the mulberry orchard. I was cooking wild onions and pussley for my husband's dinner. Elwood was loading melons at the Siding. Darwin and Olive were building a long freight train out of stovewood. We knew to leave our play when Mama called, and the note of urgency in her voice now impelled us to go quickly.

"A tramp's coming up the road," she told us. "Hurry round the back way to the kitchen, and let's shut the doors."

We were shielded from view by the fig bushes and grape-vines as we hurried around the corner of the kitchen to safety. Mama picked up the axe at the woodpile and followed us in. She closed the doors and pushed us away from the windows to which we had rushed in order to observe the progress of the tramp.

Pearl and Floyd had stopped scraping new potatoes and were sitting quietly on the workbench as bidden.

"Be still and don't talk," Mama bade us, lowering her voice. "Act like nobody's home. And maybe he won't stop."

We became so hushed and still that the silence seemed to

vibrate with our tenseness. We had never heard of tramps actually harming people, but there was a fearful chance they might. Tramps were always white men. The colored needy were not allowed to go hungry or unclothed, for even the poor white families nearest them saw to it that they had some kind of subsistence. But the indigent whites tramped and begged. It was unsafe to trust them. Over and over we had been warned to run to the house when we saw a tramp coming and to avoid meeting one along the railroad track on our way to and from school.

Often we took the short cut from the crossing, not to get to school any faster, but to walk the railroad irons and crossties and to climb the steep embankment up from the tracks. The warning about tramps did not keep us from lingering on the way home from school. We enjoyed walking the railroad irons and watching the freight train mash our crossed pins into tiny scissors. The very danger of tramps made the short cut from school all the more interesting.

The only tramps we had ever seen were along our road. There were two kinds. One tramped the railroad tracks altogether, only turning off now and then to beg for food at nearby houses. The other kind tramped the country roads.

Mama tipped to the window and listened. Hearing nothing, she pushed the curtains back an inch and looked out. Simultaneously there was a heavy knock at the back. Mama dropped the curtain and stood there irresolute an instant. We held our breath.

After a little while the knocking subsided. Mama waited until the tramp had time to get back to the road, and then she peered from behind the window curtain again.

I saw her stiffen. With something like anger she turned toward the back porch. "You all stay still," she told us firmly and then opened the door.

"What do you want?" she called out sharply.

"Give me something t'eat, please'm."

So the tramp had not gone away, as we had hoped. We crept to the door and peered around Mama. There on the woodpile sat a scarecrow. His oddly assorted clothes were tattered, and a torn felt hat more or less brimless was on his head. A gray stubbly beard covered his face, which he was mopping with a red bandana handkerchief.

"I'm hongry," he added stuffing the bandana into his vest pocket. He stood up.

"I haven't got anything cooked," Mama asserted.

"No cold bread, no scraps?" he queried moving toward the porch. "I'm hongry."

Mama's tone changed. "You stay where you are," she said, "and I'll scrape you up something."

"Where's the axe?" he asked. "I'll cut you some stove-wood."

"There's plenty cut," Mama told him firmly. She quickly pushed me back as I tried to hand her the axe. "I'll put you a plate of food here on the steps. You can eat at the woodpile. And then leave."

From a crack in the door we watched the tramp gobble the cold biscuits and ham left over from breakfast, the fig preserves and butter, the molasses teacakes. After the plate was empty he picked the crumbs off his ragged vest and ate them, hunting for more.

Then he rose and stretched. Finally he ambled off down the road. He did not thank anybody.

We were alert all day. The tramp might turn and come back by our house, or another one might suddenly appear at the little bridge near the wild cherry trees. So, off and on all morning we watched the road both ways. After dinner there was excitement in the prospect, but not fear. For Papa worked in the rockhill cotton patch in order to be close around the house.

We had chicken fricassee and new potatoes and strawberry pie for supper. Mama cut the buttery top crust off in order to sweeten the berries. This method was used in the neighborhood because it seemed to take less sugar. I was watching the tiny particles that flaked off the crust when suddenly I boo-hooed out loud. I had been seeing again the crumbs on the ragged vest of the tramp, his careful search for other flecks of cold biscuits.

My knees were aching worse than usual. The growing pains, as my constant knee-ache was called, throbbed and hurt tonight. And there was a hurting I couldn't put my hand on.

"Why, what's the matter?" Mama asked quickly.

"He didn't even say thanky," I boo-hooed.

"Who—?" Mama said.

"The tramp."

Mama looked at Papa.

"If that's all that ails you—"

Mama did not finish what I expected her to say. So often when we cried needlessly she had a way of saying, "If you don't hush I'll give you something to cry over!"

I forestalled her this time. "I feel sick," I snubbed.

"Give her a Native Herb," Papa said.

I healed fast. At one whiff of the pungent herbs from the yellow box I declared I no longer felt sick.

But in the darkness of my trundle bed I cried myself to sleep.

9

Lily Maid

LIVING AND playing life merged so nearly that we children hardly knew where one left off and the other began.

In secret I sometimes played death. I became the Lily Maid. A clump of reeds alongside our little pasture streamlet was my funeral barge. In it I floated down to the king's palace, with a lily and a letter to Lancelot in my dead hand. By the time I arrived at court, I was so close to real tears that I could not wait to receive a queen's funeral.

We played funerals otherwise. When we buried goslings and puppies and biddies, our sadness was real enough. But we found consolation in the rites we created. We sang "Darling Nellie Gray" over the corpses, set up field rocks for headstones, and made wreaths out of honeysuckle for little graves in fence jambs. We placed such a wreath over Tabby one day and labeled it, "From Uncle Paschal's sassy cat." We knew "sassy" was not a nice word and was not allowed at our house.

Refinement was the yardstick by which girls' deportment was measured, and the use of nice words was half the measurement. We had a habit of collecting all kinds of words, heard and seen in print, as boys collected arrowheads and pebbles. We divided them into funny words, pretty words, nice words, low-down words such as boys sometimes let slip. Though they did not sound exactly like the refined talk we were always being told to use, we ventured to repeat "tarradiddle" and "peccadillo" which we had heard Miss Strickland say in the schoolroom. Since Uncle Paschal had referred to his cat as "sassy," we decided to try it out in Tabby's fence jamb. Mama found the labeled wreath, and that was the end of our playing death for awhile.

In secret, though, I kept playing Lily Maid.

More often we played life, creating parts for ourselves out of the way we saw kinfolks, out of church and school life and out of picture books. We played Uncle Millard who had once been shut up in a pest house with smallpox. We played Uncle Paschal and Aunt Henrietta. Their role was sitting till bedtime with neighbors, with Uncle Paschal telling stories of sassy cats and Aunt Henrietta saying tch-tch.

Even if he had not been in the War, Uncle Paschal would have held a special place in our regard. For he spiced up everyday talk with his funny expressions and tales. He did not seem to work like the rest of the neighborhood. While other men toiled in the furrows or at tobacco barn or fodder stack, he sat on his shady bench under the spreading yard oak or on the front porch with his feet propped on the railings, smoking his pipe and encompassed in a vast leisure, as a lady teacher referred to it. One of the aunts whose husband had to dig hard for a living called it laziness instead of leisure.

Yet, Uncle Paschal and Aunt Henrietta seemed to live as well as the rest. They were genteel, the lady and gentleman of our road. She moved rhythmically back and forth in her low rocker, doing drawn-work or just rocking and calling him back from flights of fancy about varmints or wild elephants with just one tch-tch.

I played Mama sometimes, though that role did not last long. For to imitate her activity even for an hour came to seem too much like real work. In addition to her household duties, she helped with outside chores. She tended the garden, kept the yards neat and somehow managed enough time from sewing and cooking and ironing to beautify the premises and make pleasant living at our house.

Under her hands there was bounty around our place. Gooseberry bushes yielded tart purplish fruit for mouth-watering pies and preserves. There were currants and figs, scuppernongs and black grapes to enjoy at the vines and to make communion wine out of, white mulberries and purple damsons, black walnuts and hickory nuts, every kind of orchard fruit, and in the nearby meadow there were blackberries and huckleberries. There were cane patches, from which came our winter supply of sorghum. The leaves of sage bushes provided savory seasoning for sausage and tea for chills and fever. Sassafras roots from the bottom, steeped in boiling water and then lightly sweetened, gave us tonic and beverage tea, a fragrant and aromatic amber drink for springtime suppers. There were plump chickens and pigs and milk cows to supply fowl and meat and dairy foods for the table. There were garden vegetables winter and summer.

Mama ministered to the sick and suffering along our road. Like other neighbors, she and Papa took turns sitting up at night, helping nurse the sick through typhoid and pneumonia and malaria or laying them out at death. Mama shielded us from the grim details of death beds and shroudings, but Papa sometimes shared experiences in vigils and wakes, and we overheard. One neighbor who was helping at the cooling board during a wake declared the dead man winked at him. He was so scared that he jumped through the window, shattering glass and leaving a trail of blood behind him. Upon investigation it was found that the silver dollar had dropped off one of the eyes before time, so the scared neighbor had some grounds for his report.

When tired of playing Mama in her many roles, I became Christiana out of *Pilgrim's Progress*, the picture book on our center table. I had been christened Bernice Christiana for young Christiana Poole, an aunt who had died as a bride. I felt more kin to Pilgrim's wife, whom I played so often, than to my aunt. Sometimes I became Pilgrim, fleeing from the City of Destruction, as in the pictures of our big brown book.

Guano bags slung over my shoulder were my burden of sin, and the pasture bars were the wicket gate. The muddy bottom where Janet and Cousin Eldora mired that day was the Slough of Despond. A fence jamb was Doubting Castle. Mud puddles in the hog lot, which looked deep and mysterious and as darkly forbidding as death itself, were the river that had to be crossed into the New Jerusalem.

Often I acted out purely imaginary parts. Quilts hung on clotheslines to sun immediately became stage curtains as at school and the whole back yard, a stage. A wooden cracker box was an organ for concerts outdoors. Inside the house, window sills were my piano where I played Gospel hymns and Aunt Emmie's love ballads. When I was old enough to churn, the dasher kept time to the sad ballads, and many a pound of butter came to the tune of "The Baggage Coach Ahead" and "Marguerite," whose thwarted lover wandered down by a little babbling brook while I sloshed buttermilk.

I played Miss Ruth Wingate, the beautiful teacher whose tracks along our road I often stooped to kiss. It was Miss Ruth who taught me to read, when I was merely marking time at school by reciting my ABC's day after day for the man principal. I played Miss Maud Freeman, another teacher, who wore rustly purple petticoats and enchanted us with the way she held her skirt tootched up at one side. For my taffeta petticoat I used a newspaper, which rattled if it did not look piquantly purple when I held up my long skirts at one side. I even played Queen Victoria, using an old window curtain for my court train. Sometimes the Queen merged into Aunt Martha Hood of Southport, who seemed like the royalty to us children.

To act out my gentility, I dabbed cologne on my lips and went around kissing trees and porch posts, calling them cousin-this and cousin-that. "How are you, Cousin Swannanora?" I asked the maple, while feeling superior and potently fragrant. "I hope you're well, Cousin Marguerite," I said, smacking the porch post.

I wondered where the peddler's cologne came from, for Mama seemed to buy only thread and needles and hamburg lace when the peddler came around. I found it behind the clock one day while I stood on a chair to explore the mantel. There it was just beyond the blue calomel bottle from which Papa measured annual doses of calomel for family and neighbors before Native Herbs. Intermittently after that I was sweet and genteel and kissing kin. As the cologne went down in the bottle, I added water. And so the peddler's perfume and my kisses lost their sweetness.

There were baptizings in the oat patch. When cousins gathered on Sunday afternoons, we chose from among them a preacher with whom we waded deep into the rippling grain. We were lowered into the green baptismal waters, creating for those who watched from the bank a lovely illusion. Grain sufficed for cousins, but I baptized my dolls in real water under the bridge near the wild cherry trees.

In the fall we played cornshuckings, making the red ears significant beyond the usual mere count of them at these neighborhood festivals. We had cane-grindings and stored up little runlets of sorghum in our fence jambs for company that came with trunks. We chased butterflies, fancying we might have dresses the color of their wings. There were tea parties and quiltings at which scraps of gingham were pieced up into doll quilts and bits of news into gossip about neighbors. We made a stage of an upstairs room, decorating it with dog-wood and arranging rows of chairs near the door. To our performances here we invited Uncle Millard and Aunt Cynthia and our family who seemed to enjoy our version of "Demons in the Glass." Only, they laughed whereas we had meant for them to cry. Uncle Millard laughed so hard the tears fell over his smallpox scars.

So we played life and stored up impressions of people as we perceived them living it. There was always the Lily Maid to go back to when I felt sad and faraway.

· 10 ·

Love Vine

AFTER BREAKFAST one summer morning Mama sent me
to Grandpa's to find out when Aunt Martha was coming to
the neighborhood. She was company with a trunk.

It became a day of quest.

"Quest" had become one of our pretty words after our
teacher used it in her elocution pieces about Astolat and knights
and ladyloves. Today's quest was for love vine.

Love vine was a leafless threadlike plant that grew among
grass and weeds close to the ground. It was the color of bright
gold. By means of it a girl could find out her future. The
vine had only to be named and hung in a maple or oak or
sugarberry tree. If it lived, the boy for whom it was named
would be The One.

Many ways of finding out the future were being tried that
year. Some girls looked in the well the first day of May for
the face of The One to be reflected in the water. Others tried
their fortunes with apple seed and mullein. Still others
counted nine stars for nine nights to dream on the ninth about
The One.

I tripped down the hill toward Grandpa's looking for love
vine. There were detours along the way. The first was Rocky

Branch where, according to Aunt Cherry, I had been found in an old stump. The pretty scene drew me away from the path, just as in storybooks knights were often turned from their quest by the beauty of crag and dale.

The hills rose high on either side of the narrow stream, which widened at one point and looked like Niagara Falls in the geography book. Our own Niagara Falls tumbled over huge rocks before leveling off to become little Rocky Branch again. Great boulders jutted out of the hillsides above the fern-covered banks and made little caves to play in. Saplings dotted the steep slopes. Some of them were bent from the weight of young riders who had used them for horses. Suddenly I bent a litle pine and rode my steed toward Astolat.

But I remembered love vine and dismounted to continue the search. There was no love vine on the hillsides. Heart leaves and wintergreen grew under the mulch of dead leaves and pine straw. These were some of the herbs that Grandmother used in the sweet-smelling salve she made for grandchildren's fall sores. The fragrance of honeysuckle mingled with the earthy odor of wood mold over the secluded valley.

Under the big line tree I paused to search among the weeds for the bright gold threads of love vine. There were none. But I found a little flower grave I had made some time ago between the roots of the tree. Pushing aside the dirt which covered the fragment of glass over the grave, I found my flowers all withered beyond recognition. They were soon replaced with flowering weeds. After the glass was lightly covered with dirt again, I made myself count one hundred before brushing aside the dirt for that breathless view of beauty and mystery inside the earth. The wild lace did not look like weeds.

Presently I realized I was getting hungry. Would there be gooseberry tarts for dinner at Grandpa's? There would be apples reddening in the orchard, there would be Aunt Emmie's songs about love, there would be love vine in the gooseberry hedge. Remembering that it was not refined to eat hearty at meals, I foraged around and found enough wild grapes to take the whet off my appetite before time to sit down with Ina and Ethel at Grandpa's table.

Once there had been the glimpse of a chink in their refinement. Have tired of doll tea parties they had moved idly out to the back yard, out of something to do. There they found Grandmother's heifer lying contentedly on the grass. They had served themselves big glasses of buttermilk from the dairy and sat on the back of the heifer to drink it.

Taut now from my bait of wild grapes, I stood in the shade to cool off before resuming the search for love vine. I was replete, like the girl in the pretty poem. Poems came easily to mind.

> You moon, have you done something wrong in heaven
> That God has hidden your face—?

It was more refined to recite poetry than to drink buttermilk on a cow's back, I mused.

> If you have I hope you will soon be forgiven
> And shine again in your place.

Would The One expect me to be refined like Ina and Ethel and Kitty, to crook my little finger over cups as we taught our dolls to do at tea parties, to sing sad ballads like Aunt Emmie's, to hold back tears when I just had to cry?

> There was a prince with golden hair
> In a palace beside the sea—

I could say poetry for The One. I could write song poems for him. Native Herbs had already paid for music to "My Home by the Sea."

There was no love vine around the branch crossing. But there were poplar leaves, out of which I made a fine hat with a sweeping willow frond serving as plume. With it on my head I was as fine as Queen Victoria or Aunt Martha. Or the ladylove of knight or prince. I sat down near the branch with a prince and crooked my little finger over a cup of tea and made up poetry about the moon.

Just then there was the sound of running, heavy like that of horses. I jumped up quickly.

Ina and Ethel suddenly emerged from the branch thicket, looking scared.

"We just said 'boo' at Cousin William," Ethel panted. "Just one 'boo.'"

Their story was soon told. Sent to take a pail of cool water to Cousin William who was plowing Grandpa's young corn, Ina and Ethel had plotted on the way to hide behind a clump of alders at the end of the row and say "boo" when Cousin William got there. All had happened as planned, except that the horse instead of Cousin William had been frightened. The sudden emergence of the girls rather than their boo, which from them could have been only a very gentle boo, had caused the horse to run away and tear up some of the corn.

Ina and Ethel did not want Grandpa to know. It would hurt his feelings, Ina thought.

"Ours might get hurt too," Ethel added practically.

I promised not to tell on the cousins. Which made me as guilty as if I had said boo. So, like Pilgrim in the big brown book at home, I picked up my budget of guilt and continued my progress to Grandpa's house.

There I made my manners to the household. Grandpa had just finished polishing his glasses, so his serene blue eyes looked very clear and seeing as he turned them on me. But all he said was that I could go hunt for some red apples if I wanted to.

Grandmother was in the old kitchen making some of her sweet-smelling salve. But I was diverted from the bubbling ointment by the sight of a strange little woman who was bent over the stove stirring the pot. I learned her name was Kalline. She had an owlish face. Her eyes, above a beak of nose, were crossed so that she appeared to be looking at people no matter where they were standing. Toothless, her mouth stayed dropped open as though in uncertainty or surprise. Her thin hair was pulled away from her high forehead into a tight little knot at the back. She was such an odd little creature that I stared openmouthed, puzzled at the signs of age in one who had apparently not finished growing.

Her talk puzzled me more. She blabbed out words that were not nice. It was surprising to learn from Grandmother that Kalline was one of Grandpa's family connections from another neighborhood, for somehow we had never heard of her. I soon gathered that she was not company with a trunk. Her stay was to be short, I learned. Plans had already been made for her to leave before Aunt Martha's arrival on Thursday morning. With that information Grandmother sent me out to speak to the rest of the household.

Aunt Addie was in the little room where she had stored her belongings after Uncle Marcus's death had forced her to move back home. From Ina and Ethel we understood that in the little trunk there were love letters Uncle Marcus had written their Mama before they got married. It was strange to think that a mama and papa had ever made love. Had she, I wondered today as I greated her, ever hung love vine in a tree for Uncle Marcus?

Aunt Emmie was tidying the piazza room. Once this had been the bride's chamber, we had been told, where daughters of the house spent their first nights with new husbands before going off to other homes. I thought of Aunt Addie and Uncle Marcus, with their love all made and packed away in trunks— what had there been for them to talk about their bridal night? Was the young aunt for whom I was named remembering all the love vine she had hung in trees when she went into the bride's chamber with her elderly widower? Had all the love vine died, so that she had never really known The One?

Cousin William came in at twelve o'clock. Grandmother then called us to dinner. I was in such a dread I did not feel like eating even gooseberry tarts. For all that Grandmother had mothered three sets of Grandpa's children and was always pleasant and kind to grandchildren, we were just a little afraid of her. Her maxims fitted our peccadilloes so exactly. She was so knowing, she seemed always to be on to us. Would she be on to the boo we were hiding from her? Would Cousin William tell how that boo had scared the horse and torn up the corn?

After grace, Grandpa asked Cousin William about the young corn.

Ina and Ethel tensed. I felt stabs of aching nausea in the pit of my stomach. The One receded. I was sick of love vine and love.

Cousin William reported the corn was in good shape. He did not look up from his plate. The gentle boo was safe with him.

The quest for love vine glimmered again after dinner. And again detours diverted. The old well sweep, the anvil at the shop, the millstone before the dairy door, the red apples in the orchard, the pretty love songs Aunt Emmie sang, the garden herbs—

I found love vine unexpectedly along the garden path, at hand. I hung the gold threads in the sugarberry tree.

By then the stabs of nausea had sharpened into constant pain. Suddenly I wanted Mama.

I managed the goodbye rounds. Grandpa looked up from the Bible on his lap and said, "Come again, child." His eyes rested for an instant on the orchard trees where he had seen apples redden so many summers from that same porch.

Grandmother called after me, "Don't eat any green grapes along the way home."

I did not pause to wonder if she were on to me. I went straight home to Mama. She gave me a Native Herb.

Later I realized I had forgotten to name the love vine in the sugarberry tree.

· 11 ·

Sad Ballads

AUNT MARTHA arrived at Poole's Siding the following Thursday looking trim and cool, even after the long hot train ride from Southport.

She wore a black taffeta dress with a white net collar boned all the way to her ears and with a lacy jabot cascading down her front. Her clothes seemed fixy alongside Grandmother's plain print dresses and starched white collars. And her manners and pretty talk, we children were well aware, were the model to live by, to teach our dolls by.

She greeted Sister Betty and Brother Calvin, the nieces and dear little great-nieces with becoming warmth. She gracefully accepted all the little attentions showered on her. She drank fresh water out of the charming well at the back, complimented the roses that had been gathered for her arrival, tasted the cool melon picked from Grandpa's lushest vine for her, and then retired to the little room to unpack her trunk.

During the extended visit I went as often to Grandpa's as was allowed. We children dreaded the meals a little, with Aunt Martha there across the table so easily proper and fine-as-Sunday even on a wash day. But the dread was less than the fascination.

We saw that Aunt Martha did not crook her little finger over her teacup, as our dolls had been told to do. She drank her beverage with grace and ease and said pretty words about all Grandmother's savory dishes. It did not surprise us that she was too refined to laugh, at least heartily like some of the neighbors. But we began to fear that it might not be refined to cry either. Crying over Aunt Emmie's sad songs was the entertainment we most looked forward to on summer afternoons.

Aunt Martha moved in cool sweet dignity, neither laughing nor crying. And she praised everything, including the Psalms and cornbread.

She read Psalms to Grandpa. "Now, isn't that beautiful, Brother Calvin," she said after nearly every verse, "isn't that just beautiful?" Even when Grandpa was visibly moved by the majestic words, Aunt Martha read serenely on, with no hint of tears in eyes or voice.

" 'He hath founded it upon the sea and established it upon the floods—' Now, isn't that beautiful!" Aunt Martha seemed to like to read Psalms about the sea. She lived near the big waters, and she wanted to share their magnificence and educate the Wake County kin as to the magnitude of oceans that covered three-fourths of the earth. Neither children nor adults of Poole's Siding had ever seen a body of water bigger than little creeks or Uncle Joe's pond or Neuse River, which in Wake was quite narrow.

We began to instruct our dolls to be refined, not to laugh or cry. We taught them the manners and pretty words of Aunt Martha. We dressed them in whatever froth was dispensed from her trunk.

Glimpses into the trunk from Southport were a special delight. It was frothy with lace and ruffles and net collars. A sweetness rose from inside as though lavender and sweet soap and spice were part of its contents. When the lid was lifted it was like the materializing of a treasure chest, like rubbing Aladdin's magic lamp and seeing a genie appear. There were little trinkets for the children. There were basques and braided skirts and taffeta petticoats and lacy jabots. The little room at Grandpa's changed character. It was no longer the place where little underbodies were fitted and stitched, or where Ina and Ethel played dolls. It was Aunt Martha's dressing room. The clean starched odor of bed linens and of waxed surfaces was submerged in the more definite fragrances wafted from that trunk from Southport.

Often of afternoons Aunt Martha entertained herself by looking at pictures in the purple plush album on the parlor table. She turned the pages and asked questions or gave out information about the people inside. They started reminiscences or comments on propriety so that she did not turn many pages at one sitting. We gathered she didn't like pictures of loved ones in coffins or of wives standing beside sitting husbands with a hand on their shoulders. It was etiquette for women to sit and men to stand, even if not custom, we learned.

Aunt Emmie's little autograph book entertained Aunt Martha less than it did us. Most of the wishes inside it were old copybook sentiments and were properly serious and full of inspiration. Death and the golden rule were often referred to along with pleas for remembrance. The touches of originality and flippancy interested us. We never tired of reading the contents and of speculating about the people who signed their names in such fine Spencerian flourishes. We asked ourselves, which had been The One in Aunt Emmie's life at the time of the verses? Which had been the first to be forgot? Had the grave of one become his bed? Was J., an initial that appeared several times in the book, the soldier who went off to the Spanish-American War and didn't come back, or was he the clerk from Raleigh who came down to see Aunt Emmie every first Sunday? We knew better than to ask outright about love matters.

"Emmie G. Poole, presented on X-mas tree at Mt. Herman, December 23, 1887" was written at the front of the little brown book. Often at church Christmas trees, presents marked "Special" were called out for members and non-members alike. These were in addition to remembrances provided by the church. Who had been Aunt Emmie's

"Special" at Mt. Herman across Whiteoak Creek in December, 1887?

We wondered what Thad, whose autograph appeared first in the book on January 1, 1888, had in mind when he wrote: "The mill will commence to grind next Tuesday night at seven. Don't forget to be on hand." We began to apply the grinding to all kinds of things.

Just what was Codie referring to, we also wondered, by his lines: "Emmie, you are young yet and do not know what 'tis, But in a year or so more it will come with a whiz." It had been several years more since 1888, and what was the whiz with Aunt Emmie? Was it Mr. Wilder who came every first Sunday?

We asked ourselves, who was C. M. L.? He wrote on January 30, 1890: "May joy and pleasure be your lot, As through this life you trot, trot, trot."

There was this one, dated August 20, 1888: "For Emmie— To live for some good is to make heaven yours, To live for any evil is to shut to the doors. Yours kindly, E. G. Beckwith."

It seemed the young men studied a lot about death. Sellie penned these lines at Anchor Lodge Academy, February 10, 1888: "May your pathway be strewn with roses, Fresh and rosy to the end, And when your body in death reposes, May your Maker be your friend." Another wrote: "Think of me when far away, Think of me though long I stay, And if my grave should be my bed, Think of me when I am dead." Fab thought of death even during Christmas week. On December 28, 1888, he rhymed: "When I am dead and gone to rest, Think of the old boy who loves you best." Had Fab been one of those who had loved and lost?

One whose autograph consisted of a single letter, not easily deciphered because of the fancy curlicues, wrote: "If you wish to snicker, Just look where I have cut a flicker." Another erased his name after the umbrella rhyme.

E. B. J. did not sound romantic like some of the boys. His rhyme was: "To Emmie—Some write for pleasure, Some write for fame, But I write simply, To sign my name."

One young man threw away the caution quoted in other

autograph books we had seen. He changed the last line of the couplet so that it read: "Emmie—Love no man, not even your brother, If girls must love, let them love boys," which made more sense to us than the original rhyme, "If boys must love, let them love one another."

One wish drew our special attention because it was written by Cousin Will. He was not company with a trunk like Aunt Martha, but none the less he was company in Poole's Siding homes for extended visits. "May you enjoy the blessings of a long life, much happiness and prosperity unlimited is the wish of your cousin." Cousin Will made educated talk about prosperity unlimited and the stock market the weeks he stayed around with farm kinfolks.

Our choice of all the verses was Edward's. Who was Edward? Where was he now? Had the "golden time" passed for him? "Had he dreamed of Astolat?" we mused. "Oh, had we some bright little isle of our own, In a summer ocean far off and alone, There with souls ever ardent and pure as the clime, We would love as they loved in the first golden time."

With a sigh we closed the autograph album, a sigh for Edward who never got Aunt Emmie away from Poole's Siding to a bright little isle of their own, for the one whose name was erased and for E. W. S. who wrote the last lines in the little book: "Last in your album, Last in your thought, Last to be remembered, First to be forgot."

One afternoon Aunt Emmie entertained Aunt Martha with sad ballads and guitar accompaniment. We listened, tearfully entertained, as she sang our favorites.

> Oh, she never returned, oh she never returned,
> Her fate is as yet unlearned—

Aunt Emmie sang, and we sighed for the ship that must have sunk in a summer ocean or drifted all the way to China.

> But for years and years there are fond ones watching
> For the ship that never returned.

We liked the ballads about lovers wandering sad and lone among the pines, about the girl who was lost and gone forever, about the gypsy woman whose daughter had been deceived. In the stanzas the gypsy mother directed a warning to the gentle lady whose lover had broken the heart of the gypsy's only child. Later, when I changed from poetry to prose, I used ideas from this ballad. The strange ending that the story took in my development of it was beginning to shape that afternoon as I watched Aunt Martha in the cane-bottom rocker and listened to Aunt Emmie's plaintive tune. It would be more exciting, I was musing, to let the false lover be a woman in disguise, maybe the mother of the girl he was deceiving. That would move Aunt Martha. So it would be that way in my story. *He* would be a *she*.

> "Do not trust him, gentle lady,
> He is wicked, false, untrue—"

Aunt Martha seemed unmoved by the sad story of deception. Never mind, we thought, just wait till Aunt Emmie gets to the baggage coach. We braced ourselves at the approach.

> As the train sped onward
> A husband sat in tears,
> Thinking of the happiness of just a few short years—

Our throats tensed as Aunt Emmie sang about the kind lady who suggested that the crying baby be taken to its mother.

> "I wish that I could," was the man's sad reply,
> "But she's dead in the coach ahead."

We glanced at Aunt Martha who was making the cane-bottom chair seem more like throne than rocker. She listened in dignity, unruffled by the sadness we were enjoying.

"A charming ballad," she observed, not moved to tears even by baby's cries that brought memories of a fondest hope that was dead. We choked and blinked back tears from our eyes, not wanting to be unrefined in Aunt Martha's presence. Aunt Emmie sounded chords on her guitar and went into another sad ballad.

Our dream of love is over,
Today we said goodbye,
We parted not in anger, though tears were in our eyes—

Aunt Martha rocked on, gently fanning herself.

I wandered down by a little babbling brook,
Its every ripple speaks of thee—

Aunt Emmie sang.

But oh, the thought you'll not be mine
Will break my heart, Marguerite. Marg-uer-ite!

We choked and blinked. Aunt Martha moved her celluloid fan
back and forth, lightly stirring the cascade of lace at her front.
Then came the battle songs about dying soldiers.

One held a ringlet of thin gray hair,
One held a lock of brown,
Bidding farewell to the earth and sky, just as the sun
went down.

Aunt Martha opened her gauzy fan wider and waved the air
sweetly in front of her. Her hair was gray, but not thin. It was
arranged in a handsome psyche knot on top of her head, with an
elegant high-back comb under it. For all the sadness of farewell to earth and sky, she remained serene.

While shot and shell were shrieking
Upon the battlefield,
Our boys in blue were fighting, our noble flag to shield—

Aunt Emmie's voice was wistful, as though she were remembering the Maine and a particular boy in blue.

Came a cry from our brave captain,
"Look, boys, the flag is down!
Who'll volunteer to put it back again?"

Aunt Martha folded her fan and sat very still in the rocker as
Aunt Emmie sang about the young man who brought the flag
back, but gave his life all for his country's sake.

"Just break the news to Mother,
She knows how dear I love her,
Just tell her not to wait for me, for I'm not coming home—"

We tingled at the bravery of the young man as Aunt Emmie continued the ballad.

"Just say there is no other
Can take the place of Mother,
Just kiss her dear sweet lips for me—"

Aunt Martha rose from the cane-bottom chair, dropping her fan. Tears were falling down her purple front, and the lace ruffles across her bosom were trembling. She moved into the little room and closed the door.

After a brief dismayed interval the grown folks went in to see about her. We children were sent out to the shop to crack black walnuts on the anvil.

It was explained to us later that Aunt Martha had lost a son like the young man who wanted the news broken to mother that he was not coming home from the war. We were told not to ask for any more sad ballads while she was there.

One thing had become clear. It was refined to cry.

12

Excursion

AUNT MARTHA during her visit convinced Poole's Siding about the magnificence and educational value of the sea.

A Sunday school excursion to the ocean at Morehead City was arranged. Uncle Hezzie and Uncle Cana took care of the details.

There was only a little opposition to this excursion. It had been presented in a Sunday school conference as an educational opportunity to see the ocean as well as other parts of the country. One had opposed the idea because the Sunday school had never been on an excursion before. Another objected because the ocean was dangerous. Didn't enough children fall in Uncle Joe's pond and Whiteoak Creek during Easter picnics, this one demanded, without risking the Atlantic? Cost was mentioned by a father who had eight children. Uncle Cana took care of that objection. He had already arranged with the Southern Railroad for tickets to be sold at five dollars a family whether a dozen or two were in it. Uncle Hezzie pleaded the educational value of such an excursion, the pleasure to little children.

The vote was nearly unanimous. It was a vote in favor of education as much as for Morehead. For Poole's Siding believed in education. At a time when free school lasted only three months, even children knew how the neighborhood had taxed its scant resources to run a subscription school so that young people might have educational advantages denied their parents. Out of the sacrifices made, a strong loyalty for school developed among young and old. Once after an attempted arson, Papa and other school committeemen got their guns and guarded their schoolhouse just like war.

So parents scraped up five dollars for a ticket to Morehead because they wanted their children educated about the ocean and other parts of the country. They were themselves interested in seeing strange crops and gardens along the way to Morehead.

On the appointed day the neighborhood assembled early in carriages, top buggies and wagons. Poole's Siding, from which watermelons and cantaloupes were ordinarily shipped, looked like the midway at the state fair that summer morning. Everybody was dressed in Sunday clothes. Fathers bustled around importantly, lining up families covered by the five-dollar tickets. Mothers carried baby satchels and boxes of food and fruit.

Papa had eight to line up. Other families were larger. The Mundys were ten, the Britts eleven. The Southern Railroad lost money selling tickets to Poole's Siding on the family basis.

For awhile after boarding the train, the Poole's Siding families were subdued. Gradually the young people began to relax and move through the coaches as other excursionists were doing. Boys daringly snatched handkerchiefs from strange girls' hands. Away from the watchful eyes of parents, the little fellows cut up, too, experimenting with spigots of water coolers and men's-room gadgets.

We little girls thought every river we crossed was the ocean. At New Bern where the junction of the Neuse and Trent makes an impressive body of water, we ran to our mamas half scared to death at riding over the ocean on a train. The mamas were scared too.

But Uncle Cana assured us it was the same Neuse River folks went shadding in back home. We didn't believe a word of it. We thought Uncle Cana was mixed up on his geography. We cringed away from the train windows toward the aisle and remained very quiet till the long bridge was crossed.

For the most part the excursionists did not remember about education. They passed through farming and trucking areas where crops and ways of cultivating them were unlike those of Poole's Siding, where gardens and orchards varied from those at home. The men glanced only casually now and then from the windows and resumed talk about their own cantaloupes and watermelons and cotton.

Likewise the women did little with this educational opportunity of seeing some of the country. Bound by routine and habit and awed by the Atlantic Ocean they were heading toward, they clung to the known. They talked about blackberry preserves and watermelon pickles and smokehouse meat and gardens in Wake County.

After arriving at Morehead, we ate our lunches and then went to the Atlantic Hotel. A bride and groom, whom some of the excursionists knew, were honeymooning there. We were invited to rest and freshen up in their room. Before the little bride left us to our routines, we children overheard her whispering around among the older girls, and we were educated a little about honeymoons if not about the sea.

When the time came to cross Bogue Sound, the women balked. Education ended on dry land for them. They had no notion of boarding motor launches or sailboats to ride on deep water. But the Atlantic had to be viewed by Poole's Siding children, so fathers took over that part of their education.

Papa took us on a sailboat. I noticed that the side on which I sat dipped down level with the water, as though overloaded. Hastily I crossed to the higher side, followed by others with the same idea. Then the boat turned, and we were on the low side again. I knew we were going to sink. I was too scared to talk, but I prayed hard. Others did, too, they admitted later.

Safely across at last, we wandered over the sand collecting shells and watching people wading in the surf and riding the waves. The women had on bathing suits almost up to their knees. Papas looked doubtfully at them, wondering if the education business wasn't being taken a little bit too far. We overheard their funny talk about the short bathing suits.

I wondered at the ocean, not quite believing it. I was too awed to feel poetical. But I kept trying to add stanzas to my song poem about my home by the sea. It was my home by Rocky Branch that was in my mind.

A thunderstorm broke over us when we started back across the sound. We were terrified. Deep water was under us, and torrents of water began falling from above. The tempest was raging, as in Gospel hymns. It looked like the end. Papa who was always so knowing and sure about storms at home seemed doubtful now.

"We'll be there presently," he kept saying. I sensed that he did not believe a word of it. I wished I had stayed at home, forever uneducated about any waters bigger than Rocky Branch.

On that watery ride I promised, if spared, to burn up my paper dolls, to become a missionary to the heathen, to stop kicking cats. I would sin no more.

From the wharf the mamas watched in an agony of anxiety, believing every sailboat was overloaded on one side.

The landing was safely made, and we hurried to board the train for Poole's Siding. The storm raged all the way. With windows down, the train was close and hot. The odor of over-ripe bananas and wet wool suits and sour babies mingled with that of train smoke and disinfectants. Babies cried and were fed. Men laid their heads on the hot velvet seat-backs and snored. Women, cramped and crowded by drowsing children, gave what comfort they could to their fretfulness.

When we reached the Siding the tempest was still raging. So Uncle Cana directed everybody to rush to the nearest shelter to wait out the storm.

13

Haunted House

THE EXCURSION for us did not end with the train ride from Morehead. We took another excursion of a different kind. We spent our first night in a haunted house.

From Poole's Siding that stormy night some of the excursionists rushed to the nearest shelter, which was cabins alongside the railroad track. There they took refuge with colored tenants all night. Our family pressed on up the hill to the home of Cousin Allie and Cousin Troy. Since these cousins had stopped at one of the cabins, we had to shake the window stick from the upper sash of a window in order to get inside. We had no uneasiness about our welcome, so far as Cousin Allie and Cousin Troy were concerned.

There was uneasiness, though. I did not sleep that night. Through the long hours I kept thinking about the strangeness of this place, about the yard gate that clicked under unseen hands, about the tall white chimneys that rose like tombstones outside and seemed to belong as much to the vine-covered graveyard nearby as to the house.

It was called haunted. However neighbors might declare they did not believe in ghosts or spirits, they realized that a queer house was in their midst. Strange noises had been heard here ever since old people were children. Sounds as of water being poured from pails upon the floor, as of taffeta dresses rustling in the halls, as of a gate clicking and doors opening without any visible hand, all these could be heard by day as well as by night.

Most persistent and undeniable was the sound of walking. Steps could be heard in the front hall, as though being made by an elderly person in low-quarter shoes moving toward the staircase and on up the stairs. The most reliable neighbors heard them. Kinfolks attested to the sound of footsteps. They were not superstitious. They considered it ignorant and wrong to hold with ghosts and witchery. Since they could not explain the strange sounds heard at the queer house, their answer to children's queries about the strangeness was, "Hush! Don't talk about it!"

But the walking was talked about openly among adults, and we children listened. The sounds were accepted as fact, whatever they might mean. Some said it was rats, knowing rats could not click the gate and climb upstairs like an elderly person in low-quarter shoes. Others said the house was settling, well aware that houses had no business taking so long to settle. Concerning the strange walking a few declared there was a natural cause for it, though they had no suggestions as to natural causes. There was rejection of the idea, advanced by outsiders, of testing the place for hidden treasure by means of divining rods. That was sanctioning witchcraft.

There was the walking, though. It was a fact. The invisible elderly person in low-quarter shoes continued to click the yard gate, to cross the threshold and climb the stairs.

Only a baby had appeared to see something strange. Not long after her little girl died at this house, Cousin Allie was standing at the gate with her baby in her arms. The child suddenly looked toward the house and started screaming in terror. For awhile she would not be quieted. She could not tell what she had seen. Nothing at all was apparent to the grown-ups.

In time the cousins who lived there paid no more attention to the walking than if it were a roomer moving around.

Having concluded it was nothing to hurt anybody, they just let "it" keep walking. "It's used to us now, and we're used to it," they had a way of saying, "so we get on all right together." Cousin Allie added, "It's company." And we knew she was thinking about her little girl who died.

There had been a night, though, when the disturbance became too much. The walking merged into the rattling of chains upstairs. Violent, angry sounds echoed through the house. Cousin Troy got his gun, while Cousin Allie lighted a lamp. They moved cautiously upstairs, expecting to find either a burglar or a wild varmint.

Nothing was disturbed anywhere. There was an unbelievable quietness over the house that had been so full of strange sounds. Cousin Allie held the lamp, Cousin Troy searched.

Convinced at last it wasn't anything to hurt them, they went back downstairs and slept off and on till day. None of the wise of the neighborhood could throw any light on the strange mixture of angry sounds. Some who were a little inclined to superstition wondered if there had not been a reason for ha'nts to rise.

For Cousin Allie admitted afterwards that on that particular day she had thrown a nestful of bad eggs into the old wilderness of graveyard near the house. She said she could not believe the night's queer sounds had any connection with this, since her motive had not been disrespect. Nevertheless, she picked out another place to chunk rotten eggs.

The night following the Morehead excursion, we girls scrouged together on the front room bed. There were strange sounds over the house. We told ourselves the wind was blowing loose boards somewhere. But we were so scared that we pulled the bedspread up over our heads. When we came out for air, the lightning flashes revealed faces of the dead-and-gone looking down at us from the walls. The white chimneys were more than ever like tombstones in the weird bursts of light.

I was the first to hear footsteps in the front hall. It sounded like an elderly person walking in low-quarter shoes. The steps seemed to be moving along toward the stairs.

We buried our heads under the cover.

Soon afterwards Mama opened the door and spoke to us. Had the strange sounds awakened her? We asked her about the footsteps.

There had been no footsteps except hers, she said.

We wondered.

14

Livestock

Savor was added to life along our road by Mr. Claude's family and livestock.

Mr. Claude had been a preacher since young manhood. Past middle age now, he had run out of churches. With zeal he preached trial sermons, but no call was extended. Forced to retire from pastorates, he had to take up farming at his father's old home place. Mr. Perrin, now sleeping on toward his thousand years, had been his father, and so we had neighbors again in the long white house with the lacy trim.

We children loved visiting at the preacher's house. Used to being handed from the cupboard such little snacks as gunjers and cold ham biscuits, all of us were carried away by the little store cakes and blackberry cordial that were served us from flowered waiters in the preacher's parlor. Miss Katie made each between-meal snack a dainty tea party amid fine rugs and polished tables and brass fireplace pieces.

Miss Katie introduced us to the stereoscope that gave us new dimensions to life. We flinched before the ferocity of tigers that had bared their teeth directly at us, and we believed for the first time that there were elephants as big as the books said. We gasped at the daring of men and women perched on the brink of lofty crags, saw them living and breathing as surely as our family around the supper table at home. We were breathless before the trees and flowers in such strange colors and sizes. Papa overheard us comparing the bigness of elephants with the barnlot shelter, and he scolded us for stretching dimensions.

We did not see Mr. Claude as anything but farmer, different from neighborhood papas and uncles and always a little funny to us. The Latin quotations he reportedly used even to his livestock were funny. We never heard any, for he rarely came to the house while we were there. He was always busy trying to adjust to farming and to running a little store in his back yard. Our glimpses of him confirmed the impression that he was a funny farmer. For he wore even in the field a white collar and black necktie and derby hat, and he talked educated even to his farm mule and pigs.

Educated talk and Latin did not keep his livestock in bounds. They were constantly breaking out of pasture and barnlot and feeding on neighbors' chufus and corn and oats. The pigs rooted up unfenced gardens, wallowed down cotton. The mule tore up fodder stacks, the horse grazed on young millet. Mr. Claude worked mightily at mending fences and stopping holes under the rails. But shoats tunneled new places, and the mule nosed off enough rails to hop over the fence after lush fodder stacks on Papa's and Uncle Paschal's land. The horse made use of the opening too.

Neighbors for awhile held in. Papa with our help drove pigs out of chufus and the mule out of fodder stacks back to their own barnlot. Uncle Paschal, never given to exertion on the farm, continued to run the horse out of his corn and the calves out of his millet. It was said around that Uncle Paschal worked harder over Mr. Claude's livestock than he ever had over making cotton.

This lasted for awhile. Papa even helped mend fences down at Mr. Claude's. But one day when he found the preacher's mule nipping his fine young corn he blurted out words a lot stronger than "the dog's foot." Then he made us help drive the mule home, and he talked with the bark on to Mr. Claude about his animals.

"They are obstreperous," Mr. Claude admitted, removing his derby hat to wipe the sweat band with his creased white handkerchief.

Papa glanced about uncertainly and then hurriedly sent us children home. Obstreperous sounded right strong. Afterwards it became one of our funny words.

Mr. Claude's big words were generally funny to neighbors. They did not seem to go with farming and pig-raising any more than his necktie and stand-up white collar and derby did. His farming was funny. He ran his rows queer. He brought buckets of water to the field for his horse as though she were a lady. He made sunshades out of tree leaves for her head. He rested her at the end of rows, struggling with the toughest grass himself to save her strength so that she could remain a buggy-horse.

It was told that he tried out sermons on his animals. He quite early let it be known that he had a trunkful of sermons and was available as supply preacher. There were overt statements that he would like to combine farming with pastoral duties if a pastorate near enough his farm should become available. One did. The community pulpit became vacant. Mr. Claude was not called. He had impressed too many members as funny.

His son added to the impression. Swade's inclination to jest was sometimes directed at his father as though he, too, found him funny. When Mr. Claude referred to plain old winter grippe as "influenza," Swade immediately called it "hen-flew-on-end-on-Wednesday," amusing children and adults alike with his take-off on big words.

There was the time his father directed Swade to pamper the horse, as he himself always did, when she was hitched to the plow. It would not be fitting for a minister to drive a mule to preaching appointments, so continually hoped for and sought by Mr. Claude; so related to a subsistence, too, only different from cotton. The horse was a symbol of ministerial gentility. Hence she had to be allowed to set her own pace and be rested at the end of the rows. The mule, Mr. Claude explained, was to be worked hard at the plow in order that her exuberance might be cut down and she would quit hopping over fences into neighbors' fields. Swade reversed his father's directions. He raced the horse and pampered the mule. "Take your time, Mule, take your time," he was heard to say. "Or your exuberance will be cut down, and you'll have nothing to fan flies with."

"Exuberance" got around. The use the preacher's son made of it was funny to papas, who believed in blistering their own children for impudence to themselves.

They were kindly people, and later they came to see the irony of circumstances that had made a plowhand out of a scholarly minister. In mellow mood one Sunday the uncles asked Mr. Claude to make some remarks at church. The pulpit had now been filled by a preacher who had a trunkful of sermons, too. But there was time after Sunday school to spare Mr. Claude a few minutes.

Mr. Claude rose and said with dignity, "I'm like the little boy the calf ran over. I have nothing to say!"

His point was lost. The kindly mood shifted. For the mention of "calf" brought to mind broken fences and obstreperous animals that needed their exuberance to fan flies with. We were all tickled rather than impressed.

The nearness of the new preacher's family to him must have made Mr. Claude feel more than ever like the little boy the calf ran over. For it was a constant reminder of the neighborhood's rejection of his own pastoral services. Because there was no parsonage in the neighborhood, Papa settled the new pastor in our home, next door to Mr. Claude's place, and we moved to Grandpa Kelly's old house. It had to be enlarged for our family of eight. The addition of an upstairs and a chimney meant the front of the house had to be boarded up awhile, so that the place became littered with scantlings and rocks.

All this kept us in confusion the whole fall. It also kept us from going to our first circus, since Papa could not spare the time from remodeling the house to take us. We talked circus all day. We were so disappointed at not seeing live elephants as big and real as those viewed through the stereoscope that we played thundering herds on the porches.

Tired of our big-elephants logic, Papa finally hushed us up and sent us to bed early.

Sometime after midnight he woke on the crest of a prolonged snore, which had already roused some of the household, and immediately called attention to faint but disturbing noises somewhere. It sounded like the bleating of a calf in mortal distress.

Remembering he had separated the calf from its mother after feeding time last night, Papa said he had better investigate the bleating. He hurried out the back door and picked his way gingerly over the rock pile near the new chimney. The thin agony of the calf's cry stopped abruptly as Papa approached the barnlot. Suddenly near the road he halted. His heart begin to pound painfully. Cold moisture gathered at the roots of his hair.

For there framed against the lot fence stood an elephant.

Huge and sinister, the beast held in its snout the dangling calf.

The massive bulk of beast lurched forward. Papa turned. He ran to the house. Recalling that the front was still boarded up, he flew around to the back over rocks and scantlings. He had to beat the elephant to the door. It was a fearful race.

Papa dashed in, hastily locked the door and panted out the peril we were in.

Mama asked if he hadn't been dreaming.

"The dog's foot! No dream about it!" Papa blurted out. "It's an elephant. I saw him there in the road with the poor little calf in his snout dangling from side to side."

"Where would an elephant come from?" Mama queried.

"The circus. One escaped!" Papa panted. "Rouse the children and let's all get upstairs!" He hastily moved tables and trunks against the front and back doors. "Or we'll be squeeezd to death like that poor little calf out yonder!"

The children were rushed upstairs. Mama followed with

pillows and quilts. Papa loaded his gun and took his place at the top of the stairs.

It was a night of tense excitement. We kept trying to peer out the windows, but were scolded back to our pallets. We hoped the elephant would still be around at daylight.

Exhausted, we finally napped. But Papa was on guard all night. In the clear light of morning he began to look a little sheepish.

Unfastening the back door, he peered out cautiously. He ventured into the porch, the yard. He retraced the course of his midnight race. He didn't remember that rocks and scantlings had littered the path last night.

Then he saw a half-eaten bundle of fodder lying in the road. He had never heard of elephants eating fodder, but this one must have, must have dropped it there in the road in order to seize the calf.

There was no sight or sound of any elephant about the place this morning. No elephant tracks that he could see. There was the cow in the barnlot contentedly nuzzling her calf.

Calf? Papa suddenly started. Why, the calf had been dangling in the elephant's snout last night, had bleated its life out—!

An idea shaped fast. Papa walked to the road. He found tracks there, very definite and unmistakable tracks. Mule's.

It was clear enough now. The calf had been bleating for its mother. In response the cow had nosed open her stall door and hurried to nuzzle her baby. The dead calf swinging in the elephant's snout had been only a bundle of fodder. The elephant had been Mr. Claude's old mule, trespassing on a fodder stack again.

The elephant story traveled around. It became famous lore in the precincts of Wake and Johnston. Somebody was always wanting to know of Papa when he saw his last elephant. Uncles teased him about running from Mr. Claude's old mule. Dr. Hocutt of Clayton once mailed him a clipping with some faraway dateline about an elephant's escape from a circus, and he enlivened professional visits in the neighborhood with angles of the midnight race. At first Papa was sheepish about it, but in time he told the story with gusto.

Mr. Claude said nothing. In dignity he drove his horse to the rare preaching appointments he was able to secure. He followed his mule down his cotton rows. At Sunday school one morning not long after the race he volunteered some remarks, based on St. Paul's exhortation to righteousness by faith. He quoted directly, "Ye did run well: who did hinder you that ye should not obey the truth?"

Most of the quotation was lost. "Ye did run well" seemed to divert the listeners. They glanced at Papa, at us. It was as though we and not Mr. Claude were funny to them now.

15

Fleshpots of Egypt

THE NEW preacher's family added another dimension to life after he moved to our old place. Mr. Adams quickly won the respect of Poole's Siding, for all that he could talk Latin and use words as big as Mr. Claude's. Nobody thought he was funny, for he did not compete in farming and livestock and had no fences constantly needing to be mended. He went about his business of being pastor and of heading the new boarding school he was making out of Mt. Moriah Academy.

We admired the preacher's family. Royal was a Little Lord Fauntleroy. The Adams girls were golden-haired princesses. Mrs. Adams was less fixy than Aunt Martha from Southport, but like her she was always dressed to meet company. Too frail to manage housework alone, she kept a cook. The neighborhood women who did all their own work were less envious of than sorry for a woman who had to set her family down to hired cooking. However, one woman said the new preacher's family was too inclined to frills, to fleshpots like the Israelites of old.

Miss Katie let it be known that she felt the contrast in circumstances. She, too, had been pastor's wife with help in the kitchen, with honored place in communities, with a husband who had been respected and looked up to in other places. We children added to the hurt she felt. For Miss Katie's stereoscope and blackberry cordial and little store cakes no longer interested us. We liked better to play with the Adams children and to admire the frail lady who had changed as with a wand the cottage we had known in and out. White lace chair tidies, fringed table covers, rayo lamps, bookcases and a plush sofa were there now. The roof over which we had played hail-over with cousins now sheltered a man of God.

Miss Katie expressed her sense of contrast once when Mrs. Adams' cook was sent down to their store to buy sugar. Apologizing for her untidy appearance, Miss Katie said if her husband had a school and a church, too, she might be able to keep a cook in her kitchen and stay fixed up to meet the door like a lady. Word of the funny way she talked was taken back to Mrs. Adams. Cordiality did not develop between the preachers' families.

But there was cordiality between Mr. Adams' new boarding students and neighborhood girls. Romances developed. More notes than compositions were written during the boarding-school interval at Mt. Moriah Academy. The haunted house became a popular place. The young men boarded there. The angry sounds of rattling chains and of footsteps on the stairs were not heard while they were there.

Indeed, if Cousin Allie ever heard the ghostly walking again, she did not bother anybody with it—or with anything that she could help. Many years later, bowed down by the trials of life and the afflictions of body, she one morning told her son not to work too far from home that day, as he might be needed. Then she bathed and dressed in her Sunday clothes and lay down and died without any bother to anybody.

It was a lively interval for children, too, though we merely observed the strange ways of love among older sisters and brothers. We had dreamed of Astolat, of Lily Maids and ladyloves, of Marguerite about whom every ripple of the brook babbled, of Sweet Marie whose face was fair. Now we knew there were such things as sweethearts not only in song and story, but also in real life.

People in general, not just sweethearts, were our excitement. Our awareness of them was extended as we were allowed to visit in schoolmates' homes. Spending the night away from home became the chief diversion of our schooldays. We made discoveries. An old, old lady at one schoolmate's house told us the witches often rode her at night, and she kept salt by her bed to sprinkle into their skins. There was the man who claimed he could make the clock stop at his command and proved it. In another home there was a man who had trances, during which he uttered strange sounds.

There were some puzzling differences among kinfolks in whose homes we stayed all night with schoolmates. Aunt Edie was a favorite. She wore a bonnet and aprons of deep red, though only the conventional pattern of blue and white checks was used by other women. Why? I often pondered. And why did neighbors look sideways at red bonnets?

Why did Cousin Eldora expect children to do so well in life, why did she keep after us to be "Somebody"? We tried to be so dignified at her table that we never laughed or ate as heartily as at home. We felt we were in high society around her.

At Aunt Alie's we were free to laugh and talk like grownfolks. We were not ashamed to be hungry at her table. The food was not different in kind or quality, but what a way Aunt Alie had with ordinary dishes! During school nights spent in her home we studied next day's lessons, listened to Uncle John's witty stories about agents and varmints, popped corn at the fireplace, told ghost stories and speculated about our future to our heart's content.

At Uncle Paschal's there was a hammock where we could swing and dream. I was becoming less the Lily Maid of Astolat now than Mary Howard waiting for George Moreland. A white hammock hung between trees, with June apples reddening above and thistlebirds singing, seemed to make dreams surer of coming to pass one day.

I was beginning to dream of becoming a bookwriter like Mary J. Holmes. *English Orphans* by this popular novelist had been passed around among young readers at school, and after meeting George Moreland and Mary Howard in the book we girls saved our pennies and invested in Holmes' novels. They were seven cents a copy. *Darkness and Daylight, Lena Rivers, Tempest and Sunshine* and the other novels provided not only names for paper dolls, but also ideas for book heroines. In my novels I planned to use heroines with consumption who would die in the arms of heartbroken sweethearts, as in Holmes' books. In addition there would be other romantic figures like Alice Roosevelt and Nicholas Longworth. I was as glib with the names of Alice and Ethel, Quentin and Archibald and Theodore of the White House as of Ina and Ethel and Kitty and Eunice of Mt. Moriah Academy.

My dream of becoming a poet like the New England group did not subside, even after Mary J. Holmes influenced me toward novel-writing. Many little verses would continue to be stored in my crackerbox desk, on top of which now lay the words and music of "My Home by the Sea." But it took a lot of words to fill a book, and poetry was not very filling.

A novel filled pages faster. So I wrote *The Gypsy's Warning*, a version different from the song Aunt Emmie sang, but prompted by it. The story was about a mother who deserted her family to disguise herself as a man. She went around breaking hearts of trusting girls. Among her victims were the gypsy's daughter and later her own, whom she had deserted in babyhood. In vain the gypsy warned this daughter not to trust the wicked heartbreaker. The too trusting girl was drowned, and the wicked flirt lived on to break other hearts.

It was a whole tablet full of story. I had never read anything like it. Ina said she hadn't either. She was impressed. So she showed it to Professor Sackett of A. and M. College. At the time he was conducting agricultural research on a test farm at Grandpa's, and Grandmother was boarding him. Professor Sackett made some comment about the youth of the novelist. Ina and I gathered that he was impressed. We ourselves were. For hadn't I filled a whole five-cent tablet full of words?

I wanted to know for sure if I would become a bookwriter. I went to the big Bible. There I made my wish to become a writer and not a married lady like other girls. If I opened the page on "And it came to pass," then I should never need to hang up love vine in trees again. I would know my fate. Gauging the right place to open, I put my fingers between the pages.

Suddenly I closed the Book without looking inside. I might turn to "And it came to pass." But oh, if I did not!

I kept the dream, without knowing for sure about my fate. And sometimes I went along with schoolmates, who expected to be married ladies one day, to look for love vine. Just in case.

The heroines I dreamed about for my future novels were now beginning to be colored by my reading of Dickens and Scott and Eliot, as well as of Holmes. I bent over books, even when I churned.

There was an interval when everything seemed like flesh-pots of Egypt. This was after Mr. Adams talked to me about the age of accountability and about joining the church. I began to dodge the preacher. I wanted to stay where I was, in time.

Little things about joining the church bothered me. I was shy about walking down the church aisle before so many people and fearful about being put under the water at Uncle Joe's pond. I dreaded drinking wine out of the communion cup because old Mr. Mundy, who had a dirty-looking white beard, would be served ahead of us children. I even shied away from the sacrament silver, kept in our big wardrobe when it was Papa's turn as deacon to provide the bread and wine. Besides, I did not feel like giving up my paper dolls. Most of all, I wanted to write novels, and novels were considered sinful.

One day during the Maytime revival Mr. Adams preached on the fleshpots of Egypt. He outlined by exact diagrams on a blackboard the narrow road to heaven and the wide way to the Bad Place. I saw myself on the downward track, pursuing the fleshpots of Egypt so clearly listed on the blackboard.

Yet I held out. I was not eleven. One more year could not matter. I would read Jeremiah instead of Mary J. Holmes, I promised silently. I would write religious poetry and song poems of praise instead of novels. I would put aside my paper dolls. I would not kick cats any more.

From the windows I observed clouds in the sky. A thunderstorm was near. Flashes of lightning played over the congregation. Dusk settled over the church during the last stanza of "Just As I Am." I stepped into the aisle and walked the long way to the front.

Others followed me down the aisle. Women were crying. Men blew their noses as though they had bad colds. There was rejoicing over the sinners that repented.

During the days before baptizing Sunday the paper dolls troubled me. I had promised to destroy them. They were fleshpots. They were Baal. Finally I burned the entire collection, emptying J. Lynn's catalogue where they lived between the pages. I burned George Moreland and Marian Grey, Alice Roosevelt and Nicholas Longworth, Lizzie Hexam and Eugene Wrayburn and Edith Hastings and Maggie Tulliver and all their kin. My tears fried on the hot stove into which I was thrusting so much happiness I had created.

At first I felt purged of fleshpots. Play gave way to meditation. I read Jeremiah. I said many little prayers in the dark clothes closet. I wrote a sad song poem about the moon and the sod, which was a cross between songs of praise and the New England poets. I spoke kindly to the cats.

But as the losses of my paper dolls grew on me, I felt vaguely mad at somebody. I stopped hunting rhymes for the moon and the sod. I quit Jeremiah. I dressed up corncobs in bright quilt scraps and called them Alice Roosevelt and Marian Grey and Maggie Tulliver. I kicked the cats.

As the watery grave yawned before me, I grew chastened again. I was used to big white bowls and zinc tubs, but the water of Uncle Joe's pond began to seem like the ocean. With dread I saw last summer's white piqué being pressed for the baptismal rites. It seemed like my watery shroud. A big wool shawl to cover me with as I came up out of the water was borrowed from Aunt Cynthia.

The old gray telescope suitcase that had never been farther than Uncle Joe's pond was carefully dusted. Inside were placed the white lawn dress with the val lace yoke, the bleaching underclothes trimmed with the peddler's hamburg lace, the white stockings to wear with my patent leather slippers. There seemed a lot of white in the day.

On the way to the pond in our surrey Mama kept telling me to shut my eyes on "Holy Ghost" in the baptismal rite, to hold my breath and not try to fight my way out of the water as some of the girls had done last year.

Papa looked around once from the driver's seat and said, "There's nothing going to hurt you, gal."

A Sabbath hush rested over the solemn pines, the quiet waters, the subdued congregation. The meek mules and horses, tied to trees up the slope from the pond, were unwontedly still.

The candidates were grouped apart. Their mothers hovered near with shawls on their arms.

Under Mr. Adams' instruction the boys took the girls' hands. We were led down to the water's edge while kinfolks and neighbors sang.

> Shall we gather at the river,
> The beautiful, the beautiful river—?

Aunt Emmie's plaintive soprano, Aunt Alie's and Mama's sweet altos, Uncle Cana's clear tenor and Papa's gallant bass I seemed to hear above the other voices that floated out in harmony over the placid water. Mr. Adams read and prayed. Cousin Allie, who cried at baptizings since her little Mildred had been buried, was leaning against a pine trying to sing, though her tears were spilling over her Gospel hymns.

> Gathered with the saints at the river—

Mildred had been such a little thing to become a saint.

The mamas' voices faltered as their children were led toward Uncle Joe, who went ahead to gauge the proper depth of water for the children. The papas' voices were steady enough, but their songbooks shook a little. Mr. Adams moved toward Uncle Joe. The little girls, their white-stockinged legs sinking into the water, followed. The boys awkwardly held their hands.

Exum Sturdivant, who seemed not to mind water as much as he did holding girls' hands, advanced toward the middle of the pond. Roy Baucom steadied as many girls as he could.

The preacher raised his hand in ritual preliminary. I watched Myrtie come up strangled, but with that clean baptized look. I was next. My breath came fast, as though I had been running a race. I swallowed at the lump in my throat, drew one last long breath on "Holy Ghost" as Mama had instructed. I began to go backward. My eyes shut tight after that one glimpse of fathomless expanse of water I was being lowered into.

A red darkness and a mighty roaring of waters blotted out the earth. Would there ever emerge again, I wondered, the sweet commonplaces of life? The rooster crowing for day, the dinner bell, Mama's voice—I suddenly reached up from the weight that deafened and held me. I grabbed after reality. My hands were not baptized.

Then a brightness flashed into my wet face. I coughed some of the weight from my chest. Somebody wrapped Aunt Cynthia's shawl around my shoulders. The world looked sweet and clean.

I felt light. I was happy. The sweet commonplaces flashed into reality—the ham and fried chicken and pound cake in the cupboard at home, the dinner bell, Mama's voice. The water part of being a member of the church was forever over. It was true the dressing part was ahead, the undressing before a crowd of women. The wine part of it was ahead, too, the cup from which old Mr. Mundy and other whiskered men would drink before it would be passed to us children.

The right hand of fellowship was immediate. I liked standing in front of the pulpit in my white lawn dress. My unruly curls were plastered down wetly in unwonted order. But I felt that my countenance was shining below the wetness, as the uncles and aunts and neighbors filed by. They silently touched my hand, as though a bit bashful and uncertain before the new babes in Christ, they felt so humbly babes themselves.

Aunt Emmie's beau, who was used to properness and manners in Raleigh churches, spoke heartily as he passed along. "God bless you," he said to the first. "God bless you," he said all down the line.

It was all nice and grown-up to join the church. Until

Mama and Papa came along. They gave me an impartial hand-shake just like they did the others. But somehow when those calloused hands touched mine, I wanted a lap to cry on. I felt less babe in Christ than their little Bernice.

I could not play with cousins under Grandpa's sugarberry tree that Sunday afternoon. I could not frolic as long as my hair was wet from baptismal waters, or damp even.

16

Of Food and the Skies

IT WAS not strange that I came out of baptismal waters
thinking of food. At Poole's Siding, food was an important
part of the good life.

Easter picnics at Uncle Joe's pond and Whiteoak were
neighborhood feasts. Dinner on the ground at church meetings
was as hearty and bountiful as the picnic spreads. Meals among
neighbors added zest to home fare. But there was nothing
during the year like the feasting at Christmas. It was no less
a religious festival because so much time and painstaking care
went into the preparation of food. Except for a Sunday school
Christmas tree, services were not held in the sanctuary, but
Poole's Siding honored the Birthday with elements of the good
life.

Just before Christmas we butchered hogs so there might be
abundance of fresh meat along with the cured. Early in the
morning a fire was kindled under the big iron pot. While the
water heated for the hogshead, the knives were given a final
whetting at the grindstone. Wooden tubs, sausage grinders,
long red pods of pepper and dried sage were made ready. As
the men started with their sharpened knives and axes toward
the barnlot, I ran into the clothes closet and plugged my ears

with forefingers in order to shut out the piercing squeals that accompanied the butchering.

Carcasses were then dragged to the smokehouse. There they were plunged into the hogshead of boiling water and scalded before their hair could set. From the water they were lifted upon planks, their hair was picked and the skin scraped till it showed pink and clean in the early light. Carefully rinsed off, the hogs were hung by their feet to the gallows and split open. The viscera were deposited on the table in the wash-house for the women to begin work on.

Next morning the men cut out the meat, heaping the kitchen table with scraps of middling and ham for sausage meat. Mama fed the hand-turned sausage mill with these trimmings and sage and red pepper, seasoning the mixture in a wooden tub. The chitterlings, rinsed and soaked through many waters, were held open with bores, homemade from basket slats, and stuffed to hang in long festoons from the smokehouse loft. The big casings of stuffed meat were called tomthumbs.

Over an outdoor fire the fat, heaped in a big iron pot, was rendered into snow-white lard and crisp brown cracklings which later were used for savory bread and big hominy. The livers, haslets, backbones and spareribs were shared with neighbors who helped with the butchering. The pigs' feet, ears and heads were boiled together to congeal into souse meat. Sliced and placed in a crock of vinegar, souse made an appetizing and hearty accompaniment to collards and turnip greens.

For Christmas one of the largest hams was baked and basted constantly with a sauce of red pepper vinegar. A back-bone was boiled ready to brown. Poultry was roasted, a cured ham cooked. Cakes and pies and home-leavened bread were stored up.

The cakes were varied and many-layered. Pound and fruit cakes, cocoanut, cochineal, orange, walnut, chocolate, marble and teacakes were placed in cupboards and dairy. A big pan of foamy boiled custard was made on Christmas Eve, spicy with nutmeg and vanilla.

The acme of bounty was at Grandpa Poole's where we went to eat Christmas dinner. With eager anticipation we children watched for the hands of the old Seth Thomas to point to twelve, unconsciously storing up memories around this old timepiece.

Its advertisers in Plymouth Hollow, Connecticut, had printed "Warranted Good" inside the clock several decades ago. That warranty stood the test of time. It was made to keep time. It kept time.

It ticked off the birth of eleven children in that stalwart old saddleback house in Wake County. It was there on the mantel when Grandpa and Uncle Paschal went off to war in 1861, when a daughter awaited a soldier's return from the Spanish-American War. It ticked off the marriages of six daughters who stood out in the parlor floor and said their vows. It marked bedtime for bridal couples who with some impatience must have watched its hands creep toward ten o'clock, the hour for them to withdraw to the bride's chamber.

After family honeymoon customs changed and the bride's chamber became known as the preacher's room, pastors set their watches by the Seth Thomas timepiece in order that they would not be late for preaching appointments. Ministering to the neighborhood church were such pastors as the Rev. Johnston Olive, Rev. O. L. Stringfield, Dr. C. A. Jenkins and, much later, Dr. R. T. Van and Dr. W. R. Cullom.

The clock ticked equably the night of the Charleston earthquake in 1886. It was a monitor for children who wanted to stay on at Grandpa's beyond the time allotted for visits. There was no appeal from its authority. It ticked on through Aunt Martha's visit without flourishes. It was there in the silences of vigil.

It marked the hours for feasting. Men and children watched the clock while women of the household walked up wonderful meals from various quarters of the old place.

The women had to walk to the south of the big grove for smokehouse hams and sausage. The dairy with its supply of meal and flour and preserved foods was in another direction. Beyond the garden to the north there was the walk to the potato hill. Between grove and field there were plump chickens and turkeys and fresh eggs always waiting at the end of the long walk from the house.

The old kitchen where so many delectable meals were prepared was at the eastern boundary of the grove, safely isolated from other buildings because of its fire hazard. Dishes prepared there were taken up the path to the long dining hall that adjoined the living room. Later Grandmother took Professor Sackett's board money and added a kitchen to the big house.

The hands of the Seth Thomas clock pointed to twelve. We went in to Christmas dinner. The steaming brown turkey, choicest of Grandmother's flock, was placed near Grandpa's place, with side dishes of giblet and egg gravy and steamed dressing. Platters of cured and fresh ham, baked spareribs and boiled sausage were interspersed with bowls of greens and turnips and artichokes, with syrupy batises and breads and pickles. Very little of the tablecloth showed anywhere. Six kinds of cake were waiting on the sideboard.

Grandpa sat at the head of the long table. Against this lavish spread of earthly delight, his unearthiness and frailty impressed children and grandchildren anew. He had a noble face, with firmly outlined features that each year became more sharply defined, with clear blue eyes and closely clipped white mustache and beard. Always he wore a white shirt and dark blue suit. It made him seem remote on weekdays, apart from the world of work clothes.

The family closed their eyes for grace. With steady assurance Grandpa prayed.

There was a little silence, a hiatus between praying and feasting. Then Grandmother started passing the dishes.

During dinner Grandpa told again the story of his Christmas Day in camp. "I well recollect that Christmas dinner during the War, for it was the best I ever ate," he mused. "One piece of fat meat, fat side meat—that was all we soldiers had for Christmas dinner. And it was better to us than all this ham and turkey is to you all today."

I glanced at Grandpa. At that instant he was Confederate soldier more than saint. But then I thought of his favorite song, "Am I a Soldier of the Cross?" which we would sing for him around the parlor organ after dinner. And he was saint again.

Sometimes when Grandpa was past singing, he still quavered the words of his song.

> Must I be carried to the skies
> On flowery beds of ease,
> While others fought to win the prize—?

For him we continued to sing the question, "Am I A Soldier?" But I knew the answer. Grandpa had always been for the skies more than against Yankees.

Food did not seem inconsistent with being for the skies. And so we feasted on the Birthday.

· 17 ·

"Academy I Love the Best"

ONE AFTERNOON Mr. Adams made two exciting announcements at school. Governor Aycock was going to speak at our
commencement, and a photographer was coming next day. So
we were to come to school next morning dressed to have our
pictures made in an Academy group.

The following morning we spelled our words and recited
our history lesson absent-mindedly, more aware of the Sunday
clothes we were wearing than of the Revolutionary War. At
our desks we turned pages and practiced Spencerian penmanship
in our copybooks. "Labor is life; 'tis the still water faileth," we
wrote under the copy Miss Bessie had set for us the day before.
But our slants were a little vertical that morning, for we kept
looking out the window to catch the first glimpse of the picture
man.

It was my first picture. I meant to look straight at the
camera, not hang my head or flinch as my little sisters had done
in their first picture at the tobacco barn before I was born. I
meant to look sure and serene like Mama in her brown wedding
dress that day. My dress today was green flannel with a silver-
dotted velveteen yoke, pretty enough to make any girl sure
before the picture man.

After we were lined up, I glanced around to see how sure the others looked. Pearl was holding her head high, just like Mama at the barn that day. Rachel Floyd seemed serene. Pretty little Nannie Lou looked ready for anything. Gentle little Agnes watched shyly for the birdie to come out. Kitty posed in dignity. Ina smiled unsurely, as though remembering her "boo" at Cousin William one summer day. Ethel stood near, unafraid. Ava had her pretty dimples all set for the picture. Eunice, Lucille, Belle and Myrtie all seemed ready. Some of the boys looked bashful, but Frank and Roy and Hubert and Exum faced the world. Earl and Swade stood together. Elliott, the crippled cousin, waited patiently. Charlie made a funny face.

Elwood lifted his chin above his starched stand-up collar. Darwin sat sidled against him at the girls' feet. Kneeling not far from his brothers was little William Olive. He was the most dressed-up child in the row. Mama had seen to it that her baby child looked nice. He was wearing his little sailor suit. Around his neck was the starched Peter Pan collar edged with the peddler's hamburg lace. It was such a tremendous thing to have his first picture made that William Olive closed his blue eyes tight against the wonder of it.

Last of all the group that I noticed was the sawmill boy from across the creek, whom all of us shied away from in the picture. He was standing near the teachers, Mr. Adams and Miss Sue Kelly and Miss Bessie Cheatham, a lonely figure.

When the picture man went under the black cloth covering the camera, I retreated in sudden panic to the end of the third row to stand by Rachel Floyd. She was family. I felt the need of family at this moment. Almost, like Aunt Cherry at the tobacco barn, I did not get in the picture at all.

But I stood firmly in line the day Governor Aycock came to deliver the commencement speech at Mt. Moriah Academy. All of Poole's Siding assembled at the schoolhouse early that day. We schoolgirls were thinking less of education, which was the continuous message of the Governor, than of our importance in the closing exercises. Dressed in our starched white lawns with rosettes of red, white and blue pinned to our berthas, we felt very responsible for the program and rather haughtily sure because the boys wore their rosettes so doubtfully. We knew we were going to wave our colors at the right lines of "Columbia, the Gem of the Ocean," whatever the boys might fail to do. We were going to render our school song from memory, just as our teacher said render it.

Mamas stood around in groups on the school ground or strolled down the hill toward the thicket. The place to stroll was not clearly defined. On weekdays girls used the little house in the thicket, while the little house among the sheltering pines on the churchground belonged to the boys. On Sundays there was a switch. During intermissions men and boys went to the schoolground thicket, and ladies moved toward the sheltering pines. Many times on Monday mornings girls hastened to mark through their names that had been penciled on the rough walls during Sunday intermissions. Boys sometimes declared their love indirectly in this way. One boy wrote under his girl's name that she was a darling, God knew.

Today women were a little unsure as they took their stroll. It was such a Sunday occasion that their impulse was to turn toward the churchgrounds. Some remained inside the schoolhouse throughout the wait, to savor the occasion of the Governor's visit as long as possible. Others sat in surreys and buggies to keep an eye on restless children who had to be kept starched and combed and clean till after the Governor's arrival and departure.

The little governess from the river road strummed idly on the piano, trying out its tone and singing softly to herself,

> Coon, coon, coon, I'd like a different shade—
> Coon, coon, coon, I wish my color would fade,

The mamas looked at one another, not sure it was a proper song on such a Sunday occasion. They were wondering what the children's Sunday school teacher, Miss Mattie Johns, might think of a coon-coon-coon song.

Men stood around outside in shirt sleeves, with their Sunday coats placed conveniently near on the back of buggy seats. They compared the progress of their cotton and tobacco and corn. Each time before one took another chew of tobacco, he looked sharply at the road to make sure the Governor was not in sight.

Occasionally one left the group and headed toward the steep railroad embankment beyond the churchyard. He paused near Mr. Perrin's white headstone to read again the constant challenge and the answer engraved there:

> Must Jesus bear the cross alone,
> And all the world go free?
> No, there's a cross for every one,
> And there's a cross for me.

When he rejoined the crowd of men, he did not chew tobacco with them any more.

Suddenly there was a flutter of excitement over the waiting groups. Uncle Cana's carriage with the gray horses hitched to it was coming up the hill. Uncle Cana had gone to Auburn over an hour ago to meet the train that was bringing the Governor the twelve miles to Poole's Siding.

The men hastily finished their last pit-too-ees and drew on their coats. Women hurried inside. Greeting the Governor was man business, like politics. Teachers lined children up for their part on the program. We girls straightened our rosettes.

Governor Aycock alighted from Uncle Cana's carriage and was led inside the schoolhouse. Everybody stood in respectful silence as he walked up on the stage.

In our starched white lawns we marched to the front and waved our rosettes properly when we sang, "Hurrah for the red, white and blue." Then our voices blended in the school song which a teacher had arranged.

> The academy I love the best
> In all this world is Mt. Moriah.
> Her name is known in East and West
> And North and South, our Mt. Moriah.

Mamas beamed. Two aunts whispered, nodding their heads. They were agreeing, they admitted later, that a lot of territory was being covered in that song.

Governor Aycock spoke eloquently about equal opportunity and education for the children of North Carolina. There were tears in the women's eyes at the story of the poor boy who was so eager for an education that he went to school with only green apples in his lunch pail. The mamas of Poole's Siding were wishing they could have fed that little boy. I thought of the sawmill boy we had all shied away from in the school picture and wondered what he had in his lunch bucket.

The men all resolved anew that their children were going to have the opportunity and education the Governor was talking about, if it took their last ounce of strength, their last dollar. It had taken their last dollars many times already, when they had taxed their meager incomes to carry on subscription school. But it was of the future they were thinking that day, of longer school terms, of college education.

After the address, little golden-haired Helen Adams, coached by a teacher who knew about manners and politeness toward governors, went up on the stage. She handed Governor Aycock a bunch of pink roses from Miss Emily's yard. The Governor bowed his thanks gracefully.

We wondered what he did with Miss Emily's flowers on the train ride back to Raleigh. The pink roses must have been in his way.

· 18 ·

Career Visitor

EARLY ONE May morning Papa took a load of garden produce to market. He brought Cousin Will back with him.

For several days Cousin Will had been checking by the market in the hope of catching a ride out to the country, so he latched on to a seat in the farm wagon with eager satisfaction. He had been visiting kinfolks in Raleigh. But the country in springtime had its particular appeal to him. There was garden and smokehouse bounty, and there were more kinfolks to go to see in the country.

Cousin Will made a career of visiting around. Sometimes it took a year to complete the rounds, and by then it was time to start all over again.

He looked out of place on the wagon seat amid country produce. For however low his pocket change might be, he had an air of the stock market about him. He knew all about the steel outlook and cotton futures, and he talked knowingly about trade treaties with Japan and free silver and anti-imperialism and prosperity unlimited. It was educating to be around him.

Poole's Siding men listened with polite interest to Cousin Will's logic about rich people who bought cotton on the board and steel below par and made millions by closing out when the market was two points up; about how mankind had been crucified on a cross of gold; about how congressmen negotiated treaties and declared war and lived high up there in the nation's capital on the taxpayers' money; about how anarchists like Charles Giteau and Czolgosz were going to wreck the country in a dozen years if the right party didn't get control.

The women listened less patiently. Some said tch-tch at his arrival. Others agreed that Cousin Will might exert himself a little sometimes. Their own families were satisfied with leftovers from dinner, but Cousin Will had to have hot suppers every night on account of his dyspepsia. Native Herbs did not prove to be the remedy for him. They helped the indigestion, but also they gave him such an appetite that there were no leftovers after dinner any more. It was the women who had to wait on him, draw water when he wanted a fresh drink from the well, see that his changing clothes were washed and ironed, and make some gesture toward entertaining him while their husbands were in the fields.

No woman in the neighborhood minded having company. Part of the pleasure in living was to open the door in welcome, to share with visitors such bounty as there was. Rarely was any one reluctant about hospitality. The women bore with Cousin Will. What he didn't eat, the pigs would, they said, and there was plenty for the pigs and Cousin Will too.

Yet they thought he was a little too sure of himself, a little on the superior side. They felt he was looking down his nose sometimes at what was put before him at the table. None ever heard him make verbal complaint except for the spring he was served fried onions everywhere he went. His outburst then had provided many a laugh among the men who understood how a visitor might get tired of fried onions. Cousin Will might lean over in his chair and peer down at a dish as though distrustful of it, they admitted. He might remove the cover off a platter before the blessing to see what it contained. If it suited him he might pucker his lips, moistening the pucker with his tongue, and serve his plate with a choice portion before the host could bow his head. But he ate what was put before him.

Now and then he was called on to say the blessing. He had

a pompous tone, though we never understood a word except "Chrisakeamen." He never appeared humble or unsure about anything.

He did no chores. If he went to the water pail and found it empty, he returned to his rocker until somebody else got thirsty and drew some water. If the wood burned down to small chunks during winter visits, he hovered closer to the fireplace. He rocked and read and talked and educated us.

So far as we children were concerned, it enlivened our household to have Cousin Will in it. He lifted the everyday a trifle toward Sunday. For one thing, he did not look everyday to us. With other men dressed in work shirts and nondescript trousers, Cousin Will, in his white shirt and collar and necktie and with a watch chain across his vest, distinguished the family circle on weekdays. But when Papa and uncles dressed for church, then we saw that Cousin Will did not look half as Sunday as they did. One aunt said tch, he looked seedy.

Sometimes out of the hearing of grown folks we teased Cousin Will into singing. It was funny to us to hear a grayheaded man singing darling stuff.

> Will you love me, Molly darling,
> Will you love none else but me—?

he quavered forth, and we snickered to ourselves. Only in song was there ever any Molly darling in his life. As bachelor he was an oddity at Poole's Siding, which was a paired order.

Stories of places where he had visited fascinated us. Especially did we like to hear about Roanoke Island where Virginia Dare in the history book was born and where kinfolks lived now.

That first night of his stay with us Cousin Will became expansive over the platter of fried ham, red gravy and clabber biscuits. The stewed apples and turnip greens suited him too.

"There'll be a rise in the stock market," he predicted buttering two biscuits. "Steel has been fluctuating lately. It jumped up two points in one day here last month. If I had five hundred shares, I'd be making ten thousand dollars before summer's over."

"Whoopee! That's a pile of money!" Papa exclaimed.

"Why, that's nothing, Bill. Folks make fifty thousand in one day's time. Of course there's a risk," Cousin Will admitted. "Fluctuation, stocks first bullish, then bearish—that's how she goes. The time to make money is when the market's bearish."

" 'Tis?" Papa inquired politely.

Cousin Will was very educating that night. We learned how to make money and how to save the country from anarchists.

Next day Mama had fried onions for dinner. She knew how to make an appetizing dish of them. Into the hot iron skillet she minced enough cured bacon for seasoning, drying it out into crisp little cracklings. Then she added the onions, tender green tops as well as pearly roots, with enough water to steam them done. Seasoning it with slivers of hot red pepper and a dash of salt, she served the dish hot from the stove.

As courtesy to the guest, Papa called on Cousin Will to say grace. His voice, galloping headlong toward "Chrisakeamen," sounded fretted today.

"Help yourself," Papa said, passing the platter of onion greens to Cousin Will.

"Don't choose any!" Cousin Will blurted out vehemently, reaching for the boiled savory.

"Why, don't you like spring onions cooked this way?" Papa queried.

"Despise 'em!"

Mama looked quickly toward the head of the table. Plans for today's dinner had been made before Cousin Will's unexpected arrival last night. Mama had decided to boil the last tomthumb in the smokehouse and serve with it fried onions, a combination the family relished. Now she and Papa were remembering the spring Cousin Will was surfeited with fried onions everywhere he went. We children saw that they were amused, but when we started grinning there was a look from the head of the table reminding us of manners.

We might get tickled at home among ourselves over some of Cousin Will's ways, but we all had a sense of responsibility about him. We did not want him to be funny or unwanted elsewhere.

This was how Elwood and Elliott felt the summer Cousin Will took them along with him to visit the Roanoke Island cousins. The boys were strangers, but Cousin Will had visited the cousins several times before. We enjoyed hearing Elwood tell about that week on the Island.

The welcome was hearty, he said, the hospitality unstinted. At the end of a week, when Cousin Will seemed to be settling down for a long stay, the boys began to feel responsible for getting him back to Wake County. The Poole's Siding kin certainly had no notion of dropping him on their Island cousins to be rid of him themselves. Yet the boys felt a little guilty, a little afraid they might become unwelcome themselves like the innocent bearer of bad news.

So one night after supper they took Cousin Will for a walk in the moonlight and sand. The little sandbars in Wake County would be easy to walk in, Elwood said, after all these dunes in Dare. The subject had to be broached somehow.

"Lots of stars tonight," Elliott observed looking up at the sky. "But there's apt to be clouds tomorrow."

"That's right," Elwood said quickly. "Bad weather's apt to set in."

"We ought to get across the water," Elliott added, "before bad weather sets in."

"We'd better start toward home early in the morning," Elwood said. "Don't you think so, Cousin Will?"

There was no reply. Cousin Will might not have heard, the boys realized. It was taking his wind to plod through the sand.

"I don't believe they expect us to keep staying here," Elliott said directly.

Cousin Will plodded along behind, ankle-deep in sand. The boys could not seem to get a word out of him.

They tried Wake County, where sandbars were easy to walk through, where watermelons were ripe and cornfields were full of roasting ears, where smokehouses were stocked with cured hams and cleansing coops with frying-sized chickens.

Cousin Will said nothing.

Elwood and Elliott had to go back to the weather, to the stars, how bright they might not be shining tomorrow night if storms set in.

"Doggone it! Let 'em shine!" Cousin Will blurted out. And as he tottered along through the sand he used language that had nothing to do with unlimited prosperity and the stock market.

Next day he went back to the sandbars of Wake County with the boys.

19

Kalline

KALLINE CAME to our house one day and stayed on. She was out of homes.

Her homes had been along many roads wherever people would take her in. She worked like a field hand for her keep. All she asked for her labor was a roof over her head and enough food and snuff to sustain her.

Her one fear was the poorhouse.

Poorhouse had been named to her often enough by families that had grown tired of her ways. Its threat had become a fixed dread. "Why, them I've worked for all promised me a roof over my head as long as I lived and a coffin when I died!" she had a way of saying over and over, with a kind of surprise and anger in her voice. "A roof over my head as long as I lived and a coffin when I died is what they promised me!" To stay out of the poorhouse had become her purpose in life, and she worked for it endlessly.

I had seen Kalline once before. She looked even odder the morning she came to our door than in Grandmother's kitchen where I had first met her. She was wearing a rusty black hat with purple violets on one side, which somehow made her look even more owlish than when she was bareheaded. Her black sateen dress, now slightly greenish with age, was fastened together at her neck with a pearl dove. In a cloth flour sack she carried her possessions, slung over one shoulder like a peddler's pack.

Mama gave her a little wooden crackerbox to use for a trunk while she was at our house. After sorting and arranging things in her box to her satisfaction, she stood and looked down at it as though it were a treasure chest.

One day I saw her treasures. She had asked me to get her some snuff brushes from the woods. So I gathered a handful of blackgum twigs, trimmed and hammered the ends so as to form mops, and then brought the snuff brushes to her. She motioned me to the back room. There she opened her cracker box purposefully. Piece after piece she took out and laid in a neat pile on the floor.

The odor of snuff rose in a fine mist from inside, where there were underbodies of flour sacking, worn knit underwear, white home-knit stockings, spools of raveling thread, an underskirt of bleached domestic edged with odds and ends of lace in a variety of widths and patterns. Near the bottom there were two blue-checked aprons, a black and white calico dress like the one she was wearing, and the rusty black sateen she had worn on the road. Under the black straw hat there were broken bits of colored glass and pretty little rocks, black shoe buttons and hatpins with broken heads. A big bladder of snuff and several blackgum brushes already chewed into mops were in one corner. A half dozen apples from our orchard, hidden away to ripen, completed her treasures. She handed me an apple.

We learned that she made a practice of handing out apples, though to men rather than to women. Asked why she singled out men, she made it clear that she looked to them for snuff and roofs and coffins. She did not make it clear why she gave colored people on the place all the better clothes that were handed down to her. Mama said a little impatiently that she was trying to act like the woman of the house.

Papa declared Kalline was the workingest somebody he had ever seen. Mama worked continuously to get things done,

Kalline to keep busy. She dashed from hen nest to hen nest collecting eggs for the market basket or kitchen. She rarely gave hens time to finish laying before she was at their nests, peering impatiently under their feathers as though to hurry them along. She fed the pigs, watered the stock. She bugged vegetables, chopped garden rows, cut stovewood, swept yards, cut weeds, set field tasks for herself.

She had a funny way of nicknaming people and things. William Olive, always an unusually good boy, she called The Priest. Darwin, her favorite among us, was That Boy. I was Phibby. Elwood was Governor, Mama was She, and Papa was Beel.

When Papa told her not to take upon herself any heavy outdoor work, she raised her voice. "La, Beel," she cried, "where I've lived I have ditched and mauled cord wood, I have scattered compost with my naked hands, I have dug up stumps, I have plowed, I have cleared new ground. La, there ain't nothing I haven't done!" Her words became a refrain, like a Gospel hymn chorus, repeated over and over as she dashed back and forth to her field work. There was no stopping her when she set her head to do a thing. She raced from job to job with such a drive that it appeared she was being over-worked.

Her ways became irksome. She was headstrong and self-willed, not minding anybody's orders or advice. She blurted out vulgar words without regard to age or sex of listeners. Her irreverence was upsetting too. For her, God was Old Boss with Whom she was as chatty as with folks. Before waiting for the second table one day, we children hid our favorite pieces of chicken, knowing that the first table would leave just necks and backs. Left alone with Kalline, we asked her to say grace. "Thank Old Boss for dinner," she said and added chattily, sharing the joke with Him, "and we had it hid!" Another time her grace was a complaint. "Thanky for dinner," she told Him. "And peas at that!"

One day she sat on the floor to make herself a nightgown out of some outing flannel that had been given her. It was a shapeless mess. Patterns were no use to her since she could not read, and she paid no heed to offers of help. It was her goods, and she whacked into it as she saw fit. Basting the queer garment, she glanced up at me and shook her head vigorously, a way she had of showing complete satisfaction.

"I'm going to keep my hide warm, Phibby," she said. Her work seemed to have shape for her.

Uncle Paschal came by to speak to the women. The men, he said, had all been too busy working to stop and talk to him. Mama, glancing a little uncertainly toward Kalline, made him welcome.

"What are you making, Kalline?" he queried.

Mama tensed, afraid Kalline would blurt out some coarse word for nightgown. It was not a word to use in mixed company anyway.

"A circus jacket," Kalline said without looking up.

Mama looked relieved and a little puzzled at Kalline's quickness.

The quickness was less satisfactory when the preacher came. Our minister at the time was Dr. R. T. Vann. Though his arms had been amputated many years before, he managed well for himself with his stumps of arms, so that his hosts had to give him very little help. After his food was served, he was more or less independent at the table and adept in many ways.

Dr. Vann arrived on Saturday afternoon. Kalline was introduced to him. Dr. Vann moved forward to offer his brave little stump of arm for the usual handshake. Kalline did not say a word. Her mouth dropped open. She squinted up one eye and started backing away. She stared and frowned at the stump of arm being offered her, and then she whirled around and darted out of sight. Later when chided for her discourtesy Kalline said, "I wa'n't a-going to take hold of no man's nubbins!"

Afterwards Kalline seemed to become interested in Sunday clothes. She pressed her black sateen dress, sewed additional scraps of lace on her bleached underskirt and started basting up a new underbody. It appeared the minister's visit had made her decide to attend church services.

It was another kind of service, I learned, that she had in

mind. As I passed through her room one day she called me over to her crackerbox trunk. "Phibby," she said, smoothing the new underbody and bleached underskirt and black sateen dress she wore on the road, "I got burying clothes. I want to be put away in bleaching next to my hide. And you tell them that, if you're the longest liver. If I ain't fixed up nice, I'll ha'nt the whole passel of you!" Without another word she closed her crackerbox and hurried out to the hen nests.

Mama admitted she stayed in a constant dread about what Kalline might blurt out before children and men. Papa said pay no attention to her logic. Kalline was just Kalline; she was funny and foolish and ignorant and sort of pitiful and a woman. But one morning her logic was overheard by the adults. She was revealing how nature came to girls, how mumps went down on boys.

Kalline's stay with us was over. She was told to look for another home. It was the end of summer now, and it had been understood from the start that she would have to find her another place before cold weather.

She wanted to stay on with us. Mama was firm.

Kalline cried as she went into the back room to pack her possessions. Her tears fell on the faded purple violets of her hat. I cried, too, as she empied her burying clothes into the flour sack and then set off up the road to look for her another home. The violets on that rusty black hat looked wilted in the sunshine.

Off and on Kalline kept coming back, and she was always taken in. During her last stay under our roof she became high-handed about eggs. The market basket became her project. For us it had always helped to provide the nice little extras of life. Mama had used her egg money for ribbons and lace, carpets and table damask, books and cologne. Once it had provided music for a song poem.

But Kalline added eggs to the market basket as an end in itself, just to see how many she could collect. Papa praised Kalline's thrift. He said "whoopee!" over her hoard of eggs. Then she tightened her hold on the market basket, stinting us in our table uses. We were welcome to all the water we could drink, she said, but she hid eggs from us. Her bossiness became unbearable, and another home was found for her.

It became clear the following spring that her trail of homes would have to end. She was getting too old to move around looking for places to stay, too old for the hard work she willfully set herself to do. Circumstances in the temporary homes changed too fast for her to count on any staying place. So neighbors made arrangements to take Kalline to the county home.

When plans were revealed to her she cried like a child. Standing in the middle of the floor, her face twisted and her gray hair hanging in wisps down her back, she poured out her lamentation without restraint or sense.

"I don't want to go to the poorhouse!" she cried, the tears rolling down the wrinkles in her face. "I rather stay in the corncrib! Or the stable! Or the henhouse! I don't want to go to the poorhouse!"

She was assured that it was a good place for her to stay, that she would be taken care of without having to work so hard.

"I ain't too old to work. I can maul cord wood and ditch and grub new ground," she said. "I can get out and find me places to stay. I can foot it. I can foot it all over Wake County!"

It was settled, the neighbors had to tell her. They were doing what was best for her.

"Yes, but folks I've worked for has always told me I could have a roof over my head as long as I lived and a coffin when I died," she kept saying over and over as though to make it so. "They promised to bury me among folks. I don't want to die in the poorhouse. I don't want to live there!"

When finally they managed to get Kalline on the road, her protests ceased. Numb and dazed she sat in the back seat of the vehicle bearing her away from Poole's Siding, a queer little woman in a Sunday hat trimmed with purple violets. I thought how she had trudged through heat and cold along many roads. She had footed it along her trail of homes. Now she was riding in style to the poorhouse.

Later Kalline came from the poorhouse to visit us. For the

first time she was company. She brought her clothes in a valise, a battered and lopsided one borrowed from one of her friends at the home, but no flour sack or crackerbox either. The same black hat she had worn away was on her head, but the bunch of violets had been moved in front.

Bouncing into the room, she stowed her valise against the wall and laid her hat and wrap on the bed, just like regular company.

At the table she took all the room she pleased. She seemed in the mood to scrouge a little, to choose the pick of the food.

"You have plenty to eat at the poorhouse?" Papa asked politely as Kalline buttered hot biscuits.

"It's not the poorhouse, Beel!" she informed him sharply. "It's the County Home." She glanced around to include the family. "I'll have to learn you country folks not to say poorhouse. It's the County Home."

Much we learned the next two days. She was called Miss Caroline, not Kalline. Country folks had been ignorant that way too. It was Miss Caroline-this and Miss Caroline-that at the County Home.

Bet and Dilcy and others at the home often took Miss Caroline with them to the city market where they watched country people selling produce from wagons and carts. Often they were greeted by old acquaintances from the country and were given apples and peaches and grapes. Sometimes the market folks gave them nickels with which to buy bladders of snuff.

Those at the home who could read kept the others posted on the almanac and folks's ailments. "You'd be surprised how many things is the matter with folks nowadays," Kalline told us. "Doctors cut you open and take out and put in a piece just like saying howdy." She went on about strange diseases and strange remedies that country folks could not be expected to know about.

We learned that the up-to-date way to light a house was not with lamps that had to be washed and filled with oil every day, but with electricity. "You just press a little thingajig on the wall," Kalline said, "and there's light as bright as day."

She knew about a room called the water closet, where every kind of business could be attended to. In the winter a hot box traption against the wall kept everybody warm without a single stove or fireplace in the house, without wood to be cut and toted in.

Getting to bed her first night, she stumbled around in the dark noisily. She wondered why country folks didn't break their necks. The roosters crowing for day roused her too early. The water accommodations were unhandy to her. After the first day she offered to wash dishes. For the most part she sat and watched others at work.

Then she started strolling around the yard looking into hen nests, slipping to the orchard to fill her pockets with apples, going to the pasture fence to watch the pigs and cows. After these ramblings she became restless.

Before her time was up, she wanted to be taken home. It seemed she had to get back to the bright lights, the waterworks, the city market. All the folks would be looking for Miss Caroline.

After she left we laughed a little among ourselves and said that Kalline had gone off to the poorhouse and got the big head!

20

Ah, Astolat

At twelve I was in a state of love. It had no suddenness about it, no clear-cut beginning. It was as real as mumps.

All the girls my age were in the same state. For awhile we dreamily imagined ourselves floating on the stream which had borne Ruth and Mary Howard and Alice and the Lily Maid, only there was no Boaz or George Moreland or Nicholas Longworth or Sir Lancelot to float along with us.

For it was our schoolteacher we were in love with, and we realized the hopelessness of it all. We had dreaded getting used to another man teacher. It had been hard to say goodbye to Mr. Adams when he resigned as head of the Academy. Never had there been so many unabashed tears among Academy girls and boys as when Mr. Adams led us in song, "God be with you till we meet again," and then walked out the door and across the schoolyard for the last time.

But Mr. Saunders endeared himself to us the first weeks of school. For all his youth, he impressed the old as well as young with his maturity. He wore dark suits and sober neckties and a stiff wide-brimmed black hat, as though to create the proper air of austerity before his adolescent girls and boys. Just out of college, he did not look many years past adolescence himself, though he tried hard to act like a seasoned professor. He was bashful. He often blushed. His face turned red to the roots of his sandy hair, and even his large ears which angled out from his head seemed at times to blush.

For all the fluency of his Latin translations, he did not talk in everyday English easily. While he helped the advanced class with Cicero's speeches, we daydreamed at our desks and composed speeches to him rather than to Cataline.

Our love was a mixture of hero-worship and dogged devotion, and we asked nothing of it except his presence and the privilege just to love on and on. Sometimes it was a hurting thing, not because it was hopeless and unsuitable, but because it would not last forever.

For Mr. Saunders had told us early in the year that he did not expect to teach again. The parting that loomed ahead saddened us. I began to memorize Mr. Saunders instead of lessons. "Oh, the times! Oh, the customs!" he read to his advanced class. I mused toward him across the desks some words derived from my reading, "Sometimes you seem like God, and sometimes you seem like my child." It was hard to love and lose in the springtime. It would have been easier to have mumps.

April came and with it the closing of school. That last night there were wand drills and duets, songs and pantomimes. In chorus we sang "In the Gloaming." To the final strains of music we filed out.

Mr. Saunders stood at the door to say goodbye to patrons and pupils. Mama, just ahead of me, paused to thank the teacher for his interest in her children. I was too bemused with pain of parting to express myself.

As I filed by, Mr. Saunders shook hands with me as with the rest. I managed to speak goodbye, but I was musing toward him the words of the song,

In the gloaming, oh my darling, think not bitterly of me,
Though I passed away in silence, left you lonely,
 set you free.

Mama called me to come on. I lingered in his presence a little longer, thinking

> For my heart was crushed with longing,
> What had been could never be—

The words did not fit the situation, but they expressed me.

I suffered afterwards. The morning after school closed, I listened to the whistle of the train that was taking Mr. Saunders away from Poole's Siding. It blasted the woods separating our land from the railroad, and the echoes fell with harsh finality on my ears. Our dog howled at the hurting vibrations, and I felt like howling with Madge. The train gathered speed to make the grade beyond the crossing. Then there was silence.

I looked up despairingly. There were no nine stars to count, in hope. The sky had never looked so out of reach.

Dazed by the sense of loss, I started purposelessly walking the rungs of a ladder that happened to be lying on the ground in the back yard. I stepped each rung, turned and walked the length of the ladder over and over. If it had been upright, I would have climbed enough rungs to reach the sky.

Mama called me away from the ladder. "Come fill the lamps with oil," she bade me, as though I might have been a foolish virgin.

We never saw Mr. Saunders again. Later that summer he sent me a copy of *Kenilworth*. I identified myself with Rebecca, another leaf on the stream that had borne Elaine and Ruth and Alice Roosevelt. Only Mr. Saunders and Robert Dudley did not float in rapport with us.

I made up my mind never to love a schoolteacher again.

The following fall Mr. Francis came to head our school. I was soon in love with him. Like Mr. Saunders he was young and only recently graduated from college. He boarded at Uncle Cana's. All the girls fell in love with the handsome teacher, and all of us became a little jealous of one another, especially of Ethel because she was the prettiest. Once after the music teacher finished my piano lesson, she had a heart-to-heart talk with me about Mr. Francis, and I found out she was jealous too.

Mr. Francis was not austere or bashful either. He did not blush. His ears angled out from his head as Mr. Saunders' did, but they did not turn red except from cold weather. His reddish brown eyes, which could look sharply enough at a culprit, were not without a merry glint. Aware of those brown eyes, we girls became vain over ruffles and laces and fancy combs.

It was a jolly year. It was fun to be in love with the school-teacher. Mr. Francis was not a book-hero, apart and awesome. He teased and joked and laughed just like Uncle Millard and Uncle Paschal.

The smallpox scare drew him still closer to Poole's Siding. Before he came to teach, Uncle Hezzie and Aunt Lillie had bought the Clayton hotel and had moved away from the neighborhood to run it. There they had been exposed by drummers to smallpox. Not aware of it at the time, Earl and Kitty had visited at Poole's Siding and thus exposed the school children to the dread disease. As soon as the danger was apparent, plans were made for compulsory vaccination.

Fearful stories were circulated about the dangers of this new treatment. Vaccination meant inserting smallpox germs, maybe from dead victims, into arms by means of needles. It meant swelling and inflammation and high fever and gangrene. Sometimes it meant amputation of arms.

Uncle Millard, who years ago had survived the horrors of smallpox and pesthouse in Raleigh, advised kinfolks to submit to vaccination. His own pock-marked face was a strong argument in favor of risking the new preventive. Uncle Hezzie advocated it too. Papa had allowed him to move out of the hotel into our old home, while he and his family waited to see if they were going to take smallpox. We thought of it now as pesthouse rather than parsonage. All who ventured in talking distance of the quarantined family from the Clayton hotel were advised to be vaccinated.

Olive and Darwin were not convinced. They collected field rocks and hid them in our front hall closet. From there they aimed to let the compulsory doctor have it, if he came to scratch smallpox scabs from dead men into their arms.

We were all soundly vaccinated, and sore arms and scabs

were the excitement of the neighborhood while school was suspended.

Only Mr. Francis did not have a sore arm. According to reports circulated around the neighborhood, he hid out in the woods every day in order to avoid the vaccinators. At night under cover of darkness he returned to his boardinghouse. Neighbors chuckled over it, liking the teacher all the more for his timidity.

There were no chuckles as school closing drew near. Mr. Francis was about to leave not to return. I was miserable over the parting at hand. I ached. I felt chilly and feverish and nauseated. It turned out I had something to ache over. For after school closed I had a serious attack of malaria. My family thought I was going to die. Aunt Edie took my white lawn dress and Sunday underskirts to her house where they were freshly starched and ironed to bury me in. I often pictured Aunt Edie in her red bonnet taking the white shroud to the little corpse everybody thought I would soon be. Amid the white order of the occasion so vividly envisioned, the red bonnet was an odd comfort. When I wore the clothes afterwards, I felt no vanity over laces and ruffles.

The following fall Miss Nina Brown, a lovely young woman with an enchanting voice, came to head our school. Miss Euzelia Lassiter taught me music that year. Attractive blonde and brunette respectively, they fascinated us. Always immaculate even after a day of chalk dust and wood smoke, Miss Brown wore crisp white linen shirtwaists and neat gray skirts, and always she smelled of violets. The sweetness of spring violets became her essential essence for us.

I decided I wanted to be a teacher just like Miss Brown.

But there was a lost, unsure interval when I wanted only to hold on to Astolat. A butterfly over the sage bush one morning vaguely symbolized it all.

I looked in every direction before starting after the butterfly.

Nobody was in sight. Mama had left the clothesline and was ironing the parlor curtains on the back porch. Rachel Floyd was still busy putting down the new carpet in the parlor. Pearl was helping her. Papa and the boys were at the lower field.

I knew everybody thought I was getting too old to chase butterflies, too old to play at the claybank, too old to have paper dolls. For months now I had played paper dolls in secret, feeling a little ashamed and disloyal, too, at having to hide Mary Howard and George Moreland and Rebecca and Robert Dudley and Elaine from the world. I was ashamed now that I wanted to catch the butterfly and bite off its head. A gorgeous maroon with intricate designs on its wings, it had impelled me to the chase from the minute it flitted above the sage bush. It was as though it were the last butterfly.

So I had dropped my pail, only half filled with the young sage leaves I had been told to pick, and reached out my hand for the butterfly.

But this Saturday morning I could not seem to find any delight in the chase. If I caught the butterfly and bit off its head, I kept telling myself, I would have a dress the color and pattern of its wings. In this assurance, confirmed by Aunt Cherry, I had caught many a butterfly during childhood and had marveled at the winged beauty with which I would be clothed. Only, I had always let the butterfly go, unable in the end to test my faith or to still the graceful wings, even for the most beauteous dress in the world.

It had never been just dread of the physical act itself. Unflinchingly I had tasted mud pies and bitter weeds. In fence jambs where, as Aunt Add, I had prepared meals for Uncle Cana, I had eaten sheep grass and pepperweed and sour sumac berries. I had tasted pussley before feeding it to the pigs. I had chewed bitter rabbit tobacco with the boys. So I could have bitten off a butterfly's head.

Or could I have? I asked myself. Wasn't this a chance today, a last chance maybe, to find out? I might never know why Aunt Edie wore red aprons, but I could find out if biting off a butterfly's head had anything to do with red dresses. The impulse was to go back in time, to act out a childhood fancy as though that could keep us all as we had been, securely beyond change.

Change had been edging closer. I had felt it coming. The new carpet for the parlor made me know its nearness.

The wish for pretty dresses was still real, even if the impulse to act out a childhood fancy was forced. Always I had craved bright colors. There had been only pastels and white and brown, with just one green flannel, in my wardrobe.

Red had been my craving. I had gathered red rose petals to color the girls' dresses in my Reader. I had made little necklaces and bracelets of red honeysuckle. I had watched fires leap against the soot of chimney backs and imagined myself playing hopscotch in a flame dress.

Even as I seized the butterfly now, I knew it would make no difference if I bit off its head or not. It would mean just one more butterfly dead and a bad taste in my mouth.

I opened my hand to seize the butterfly and raise it to my lips. It flew out of my fingers. Wobbly in its flight at first, it soon rose above my head. I stood watching it circle out of reach. It was a lonely dot of red against the big blue sky.

I felt lonely. So much was flying away on those beautiful wings.

Turning, I moved quickly down the hill at the back of the house. Screened by the orchard, I cut across the plum thicket and was soon hidden by the incline that rose from the branch woods. I ran down the wooded slope to the little branch that meandered all the way to our Niagara Falls. Moving along the edge of the stream, I came to the claybank. The pounds of butter I had left to harden among the ferns were broken and scattered now. I seized handfuls of fresh clay, kneaded them together, shaped them into pound molds and imprinted a pine cone on the smooth round tops similar to the wheat sheaf on Mama's butter.

When I had molded my last pound of butter, I looked down at my handiwork. It was just foolish lumps of clay.

I bent one of the pine saplings which had been my steeds for the ride to Astolat. It was nothing but a scrub pine. And Astolat—oh, where was Astolat?

I followed the branch to Niagara Falls. There the water tumbled over big rocks before leveling off to become the little branch again. Great boulders jutted out of the hillsides above the fern-bordered banks and made cool little caves to play in. But it was not Niagara Falls today. And I did not care about playing in little caves.

They would be uneasy about me at the house. I hurried up the hill.

Back at the sage bush, I realized nobody had missed me. They were all too busy about the parlor.

When I had filled my pail with sage, I spread the leaves on the pantry roof to dry. They would be the sausage seasoning next winter and the sage tea for fevers. Only, Rachel Floyd would not be under our roof to eat sausage with us. Or to be doctored for fevers. I suddenly boo-hooed. And it was for my paper dolls and clay butter and Niagara Falls and Astolat. It was for my big sister who was about to get married.

· 21 ·

Sacrament

RACHEL FLOYD was going to be married on Thursday. She was going to leave us for good.

Leave-takings of any kind upset me. Cousin Will and Kalline might wear out their welcome with others, but I was always sorry to see them go. It hurt to say goodbye even to the peddler or Native Herb man. Once I had cried myself sick when a ragged tramp trudged off down the road alone. It might not seem like goodbye for Rachel Floyd to move just across Little Creek from us, but it would mean telling her good evening and good morning, just like howdying Miss Emily. It meant change. Already I could see vacant chairs all over the house.

Besides, Rachel Floyd was leaving me an unhappy place to fill. If only I could hold on to where I was in time, I thought, or else just skip a lot of years and be an old woman. For now I was going to have to sit in the parlor when boy company came to see Pearl, I was going to have to play talk-music or else just mope and watch the clock for bedtime.

It was Papa's rule for his girls not to entertain boy company alone. He did not think much of such company anyway. Sometimes he blustered through the rooms, knocking over chairs and slamming doors. Sometimes he moped and watched the clock. Once I saw him move the minute hand up to ten o'clock. Ten was bedtime for all boy company. Papa began to drop his shoes with a heavy thud at nine-thirty, and if the boys did not take the hint and leave on the dot he called out, "Bedtime!" Even in the darkness of my bedroom it made me sick to hear "bedtime!" blasted out at company. Now I was going to have to face it in the lighted parlor.

I was hurt and mad; mad at Rachel Floyd for bringing all this to pass, at Mama for buying a new carpet for the wedding, at Pearl for looking so pleased about it all, and most of all at Will for asking Papa to let him marry his daughter. The asking had not been easy. Papa had dodged Will every time he had tried to ask, until that final night when he had been cornered in the barnlot and could not escape. Papa had come to the house with a chill. It was as though he was the one that had had to do the asking.

I had a sense of chill as the hour for the wedding drew near. Marriages did not seem like happy occasions to me. All I knew about had something scary or queer or sad connected with them. Ava had cried her eyes out when she played the wedding march for her big sister.

There had been the queerness just after Mr. and Mrs. Spillars had finished saying, "I will." To break the ice a neighbor woman had placed two chairs in the middle of the floor and had bidden the couple to sit down. This had only seemed to freeze a roomful of people, until somebody rushed in and said Mr. Spillars' horse was cutting up and would he attend to her? "I will," he said and dashed out to stop the pawing outside. Weddings were horses' hooves for awhile.

The deep vibration of Mr. Stringfield's voice as he slowly intoned, "Della Poole, Bonnie Daughtry" below the white wedding bell over the altar had been like echoes from the Lambs's book of life in the Bible, calling the bridal couple to heaven, but ready also to call others to the Bad Place. Weddings were reminders of death and Judgment Day.

They were the old clock on the stairs chiming forever-never, never-forever when brides came forth on their wedding night, clothed all in white like a corpse under their wedding veils.

I was beginning to feel sick, more than hurt or mad. My sickness was like Solomon's in the Sunday school lesson. I did not understand what it was to be stayed with flagons and comforted with apples, but like Solomon I sure was sick of love.

I knew I was going to throw up. I hurried to the wardrobe room.

Mama found me there. She looked at me sharply, then felt of my cold hands. I saw her glance toward the wardrobe.

It happened to be Papa's time as deacon of the church to furnish the elements for sacrament. On first Sundays when communion services were to be observed, Mama always prepared unleavened bread to accompany the homemade wine, sacred to the church observance.

Mama opened the wardrobe door and took out the sacrament wine. She carefully measured out a little of it into a glass on the washstand. I took it. It warmed me.

Later when I started whispering around among the cousins, Mama told me to hush. I had not named flagons or apples at all, but Mama looked at me as if I had.

A new idea was added to horses' hooves and Ava's tears and white bells and shrouds. Weddings were sacrament.

So Rachel Floyd and Will stood out in the parlor together and said their vows. Afterwards they went home across the creek. Some of the wedding guests beat them there and had the house lighted for the bride. They talked awhile and inspected the new rather empty little house. Finally Will called out, "Bedtime!"

The girls put the bride to bed before they left. In her pretty new nightgown Rachel Floyd knelt at the side of the bed. Lucy Poole tipped into the hall and with a loud masculine har-umph approached the bride's door. With a bound Floyd sprang from her knees and jumped into bed, turning her back modestly toward the door. Will put a stop to the pranks and sent the merrymakers home.

The following Sunday the newlyweds came to visit us. We said good evening to them. Rachel Floyd moved through the rooms as though to refresh her memory of home. She walked on the new carpet. "I'm happy as a queen," she murmured.

I was not that happy. I said so in a poem. "Our home is filled with vacant chairs," it began, "My heart is bowed with heavy cares."

Mama thought it was good. She asked Papa about money to send off the song poem, by way of encouraging the child in case she might sometimes write hymns. But Papa said the child would outgrow poetry, like knee-ache.

So my song poem was not sent to Chicago to be set to music this time. Since the new carpet had taken all the Native Herb money, we needed the two dollars more than we did Mr. Jacobsen's music.

· 22 ·

Halley's Comet and Drama

I GREW up, but did not outgrow poetry for awhile. Even while preparing myself to be a teacher like Miss Brown, I still felt inspired to write poems. At Meredith College, where Latin, English and science courses took all my time, I managed to spend some minutes every night after light bell on my rhymes.

In the darkness of my room, after retiring, I sat up in bed and put words on paper as they came to me. Though the lines were crisscrossed and phrases overlapped, I was able to translate them next morning into couplets and stanzas to be continued after bedtime.

Halley's Comet checked the poetical inspiration.

At this time Halley's Comet was exciting fear and dread among people everywhere. There were those who believed the end of the world was at hand. Preachers used its imminence to conduct crusades. Quacks profited by sales of scare pamphlets. There were some suicides, prompted by the tensions built up over the dire possibilities of the earth's contact with the tail of the comet.

The calm reassurances of our science teacher, Professor Boomhour, percolated through the student body during the daytime. But at night we gave way to fear of the chaos that prognosticators were predicting. Girls from other buildings joined us on top of Old East to watch the comet and to speculate on its electric potentials, on its dire impact upon the earth. Nightly we watched for encompassing darkness. On top of East Building we became Paul Reveres to sound the alarm if the world should ignite from contact with the comet's tail.

After viewing the heavens until late one night, I came down from the roof feeling the urge to write poetry. Stars and sky receded, though, and my thoughts turned in dread to tomorrow's schedule. The everyday suddenly encompassed me. The rising bell, ringing early each morning, was a signal of doom to students unprepared for the day's activities. I had to express in rhyme the way I felt about it.

So I carefully tucked dresses, including my suzene silk from last spring's high school commencement, around the electric cord and light fixtures. Then I turned on the current. I sat below the narrow jet of light, too dim and restricted to disturb my roommate or to alert any vigilant hall proctor outside, and wrote an ode to the rising bell.

Everything remained quiet as I composed the first lines. There was no proctor's tap on my door to warn me of student government rules about the light bell. I wrote, "Oh, bell, that pealest forth discordant sound—"

Then all at once the jet of light flashed out. A thick darkness pressed down on me. There was no reflection through the transom of the dim night light outside. It seemed the whole world was completely blotted out.

At first I thought Halley's Comet had hit the earth and chaos was at hand. But even in that instant of awful fear an instinct warned me to be quiet and let some other Paul Revere sound the alarm. For one thing I was aware of the smell of scorched goods, and it seemed to come from over my head.

Not knowing much about the properties of electricity, I realized I might have caused the darkness by too much protective covering over the light bulb.

Quietly I investigated. The light switch over my head had melted. The fixtures were sizzling hot. My skirts were burned. The scorched odor and the slit under my probing finger confirmed the damage. The suzene silk could never be worn again. How was I going to explain about that scorched dress, the first silk there had been in our family, the silk Mama and Rachel Floyd had so carefully made for my Cary High School commencement?

There was another dread more immediate. What if some girl in Old East, trying to turn on a light in the middle of the night, should give the alarm we had all been waiting for? Should I keep silence, or admit the encompassing darkness was caused by poetry instead of Halley's Comet?

How could I know that the college president and his family who lived downstairs would not notify the police? There was such a sense of complete blackout over the city that my responsibility might extend beyond Meredith, I feared.

There was no sound from downstairs. My roommate slept peacefully on. No hall proctors stirred.

I could not sleep. It seemed right to sit up with the havoc I had caused, to keep watch just in case Halley's Comet had something to do with the light failure after all.

Sometime before day as I crouched in the darkness, I completed the ode to the rising bell. The lines were up and down, the words jumbled together in the light of morning. But I could read the poem. It began: "Oh, bell that pealeth forth discordant sound, When thou, oh fateful hour, approachest nigh—" Those who read it later in *Oak Leaves*, the college annual, could not know how fateful next morning's rising bell really seemed in prospect.

The bell rang as usual. There had been some fuse damage, the girls in Old East learned, but it had been repaired. Lights were on again. I kept silence. Later when I became an officer of the Student Government Association, I was very patient and understanding when freshmen blew fuses.

At Meredith, writing continued to interest me. But I lost my taste for poetry. Instead, I tried my hand with short stories, some of which were used in college publications. "Six Christmas Hats," "Miss Jeannie, the Boys and Bud" were published in *The Acorn*. "Cupid on Toast" was used in *Oak Leaves*.

After college I did some preliminary teaching in Duplin and Catawba counties and then came to Seaboard High School to teach English and dramatics. For awhile I taught both winter and summer; in winter at Seaboard and in summer at Washington Collegiate Institute, where students sought certificate credit to teach in Beaufort County schools.

There were alternate summers of study at Chapel Hill, so that I had only brief intervals at home during vacation months. I became interested in what was being called at Chapel Hill the new folk-play movement, and as soon as a course in folk playwriting was offered at the university, I took it. After classes under scholarly Dr. Chase and Dr. Greenlaw, we teachers were unprepared for the entrance of the little man of boundless enthusiasms that the catalogue called Frederick H. Koch. On our first day in his class he sat on the table and dangled his feet and talked with eloquence and zest about the unwritten folk drama of America. Staid principals, sedate classroom teachers and experienced supervisors all fell under the spell of "Proff." His class was like an oasis in our quest for credits and pedagogy.

Proff opened our eyes to the dramatis personae we had known all our lives, to the drama along little roads. He did not teach techniques or facts or book lore. The little man in the Norfolk tweeds inspired, evangelized. He dispensed folk-drama propaganda that echoed around the land in Thomas Wolfe and Paul Green. Never a class went out from him without handfuls of pamphlets, never a letter without its tracts.

He might well have been called evangel. For he tried to convert a region. At a state drama festival Barrett Clark once said in graceful compliment that in heaven Proff Koch would hand out folk-drama propaganda among the angels.

My interest at the time was in relating my playwriting course to classroom English, in inducing my Seaboard students to write folk drama in place of routine compositions. Aldie Kinin wrote "Old Lishe," based on a legend of her native Beaufort County. We took this one-act folk comedy from Seaboard to the drama festival at Chapel Hill, where it had a realistic production. The script called for a featherbed, and our leading man secured the plumpest one in his mother's house.

At the time indicated in the stage directions, the featherbed was opened, and feathers floated over Chapel Hill for days.

Next we produced William Long's "Walnut Boards," which won an award for us at the state drama festival at Chapel Hill. After these successes, every student in high school began trying to write plays, and we organized the Seaboard Players to produce them.

While other teachers were being squired around, I spent my nights in rehearsals and revisions of high school plays. My life was lessons and drama. Willie, our dormitory cook, chided me for my dedication to teaching. "How come you don't take company, too, Miss Kelly?" she demanded. "How come you don't court some like the other teachers is doing?" She listed certain credentials of town bachelors. "There's Mister Ben Stancell that's got a store, Mister Elmo Crocker that works in the bank, Mister Hub-but Harris that has a cotton gin—"

I interrupted the credentials to return to drama. At this time we were producing Shakespeare along with homemade folk plays. It did not seem venturesome to us to stage "Taming of the Shrew," "Merchant of Venice," "Hamlet" and "Macbeth." The students learned their lines, pronounced final consonants, used broad A's and spoke with conviction. From a costumer in Philadelphia we ordered costumes. There was no lack of authentic and fine array.

On one occasion I took a whole class up to Norfolk to see Robert Mantell and Genevieve Hamper in Shakespearean roles. The students were entranced by the possibilities of Portia and Brutus and Macbeth and MacDuff and Banquo's ghost. Afterwards one of the students upset the quiet halls of the Monticello Hotel where we were staying overnight. Rounding a corner of one corridor we met a man in a voluminous white shirt which looked ghostly enough in the dim light to be Banquo's other-world outfit. Selma Bradley screamed, and for an instant Banquo's ghost was very present in the Monticello.

We took our productions to four colleges in North Carolina and had good notices in newspapers. My characters never let me down, though they sometimes surprised me. Once at a county fair in Woodland, where we competed with merry-go-rounds and horse racing, Walter and Clarence decided to improve the production by ad-libbing a bit. As servants of Petruchio, they introduced some slapstick dialogue and good ole South'n clog, prolonging their scene and spicing it up, in spite of my frantic whispers from the wings to stop. Weren't they getting laughs, they defended themselves, weren't they getting more laughs than all the other characters put together?

This mingling of minstrel show and classic comedy set a record even for the Seaboard Players. The merging of the folk and classic theme was incidental to another record. Miss Kelly at long last began to take company. The company was Herbert Harris.

· 23 ·

Trunk Packed and Waiting

I SPENT my vacation at home in the summer of 1920. Out
of a clear sky one day Mama took me to her trunk and lifted
the lid.

In the top tray there was a neat collection of underclothes,
exactly pressed and folded. There were ruffled underskirts,
carefully finished in Mama's pretty stitches. There was a new
pair of stockings. At one end were crisp muslin sheets. Near
them were bath towels that had never been used and a cake of
unscented soap. Everything was white, except one black dress
with white ruching at the neck.

As the items were identified, I became uneasy. I felt like a
little girl here with Mama, not a woman to be told things to.
Even before Mama made it definite, I sensed the meaning of
the moment.

"Everything's here that will be needed," she said with an
incredible serenity. It was as though she were packed for a
trip.

As indeed she was. And so I had to tell them where to find
Mama's things the morning they were needed. They were all
there, neat and sweetly starched and waiting.

Mama seemed better that Saturday morning. She had been

more like herself all week, more interested in the tidiness of living. The day before Dr. Hocutt had made his regular call and was pleased with her condition.

It had been an anxious summer. For several months we had watched Mama fail. There had been several heart attacks. But always she improved rapidly and insisted that all of us go on with schedules we were involved in at the time.

Through anxieties and tensions during World War I, Mama had remained outwardly calm. Elwood had been with the Atlantic Fleet overseas. Darwin had been stationed at Camp Jackson. As soon as William Olive was twenty-one, he had been drafted into service and taken overseas "somewhere in France." Mama bore up under the stress and strain. She attended church services the day William Olive left and sang alto as usual. But that night she had a heart attack. The attacks recurred. This last year, with all the boys at home from the war, she was content. But she was leaving home, and she knew it.

We thought she would be with us awhile. Yet I had been startled by the sureness of one of her statements. When I mentioned that Elwood would be bringing his new bride to see her Sunday, a brand-new daughter-in-law, she had said as matter-of-factly as though predicting weather, "I'll never see her."

Throughout that Friday Mama had been free from pain. She had been casual, even chatty. Then on Saturday she ate the breakfast I took her, managing it well enough without help. I was a little puzzled at the way she stared. Not once while I was waiting for the tray did she take her eyes off me. She was oddly silent.

She had nothing to say to Aunt Ella who crossed the bottom early to find out how she was feeling.

Dr. Hocutt came at the usual time that morning. He stood in the yard talking to the men who were getting ready to go to work.

Mama suddenly asked me if the doctor planned to come back today.

"He's in the yard now," I said reassuringly. All at once I was oppressed by the sense of a strange presence.

"He's not in here."

They were Mama's last words. Casual, factual, chatty as mine had been to her. Mama died before the doctor could get to her room.

I knew afterwards that even in death Mama had somehow managed to go through the gesture of eating breakfast, had for our sakes kept up the sweet routines of living to the last. I knew I had been a little girl to her again.

It was suddenly a strange world. Neighbors and relatives began to come in. I saw them all through a haze of unreality. I knew they were kind. But I was too numbed by the strangeness of a world without Mama in it to feel even gratitude.

They saw to the composing of the tired body. I told them where to find Mama's things.

Neighbor women dressed her in a black shroud with white ruching at the neck.

She looked as nice as when she had dressed up to have her picture made at the tobacco barn that day.

PART TWO

· 24 ·

Something Borrowed, Something Blue

HERBERT AND I were married at Mt. Moriah Church the last of May, 1926.

Papa, who had married Miss Myrtle Wilder a year after Mama's death, was in mellower mood than when his other daughters were married. Still, he had cold chills now as then. Herbert had appeared at our house three weeks after school closed and announced he had so arranged his business that he could be away for a few days, and it was his wish that we get married right away. There would be a quiet wedding and a brief honeymoon wherever I wanted to go, he had said, as brisk and businesslike as though settling with a customer at the Bradley and Harris cotton gin. The casual briskness had been temporary. It had been a tremendous moment.

It had made a commotion in the household when I announced our decision to get married at noon the next day. The family hastily rallied and organized the wedding. Miss Myrtle, expecting a child in October, was feeling far from well, but like a real mother she joined with the others to get me ready.

We were awake most of the night packing my trunk that had made so many trips up and down the railroad and that was now going to be checked for the last time.

Next morning Olive took us to Raleigh to complete arrangements. At Herbert's request he picked out the wedding ring, saw to the business details. Those who helped me select my wedding dress saw to it that I had something old and something new, something borrowed and something blue in my outfit.

While we were gone to town, Mrs. Hall, our pastor's wife, got the church in order and arranged flowers at the altar.

As I stood before the altar at noon, I was vaguely aware of much clearing of throats among the kin, of sniffling as though somebody had a bad cold.

"—until death do you part?" Mr. Hall was asking now.

I hesitated for one instant. In the solemn joy of the moment I rebelled at the limitation set by the phrase, at the idea that loving and honoring and cherishing were not infinite and limitless. Forever should have been in the phrase.

"I do," I said without emphasis.

When we left the altar I saw tears in Miss Myrtle's eyes. The others were being very bright and chatty.

We had settled on a brief trip to Washington and New York. What was place?

Place for Rachel Floyd's children, who heard us mention going to New York, was seeing the Statue of Liberty and Grant's tomb and subways and skyscrapers. They knew from their schoolbooks what we ought to see.

Carey slipped out from the rest and in adolescent zeal wrote "Just Married" all over the family car in which Olive and Mary Coats were to take us to the train in Raleigh.

When I looked back from the station door, I saw the huge white letters chalked on the back and sides of the car. Olive and Mary would be riding under that label down the Poole's Siding road, past the church, past Aunt Edie's house.

Already Poole's Siding was receding, becoming remote. Now I was thinking with odd wistfulness that I would never know why Aunt Edie wore red bonnets.

I glanced at the businessman standing by me. He was remote too. For all his handsome wedding suit he did not look like a bridegroom. He looked Bradley and Harris. He looked cotton gin and land and timber. And he looked a little lost.

In that instant I moved close to him. We walked arm in arm to board the train, shamelessly "Just Married" before the world.

We did not see New York. In Washington we stayed first at the Wardman Park Hotel and then transferred to a more convenient place uptown. At the start we were conscientious about points of interest we were supposed to see. We went through the Capitol, the halls of Congress and other government buildings. We stood before the great memorial to Lincoln. We took some of the guided tours around the city and out to Mount Vernon. But Herbert decided we could see the zoo and the art galleries and the site of Ford's Theater where Lincoln was shot and the museums another time. I realized he was beginning to be a little homesick.

He started searching the newsstands for copies of the *Raleigh News and Observer*.

I mentioned New York and the Statue of Liberty and Grant's tomb and skyscrapers. Herbert collected travel folders at the newsstands, some of which had information about skyscrapers and the Statue of Liberty. But it was soon clear that we were as far north as we were going.

The afternoon train which was bringing us back from our honeymoon neared Seaboard. I began to dread arrival. Would a crowd be gathered around the station, would merchants be staring from doors and windows, would a self-appointed welcoming committee be on hand? The chief recreation of the town at that time was meeting the afternoon passenger train.

We were not met. Nobody knew we were arriving, of course. Or did people know, and were they watching us from inside buildings today? The town where I had felt at home for nine years suddenly looked strange and unreal as I got off the train. I saw it with new eyes.

We were not met, but there was a welcoming committee of a bizarre sort. Herbert recognized a group of colored sharecroppers from the Harris farm, and he stopped to speak to them. He patted the mules that were hitched to farm wagons beyond the railroad tracks. The mules seemed fatuously affectionate, rubbing noses and stretching necks over each other as though for reassurance. They were acting more like honeymooners than we were, I thought.

For Herbert was so preoccupied with the group and the wagon load of farm supplies that he forgot me and the luggage. It was as though back in Seaboard he had momentarily forgotten he was married.

He was reminded. I overheard one of the sharecroppers say in an undertone to him, "Is it so you-all is married together, Mr. Hub-but?" Whereupon Herbert collected me and the luggage and took us along a side street to our quarters.

Since I had already signed a contract to teach another year, we were staying in the teacherage. As we drew near, the familiar white building looked solid and welcoming. The rooms were empty, the halls echoed, the air inside was stale. But we soon adjusted to the empty spaces of the big house and were at home.

Our apartment on the east side was cool and comfortable, though inconveniently detached from the rest of our living quarters. The dining room was a long walk from the kitchen. The big wood range, when heated to cooking capacity, made any eating nooks in the kitchen impossible during the summer months.

There was no water system in the teacherage. The pitcher pump was opposite the dining room and quite a few steps from the kitchen. The supply of wood was some distance away. The pantry was a good walk down the back porch.

So we had to adjust to spacious living.

I felt challenged by the distances involved in the adjustment. They brought to mind the wonderful meals that Grandmother and Aunt Addie and Aunt Emmie used to walk up from different quarters of the old Calvin Poole place in Wake County. It was in me to do as well here, I resolved, on Northampton soil.

Northampton was home now. Seaboard was my home

town. I wondered what its essential composition was, what the composition of life here would be for Herbert and me, how its savor would be related to everyday living.

It was little surprises for one thing, I soon learned. Herbert had a way of making drama out of very simple situations. Under his impact the nothings of everyday were climactic, and consequences were denouements. One July morning two months after our marriage he came home looking so solemn and bothered that I was uneasy. It was a good while before lunch time, and I knew Herbert was not in the habit of taking mid-morning breaks like this. Always he was busy on the farm or with fertilizer sales or gin accounts, so that his summer was as crowded with activity as his ginning season.

I waited, searching his face. Already I was learning not to guess his little surprises and thus spoil his effects.

"How about riding over to Gay Street with me?" he said. "Right away. I'm in a hurry."

Gay Street, I reflected, was where the Bradleys lived, the Bullocks, the Lem Harrises, the Kees, the Maddreys. Had something happened to any of them? But I noticed that Herbert's solemnity was crinkling a little now, that he was beginning to look important rather than bothered.

"Well," I said. The response was just tinged with question, for I was not going to let my curiosity queer whatever little drama Herbert was setting the stage for. "I'm ready."

We passed the brick residence of the Russell Harrises and turned into Gay Street. It was so called from a family of Gays who had once lived at the end of the street. It was an unpatterned drive where pines and maples and dogwoods mingled their shade with apple and pear and pecan trees. An informal and comfortable kind of street, it had gardens flourishing at the side or back of well-built homes, with corn patches tasseling on some of the vacant lots, with a cow grazing contentedly on a grassy slope alongside the big brick house where Bettie and Lem Harris lived.

Herbert was driving very slowly toward the end of the street now. I looked searchingly toward the Bullock house for a reassuring glimpse of some member of the family, five of whom I had taught. Mrs. Bullock, invalided with arthritis, was beloved by the whole town. I hoped fervently that nothing had happened to her, that Herbert was not withholding some bad news. A glance at his face assured me the surprise was elsewhere.

"You're looking the wrong way." Herbert spoke a little impatiently, as though he expected me to be seeing what he saw. He stopped the car. "This is the side to look at."

I glanced quickly at him and then focussed my eyes on the slope he was gazing at. The land rose gently from the street and leveled off into a lovely vacant lot.

"A thousand dollars is right steep to pay for a building lot in a town the size of Seaboard," he said.

"That lot?" I queried, still gazing at the slope before which he was parked.

"And what's there? Just dirt. No gold in it! Just crab grass and a few orchard trees. A thousand dollars for that?"

"It's beautiful." I was seeing the slope with new eyes. It was a building lot, a home site. Not ours, since Herbert said the price was too steep, but a matchless place for a white house and green lawn and orchard nooks for children's play. If only the buyers, whoever they were, might see it so!

"I hope the right people buy it," I mused.

"What's beautiful about it?" Herbert challenged.

"The grassy slope, the peach trees, the little apple orchard—" Just then I noticed a butterfly flitting above the ripening peaches.

"It will wash. Rains will make gullies up and down that slope!" he said.

"Children would love that. They could baptize their dolls in gullies. Or wade in them. Or make clay butter like I used to." I was watching the progress of the butterfly. "Or bite off butterflies' heads, so they could have yellow and red dresses—" Impulsively I explained the childhood fancy about butterfly wings, pointing out the gorgeous yellow creature above the peach tree.

Herbert did not see the butterfly. He was gazing at the

land with singular concentration. "A thousand dollars!" he said. "Why, it's just dirt. No gold in it."

"But if it's a home site—" It was, all right. The place just asked to be lived on. I took my eyes from the home site where I had envisioned a white house with children chasing butterflies around it and looked at the dirt that had no gold in it. "If only the right people buy it!" I added.

"It's bought," Herbert said.

I perceived his little drama, knew the truth. I felt I should be homed on any dirt with Herbert, but it was wonderfully satisfying to realize that we both knew our home site when we saw it. Herbert had managed his denouement deftly. "It's just as well," I sighed. "Otherwise I'd be hankering after it myself."

"Just suppose the right people didn't buy it."

"They would, though."

"Make a guess who."

I named two or three.

"Where would they get a thousand dollars from?" Herbert's voice, a little boasting, quickly became calculating. "I jewed Bradley down from his first price. A thousand dollars was my top offer, take or leave it. I made him throw in an acre at the back for a garden."

"Herbert, do you mean—?" I knew. Even so, I caught my breath. It was no act. "Is it our home site?"

"It is. I had an option on it when we were married. I wasn't going to bring you here without a building lot in prospect. Bradley said he wouldn't sell this piece of ground to anybody else but me, regardless of price. Well, I've bought it. The papers are fixed up, and here's where we'll build."

I was silent in prayerful exultation a minute. In mood I was like Peter who impulsively appropriated a home site on the high mountain a long time ago and wanted to build there three tabernacles. I was thinking of a place of abode, too, for myself and Herbert and our children who would chase butterflies under the peach trees and deck the halls with holly and pass on the savor of life.

"Our home site." I kept trying to realize it. Then briskly I added, "Let's walk on it."

We walked on our earth. Herbert was preoccupied with boundary lines, with the iron stakes he had already driven deep into the ground to define the limits of Harris property. I just walked.

Ashes and Light

I WAS aroused early that spring morning by loud talking somewhere around the teacherage. School had just closed, my last year of teaching. The teachers and matron had gone, and Herbert and I were moving into our new home as soon as we could finish it.

My first drowsy thought, after becoming aware of the confusion of voices, was that a picnic was being organized and we were about to be left behind. In my state of half-sleep I could not seem to plan what clothes to wear to Jordan's Mill or what food to take along for the picnic.

Then I heard shouts of, "Fire! Fire!"

Herbert and I dashed into the hall. Before we were told, we knew one of the gin buildings was on fire. Through the door and windows we saw the blaze lighting the sky. The darkness of predawn had become a terrible daylight just across the road from the teacherage.

With incredible speed Herbert dressed and rushed toward the burning building. I followed quickly.

There was no volunteer fire department then, no fire-fighting equipment in Seaboard except water from pitcher pumps. But the town assembled and helped with such resources as there were. Neighbors hurriedly brought buckets and tubs of water in an effort to keep the fire from spreading. Mr. Bob Crocker kept dipping his derby hat into a ditch and throwing ditchwater upon the blaze.

Heroic measures were used to save some of the machinery, but the fire had already progressed too far when it was discovered. Farmers, rising early to get their work underway, had first given the alarm. Word had spread from house to house, and the town gathered. Some of the people were only partially dressed. Their faces looked tense and white in the glare.

Smoke rose like an angry cloud. Great sheets of flame shot up toward the sky. Blazing rafters fell. The roof of the gin crashed in. Herbert and Mr. Bradley were everywhere, fighting the fire themselves and directing the efforts of others. Highlighted by the reddish glare, these two partners were heroic figures. They looked immense and dedicated.

Efforts were directed toward saving the other buildings close to the one on fire. Water was dashed on the roof and facings to temper the awful heat and to keep live sparks from igniting exposed wood. Sam Vassar, who some years before had lost a leg while working at the gin, hopped around, trying to help. Walmus, another faithful colored hand, pumped water for the fire-fighters. Neighbors brought tubs and barrels of water from their own homes. Mr. Bob Crocker kept bringing ditchwater in his derby. The doctor came, the minister.

The spirit of the little town was revealed in that fire. All families were one family and all business partners, one partnership. They rallied to Bradley and Harris. The fire also revealed purpose beyond business dividends motivating the man I had married. Herbert literally risked his life that day for his customers as well as for the partnership. What would the farmers do without Bradley and Harris? Where would they get their cotton ginned?

I caught something of the spirit. Suddenly I dashed into the ell of the burning building where a few cotton-seed bags were stored. With a challenging wave I motioned on-lookers to follow me. We had to save the cotton seed!

Cotton seed was a minor item in the loss suffered that early morning. It had a little more value than last year's calendar that is proverbially snatched out of burning buildings. I was extricated safely from the foolish dash into the ell, though the cotton seed was lost.

Day came. People went home. The wind blew through Mr. Bob Crocker's gray hair as he carried his wet derby hat at his side.

A few of us lingered around the ashes. They were not ashes altogether. They were reminders that neighbors had been there. For the other gin building stood safe and sound to validate triumphant neighborliness. There were reminders, too, that the cotton gin was more than machinery for Herbert. It was a calling. It was teaching and preaching and writing books. It was creating, and Herbert saw that it was good.

There were further revelations of the businessman.

Later that spring Herbert and I went to Norfolk to buy furniture for our new home. It was a red brick rather than the white frame house I had envisioned for our home site. Brick was less expensive in the long run, Herbert had decided, since it would not require continuous painting. I sensed he just wanted us to live in a brick house, since neither of us ever had. I was suited fine with the decision.

Life was good that spring. My family was well and happy. Haywood had been born to Papa and our Miss Myrtle, Rosa Jean to Darwin and Viola, and Gorden Bennett to William Olive and Mary, both of whom were now teaching in Wingate Junior College. Pearl had moved back to Poole's Siding with her family. Rachel Floyd wrote frequently to keep me informed about the old neighborhood. Elwood and Mary Belle were living in Rocky Mount, near enough so that we could see them often. Poole's Siding had composed one package of life. Seaboard was going to become another.

It was an unforgettable May day. For the first time I did not have to base my shopping choices on a specified sum out of my teacher's salary, which always in the end had forced me to have to look somewhere else for something cheaper.

When we began our rounds in Norfolk that morning Herbert said, "We're not going to pay the world for furniture, but we'll keep looking till we find something that suits us."

I still felt tentative. "If you'll give me an idea of the price range—"

"Let's find what we like first and then talk prices," he said.

It was a refreshing experience to be suited first and ask for the price second. I was not yet adjusted to the solid security that Herbert represented.

I knew our furniture when I saw it, as I had known our home site. Out of a city block of tables and sofas and chairs and beds, I identified ours.

Herbert was tentative. He liked my choices, he said. But there were many furniture places in Norfolk, and we were going to look around further before closing any deals. He was businessman with the dealers, and he spoke their language before me. The colloquies often became little comedies before prices were agreed upon. I came to believe that the rock-bottom prices Herbert held out for were not motivated by the saving involved so much as by victory over the other business-man.

He made a big production out of buying a pair of shoes. From the sidelines I watched the little drama.

At the outset he would select shoes of value and then point out flaws in them that justified a cut in the original price. The dealer would automatically reject the lowered bid offered, after which Herbert would leave with a great show of finality. Sometimes the dealer held out, but usually he called his customer back and in mock exasperation agreed to the cut. It never seemed to dawn on Herbert that the dealer might have learned to play the game too, that he might have upped the price as soon as this particular customer appeared so that he would have leeway to fall.

Their manner of dealing reminded me of the days of peddlers when families at Poole's Siding bargained over wares, not in the interest of victory over businessmen, but because of scarce butter-and-egg money.

We went to a seafood place for lunch that day in Norfolk. It seemed odd not to have to check in my pocketbook to see what I wanted to eat that there was enough change for. On our shopping trips we teachers had always done that. I noted there were no teachers in evidence today. People were all in family groups. Out of my sense of well-being I spoke idly, impulsively, "Family is so right!"

Herbert looked up questioningly from his seafood platter, a little startled.

"Us," I said. "Married folks."

His face cleared. He nodded. "He knew what He was doing, didn't He?"

I had never heard it said better.

After lunch we looked around in other stores. "Let the furniture man get anxious," Herbert said.

In the end he paid the original price of the furniture, less the cash discount. The furniture man did not seem anxious. Herbert made him throw in a smoking stand.

Later as I placed the tables and beds and chairs, they became more than things. They seemed animate and dear. They were home.

Finally there was the miracle of completion. That first night while I waited for Herbert to come home, I turned on all the lights of the house and slipped out into the darkness to look.

I was still looking when Herbert drove in. Hastily I turned out the lights and slipped into the kitchen to finish cooking supper.

After supper Herbert said, "Let's see how it looks from outside with all the lights turned on."

I followed him out. We stood wordless and looked. In every window the lights gleamed softly, outlining the house against the night.

He knew what He was doing, I mused in that moment of sharing. Then aloud I said, "There'll be spring and summer and fall and winter. And Christmas. And weekdays and Sundays—" I was keeping my voice low, containing myself. "There'll be rain and snow and hail and wind—"

"I took out wind insurance with Rip Foster today," he said.

We went in and turned out the lights. There would be hospitality in time, there would be sharing with friends and neighbors and relatives. But tonight Herbert and I were at home to ourselves.

We sat awhile in each unlighted room.

· 26 ·

Silent Night

THERE WERE spring and summer and fall and winter. There were weekdays and Sundays. There was Christmas.

One December morning Herbert and I rode to the Harris woods to gather greenery for our first Christmas. We drove along the road bordering fields of dead cotton and corn stalks and came to the pasture enclosure. There mules moved around in the sunshine, some of them looking incuriously over the fence while others picked at oddments of green. Most of the thirty mules seemed detached and aimless, but two at the fence kept their heads close together with such remarkable evidence of attachment that I commented on it.

They were Fanny and Brown, Herbert told me, and if separated they whickered so distressfully there was no peace on the place. When he stopped to fasten the pasture gate more securely, I moved over to Fanny and Brown and patted their necks. They had been our "welcoming committee" the afternoon we had arrived newly Mr. and Mrs. Herbert Harris. Nothing seemed bizarre that related us to the world around us.

The mules were not handsome or groomed. Their hides were tough and scarred, and blood vessels stood out like ropes along their sides. Fanny leaned her neck over Brown's, and

Brown stood motionless receiving the awkward caress. Herbert called them old fools, adding they were good mule flesh.

Mule flesh sounded so mortal. Animal devotion, I was thinking, had harsher limits in time than human. There was something moving and lovely here between the ugly work animals.

The woods looked dense and impenetrable. Green vines festooned the trees. The mistletoe high up in an elm reminded me of childhood Christmases when my brothers had vied with one another in shooting the prettiest mistletoe out of trees. Today Herbert was as intent as the boys had been on getting mistletoe with the waxiest balls and holly with the reddest berries for our first Christmas.

Gathering greenery was commonplace preparation, yet I knew this was an experience in time. Herbert and I were extending our areas of sharing. We were encompassing the land with our happiness, leaving little fragments of it as reminders, relating ourselves richly to the world around us. Forever afterwards now this standing timber would be where we had gathered holly to deck our home, where others would gather it after us, where a little fellow with sharp brown eyes would look for holly with the reddest berries.

That afternoon I completed arranging the sprays of pine and running cedar, the holly and mistletoe. Then I placed a white candle in each window.

At suppertime I watched for Herbert's car, wanting to observe on him the impact of white lights gleaming softly from our windows. Other houses were all-blue, all-red and multi-colored this year. But altar white seemed right for the new house among them. Lighting the candles had been a rite.

Herbert slowed his car as he approached, stopped an instant in front of our driveway, and then without turning in rode on down the street.

My heart sank. Hadn't Herbert liked my choice of white lights, when bright colors glowed from neighbors' windows? Had twenty-three electric candles seemed unnecessary expense? There was growing concern over local as well as national economy. Groceries had gone up to seven dollars a

week the past month. Was Herbert upset over the cost of our
first Christmas?

Then I saw him turning the corner again very slowly,
creeping along in front of our house, driving unevenly and a bit
zigzag because his attention was elsewhere than the street.
Several times he drove by in this fashion, observing the soft
gleam in our windows. Or was he counting the candles?

When he came in he said we had the prettiest lighting in
town. For all the wreaths lighted in a riot of colors, the yards
splashed with green and red, the all-blue Christmas trees and
Santa Clauses at chimneys, our house was prettiest to him.

Christmas cooking was a rite, like lighting the candles. It
began the day after Thanksgiving, when one festival of bounty
merged into preparation for the next. White and dark fruit-
cakes were baked, and over the town like incense there was the
aura of spices and fruits and homemade wine.

The pattern of bounty, followed and shared by neighbors,
varied little from year to year. The turkey, whether cooked
dry in aluminum foil or under buttered cheesecloth or in steamy
roasters, varied only in size and sex. There were the oyster and
chestnut and cornmeal dressings. Old bacon ham simmered in
its savory juices. Fresh ham, with the rind crisply brown, was
basted with red pepper and vinegar sauce. Apples and yams
were glazed. Greens were cooked richly in ham broth. There
were the casseroles and souffles, the endless salad combinations
and sweets.

Each hostess had a specialty. With one it was a squash
souffle that baffled and delighted guests, baffled because the
exact ingredients were not shared with recipe seekers. It had
something beyond squash and eggs and mushrooms and cheese,
as women found out when they tried to imitate the souffle and
turned out a soggy mess.

With another hostess it was orange-cocoanut cake. Un-
hestitatingly she gave the recipe and minute directions, though
results were varied according to skills. The almond-asparagus
casserole was easily put together by all hostesses, but it was
distinctive only with the right sauces and seasonings. Chicken
creole and lobster newberg were occasional specialties.

Meringues and tortes were beginning to appear on local menus. Preoccupation over food seemed second-rate to one lady who belonged to the Literary Guild and who read more than she cooked. But with Seaboard hostesses generally the preoccupation was imaginative and creative.

On Christmas Eve, Herbert and I sat in the candlelight of our room and listened to radio music and ate white fruitcake and candied ginger and toasted peanuts and had no sense of being second-rate. Through candlelighted panes we looked at the snow swirling outside. In the lighted space under the street light the flakes skittered across the night, covering the familiar sidewalks and driveways. The blue and red lights of Christmas trees along the street looked soft and mysterious under the animated white veil.

> Silent night, holy night,
> All is calm, all is bright—

a radio quartet sang. The muted notes of "Silent Night" seemed no less sacred because we savored our bounty.

Another evening another year we sat near our windows again looking through a veil of snow at lighted Christmas trees along our street. At intervals little children made quick stealthy excursions into front porches, as though looking for a beauty beyond tinsel and bright lights.

A radio voice had just quoted from the Magnificat, and echoes of the Annunciation seemed very present.

> For the beauty of the earth—

a radio chorus sang.

The beauty of the earth, I was thinking, the animated white beauty which held inherent meaning and delight for little children. To channel the savor in living, to pass beauty on from heir to heir, to pass life on—

I voiced my thoughts. Tonight it was an ultimate plea for accord.

There was such a stillness after my words it seemed odd that the feathery flakes were not suspended motionless, that they were still swirling across the path of light. It was as though synchronization had lapsed, as though the sound equipment had failed with the screen still animated.

Herbert was suddenly very tense. I sensed that he was startled by my mood. For I was trying to make the little fellow with sharp brown eyes like his own very real to him.

We had been over this before. Tonight the essential meanings had to be faced together, the equivocations had to be shunted aside. Another veil briefly dimmed the Christmas lights, for my eyes misted so that the swirling whiteness was not single flakes but solidified gossamer. It was a solemn moment, with no room for evasion or pleasantry in it. He could not be spared.

"Don't you want him, too?"

"No."

The synchronization began. "No" blasted the stillness. It was as though the animated flakes pelted noisily against the blanket of white on the roof outside the window, as though the cosmos reverberated.

He turned from the window and went to bed. I sat alone by the radiator, trying to understand the rejection, to adjust to the final relegation.

The animated whiteness did not turn back into the beauty of earth that night.

27

Savor

THOUGHTS OF passing on inherent meanings and delight from heir to heir receded, but my savor of life found a new channel. Without any particular direction I started writing.

Sometime after Christmas Eve I began to record my impressions and observations in diary form, calling them "My Days." The diary, in contrast to *My Day* by Eleanor Roosevelt, was not designed for publication. It served at the outset to fill a void, and in time it gave me a new awareness of the drama of the everyday and of people.

The afternoon Herbert and I arrived in Seaboard after our honeymoon, I had wondered what the composition of life would be for us in this little town, what its savor was going to be. The savor was people. Among them were my cooks and their families, whose manner of life and of expression prompted me to write their stories in their own idiom. In the process, they became individuals meriting respect and understanding, not just domestic help.

During the three years that Ethel Vassar cooked for me she remained an individualist, defying classification. She looked the fictional Mammy of the Old South, though rarely were there intimations of the character. Vague resentments seemed always to seethe in her just under the surface, so that during her stay with us I never quite knew how we stood with each other. Just when some warmth seemed about to break through the surface, Ethel suppressed it quickly and became aloof again, as though distrusting the usual attachments in our kind of relationship.

One morning after she had been among the garden flowers and vegetables she came into the kitchen with her face all lighted up. "It's so pretty outside," she said, "that I pure feel like getting down and wallowing in April!"

I tried to communicate my own sense of delight in April. Ethel closed the door. Her mood remained darkly introspective. As she related bits of her story, I came to understand why she was so moodily self-contained. Her parents had been slaves under extremely hard masters. The cruelties they had experienced colored their attitudes, and they transmitted them to their children.

"Papa was always bitter about the way he was treated as a slave," Ethel said in a talking mood one day. "They didn't burn him at the stake like they done old Ephraim yonder on the Woodruff place, but his master was mean to him. I'd kill myself before I'd submit to slavery. And looks like it's coming back. If these compulsory shots ain't slavery, what is they, do-pray? They say all we cooks is got to take shots, or we can't hold our jobs. Here's one ain't going to take no shots, job or no job! Me, I'm going to stay free!"

After freedom, Ethel's father acquired land and built a home on it, which Ethel and her sisters maintained with fierce pride of possession. Only Little Sister lived at the old homestead with Ethel then, though their brother, Sam Vassar, was in a house nearby with his family. The oldest sister, Melissie, who had been cooking in a Norfolk boardinghouse for nearly three decades frequently sent money to help pay for the upkeep and personal needs of her family in Seaboard. Their yard bloomed with an incredible variety of flowers. Their garden flourished under their own hands. Their house had conveniences secured on down-payments. They scuffled and scrimped and mauled cord wood from their little acre of timber. They did their own medication and surgery. But they owned the roof over their heads.

Owning was a badge. It made them of the taxed and free.

"It costs a poor person to own a home," Ethel said. "Our three-room house is 'bout to fall down on us, it needs repairing so bad. The wind blowed the paper top off the kitchen this last week of March, and something is bound to be done about that. I'm trying hard to save up enough money to buy some lumber, but my wages just don't stretch far enough. I have to pay out sixty cent a month for insurance to the burial league, fifty cent a week for straight life insurance for myself, fifty a week for sick benefits for myself and Little Sister and ten cents for her two children. There's clothes and groceries and church dues. There's school tablets and books for Little Sister's family. All that has to come out of the three dollars a week I'm paid. Then there's taxes, nine dollars a year. Taxes has got to come, if the whole passel of us goes hungry! They sha'n't take our land and our roof for taxes!"

I agreed that it was important for her to hold on to her home. Unschooled though she was, Ethel was managing her resources better than I could have. I had been to college, but I could not figure how she made ends meet. I marveled that she did so much with so little. Yet at that time three dollars was the local top price for regular domestic help six mornings a week, and cooks were glad to get it during off-farming seasons. At least they were fed and their family partially provided for with leftovers and old clothes. They joked wryly among themselves about arm-crooking, which meant "toting home all they could carry." Ethel was not habitually an arm-crooker.

Sometimes when taxes were due she had to borrow on her month's wages. "They sha'n't take my home from me!" Ethel said, explaining her request for a loan. "Course there's plenty folks my color that wouldn't own a home if you'd hand it to them on a silver waiter. If they own, they can't get on the Welfare. Look what happened to Little Sister. The doctors told her if she'd get shots in that clinic, the Welfare might give her some clothes and stuff. So Little Sister went to the clinic and let 'em stick that needle in her arm. In a few days the report come back 'twa'n't nothing ailed her. Course nothing ailed her. She hadn't done nothing to get shots for. Next word we got was that the Welfare couldn't help Little Sister because we own our home!"

I tried to explain the wonderful work our Welfare agencies were doing for the underprivileged, but I made no headway.

"You got to be low-down to get on the relief around here," Ethel went on. "One sorry gal that had to take shots is now getting fifteen dollars a month and not doing nare lick o' work, no more'n them in a house of ill flame! They'll all get help for their sorriness if they don't own no home. But Little Sister, making just a dollar and fifty cents a week for washings, crippled and needing bought-medicine, why she can't get on relief because we own! We'll keep on owning. We'll scuffle along somehow under our own roof. At least we'll perish free!"

The weathered cabin they paid taxes on made the sisters of the free. And a broken-down typewriter made their brother of the literate. Sam with his family lived in an unpainted shack amid bleak surroundings. He had been to college in Greensboro. On a job at the cotton gin following his college year he had injured a leg so that it had to be amputated. Bradley and Harris gave him a wooden leg. Though his schooling in Greensboro had not lifted him out of the economic bracket of ordinary gin-hand among unlettered co-workers, he remained until his death of the literate. His second-hand typewriter had made him so.

Somehow out of his scant wages he had managed to buy this used typewriter. On it he often typed notes to Herbert asking for money to buy groceries with. It seemed to make him feel he was a businessman soliciting business favors, not a cripple with a wooden leg asking for a handout. He always handed the typed notes to Herbert himself, in secure pride of composition as though certain of an "A."

When Ethel stated directly, without benefit of typewriter, that she was naked for wearing-clothes, I suggested that she go ahead and use the pretty uniforms I had given her at various times. I noticed she had been wearing the nice black taffeta uniform I had bought for her to use only when we had dinner parties.

"I had to put on black when Sis Julia died," she said. "It ain't proper to wear them green and blue uniforms. We was brought up to wear mourning, ourselves."

So, I reflected, the black party uniform had served as mourning. Wasn't mourning a badge of the taxed and free to Ethel?

Though not believing justice would prevail on earth, she looked forward to it in the hereafter. She felt close to hereafter, for she had seen the dead walking around their old haunts more than once. "Oh, yes, the dead do come back," she often affirmed. "I've seen them with my own eyes. One night around dusk-dark when we was coming from the field, a woman suddenly appeared out of the side woods and walked along the thicket edge near us. She had a shawl over her head, and her arms was folded over her chest just like they was in her coffin. She hadn't been dead long. She moved along with us, not making a sound. If we peartened up our steps, she was right there with us. If we slowed down, she slowed down. When we got to our house, she just vanished away. I've looked on the dead that come back and been plently scared. But I'll say this, they don't harm you like the living sometimes does."

Ethel told many tales about how her family had suffered under conjuration. Graveyard dust, thrown under their house, had once made her father and mother nearly cough themselves to death. They had been tricked many times because of grudges harbored among their own people. Ethel's faith in necromancy was as firm as in freedom.

In romance it remained negative. "It ain't that I've not had chances a-plenty," she declared. "When I was a girl I loved a man my mother and father objected to me marrying. I ain't cared much for nobody since.

"There was this man from Franklin I finally give a date. He wrote me to meet him at the train, declaring he'd know me. But I wouldn't go. He found his way to our house. Sis Julia met him just like she was me. But it didn't fool him. 'This ain't the young lady I've been writing to,' he told Sis Julia.

Soon as I went in he knowed me—the first time he ever laid his eyes on me. He was dressed to kill and talked like it was good times with him. But every time I tried to make up my mind to have him it seemed like the man I first loved would come between us. So I quit. I don't never 'spect to get married now, for I'm too old and too many's depending on me.

"All I've got ahead," Ethel concluded, "is working in the field and cooking for white folks. I wish them that pays us had to stretch the ends to make 'em meet like we do. If they saw what I've had to do, with near 'bout nothing to do with, maybe they'd open their pocketbooks a little wider."

Ethel lived to see the pocketbooks opened a little wider. Cooks' wages were more than tripled after a few years. Ethel was not with me then, though we had become friends again.

Ethel left me in anger. When Sam died she sent to borrow my one and only black coat to wear to his funeral services. Ethel was fat and squat and broad, and she could not have squeezed herself into my coat even if such a loan had been proper. I thought of what the Bible said about giving one's cloak also. I compromised by sending my blue spring coat which was roomy and loose-fitting, specifying that she might keep it permanently. Ethel wore black to the funeral. And she did not work for me any more.

The articulation of her discontent was some years before that happened. She poured it all out one day after a moody silence. "All you white folks wants with us is to work in your kitchens and then soon as work is over to get out the back door. Them that goes up north don't have much better luck, they tell me. Aah me! That's all 'tis for us here, just dragging along. All I hopes is, when my time comes to leave here I'll die right off in my working clothes and not have to linger for somebody to wait on me."

Years later Ethel was to have her wish. She left her job at noon and died in her working clothes.

I like to remember that one day she had an impulse to wallow in April.

Mattie Ferguson succeeded Ethel as cook. She prepared food so appetizingly that a Yankee editor who was once our guest during Mattie's stay with us declared he was going to take a place on the Richmond Pike and call her from my kitchen to cook for him. Before the end of World War II she moved to Norfolk and died there not long afterwards.

Then Ethel arranged for her older sister, Melissie, to cook for me. During Melissie's "incumbency," as she called her stay with employers, I had no worries about household routines. Undaunted by her physical limitations, she carried on adequately. Her coming was a relief otherwise. She inherited one of my wartime projects.

There had been participation in several projects during the war. With Josephine Parker I had spotted airplanes one morning each week, had flashed identification of fighters and bombers to our Filter Center and learned to speak as easily of dihedral swept-back wings and fuselage blisters as of cotton and peanuts. I had basted garments in the Red Cross sewing room where with one accord we all sewed for the Russian women, for the besieged of Stalingrad who were in our admiration and affection then. I had worked on rationing boards and co-operated in drives for tin and household grease. To help morale on the home front I had organized a reading circle for the days and nights of restricted activity.

Generally all of us had stayed within all our ration quotas. Allegedly some sugar was bootlegged into Seaboard. There were isolated reports of gasoline trickery. Before sugar rationing went into effect, some local housewives had made gallons of syrup out of granulated sugar and canned it against the approaching sweetless days. But generally the stringencies of sugar and meat and oil rationing were accepted with patriotic good will.

In this spirit I had set about relieving meat shortages. I had decided to help the war effort by raising chickens, in this way releasing our own meat quota to the total need. So I had ordered twenty-five chickens from Sears and Roebuck. After this start I had expected to expand.

Herbert had blown up when the biddies arrived, for we had no place to put them. It had been my idea to start them off in big pasteboard boxes on the back porch and then fence in our

little orchard for a chicken yard. I had forgotten about pasteboard and steel shortages.

After the explosion, though, Herbert had met the situation
by taking down the garage doors for a shelter for the biddies.
Building materials were as short as steel wire and meat. I had
forgotten that too. But Herbert was equal to the need. He had
taken down enough garden wire to make an orchard enclosure.
At first he was fretted over my bright idea for relieving shortages. Then he had begun to feed and water the biddies and
buy medicine for them as indicated. Often when their needs
had been attended to he had made his way, slyly at first, to the
fence just to watch their cunning ways.

Later he had begun to go inside the enclosure and sit with
the biddies, pet them. We became partners in the chicken
venture. We watched their growth, their individual differences. One from the start had been forward. He grew lordly.
We called him Big Un. He knew his name. He knew us.
When we called he came running, as though to receive our
commendation or to absorb our petting. Other chickens caught
on and followed their leader. A lot of petting went on in our
orchard enclosure.

Time passed, and inevitably our biddies became fryers. A
sense of their destiny was in our greetings, a growing conviction
that our lordly Big Un deserved a finer end than the frying
pan. Herbert kept his balance about it, though. When Olive's
family came to spend a weekend with us, he directed Melissie
to kill Big Un.

When that platter of nicely browned chicken was placed on
the table, I burst into tears. It had not occurred to me such a
thing would happen. I knew beforehand I was not going to
eat any of Big Un, but I aimed to offer it proudly to guests. I
queered the *pièce de résistance* that day. Olive and Mary and
Gordon and Alice Jo ate tentatively, as though apologizing for
being the occasion of the slaughter that had provoked the tears.
Herbert managed his drumstick with every appearance of brash
enjoyment, but I saw a look in his eyes that belied it. Pet meat
did not eat good to anyone.

I did not cry again when our biddies were served. Neither

did I eat them. Herbert lost his taste for them altogether and decided that eggs would do us as much good as chicken meat. Hens needed roosters, he said, so he rationalized his decision to keep pullets and roosters too.

They became out-and-out pets. Then one night a weasel destroyed all but two. These two grew into pullets, then hens. They were our constant care and pleasure. Herbert sat in the orchard with them, talked to them, fed them from his hand. They were at home on his knee, his shoulder. When he started downtown they followed him, exactly as a puppy follows his master. He might shoo them back toward the house, but as likely as not when he turned to join a group of men at the filling station one hen would be there at his heels.

Whether it was because he actually feared his pet would be run over by a car downtown, as he declared, or because the hen was out of place among men at the filling station, he decided to let Melissie take the last of our flock.

Our last Barred Rocks, alas, I thought. I watched Melissie in her flowered kerchief and dull winter coat move toward the fenced enclosure. Not that fences had kept our chickens in. They had learned as biddies to fly like birds, and they had always come and gone as they pleased.

With eyes a little misty I watched Melissie stoop to pick up our last Barred Rocks. "My Last Duchess" came to my mind, but I hurriedly rejected any application to Browning's monologue.

There was no need to fear. For Melissie had promised to keep our last two Barred Rocks to lay eggs. "If the time comes," I told Melissie, "when it wouldn't make sense to keep them any longer, you just go ahead and do what has to be done. But never let us know. Let us think of them as alive and laying eggs."

She said she would. With her a promise was a sacred trust. I never knew how long the hens lived.

Melissie was a woman of her word. And she was a lady. She bore with Herbert's expletives, but not with mine. She was sternly exacting toward me. I was permitted no expletives in my house. If I tried to damn something in Melissie's hearing, she quickly reminded me I was too much a lady and a Christian to use slack words.

She was a Christian. She slighted her job to read the Bible. Its assurance gave her more bounty than wages did. She was reading it through for the third time now, having arrived at Job again while she was with me. The impact of the beauty and majesty of the passages was so overwhelming that sometimes Melissie called out to me in a kind of transport, as though she had just received some good news that had to be shared. At times I found her gently swaying back and forth in her chair, forced to move outwardly since she was so deeply moved by her reading.

Under different circumstances she might have indulged in shouting, as many of her neighbors did, but her sense of fitness did not permit outward exultation. Once when a relative, less inhibited than Melissie, pantomimed her religious exuberance as she sang in the choir, Melissie shook her head at her with all the sternness she had mustered at my expletives.

But she exulted in the Bible and in claiming the promises of her Lord. I have seen her face when it looked transfigured. Every promise in the Word for her was as literal as sunrise. The imagery and words were a fresh delight to her. She peeled potatoes and talked to her Lord as though He were there in the kitchen.

At first I used to call downstairs to find out who was there. The muffled talking below stopped instantly. "Just me," Melissie answered. I soon learned Who it was she talked to.

A long time ago she had been to school in Elizabeth City, where she had received some teacher training. She had taught, married, been widowed. Then leaving her native Northampton, she had gone into domestic service in Norfolk. There she had held a job as cook for over thirty years. Broken down in service in Norfolk, she had returned to her old home in Seaboard for lighter work.

Melissie could not shoulder the heavier work that went with domestic service in Seaboard. Only the minimum she managed. Friends sometimes teased me about the minimum I accepted, asking who served whom in our establishment.

Melissie was a blessing to me in ways that had nothing to do with work, light or heavy. We shared many experiences together. Her sound sense of philosophy gave me balance and poise sometimes when my own equanimity was lacking. In stress and trouble she remained serene and undaunted.

She shared my pleasure in the prospect of company. Many cooks were inclined to grumble over the extra duties that guests involved, to feel uncompensated even by generous tips. The degree of pleasure, with Melissie, depended on the importance of the company.

To be important, people did not have to be rich. They might, indeed, be poor. But it was essential for them to be upstanding. That was Melissie's word for quality in people. That she required of them. She was a snob so subtly that I discovered it only in the cool reserve shown toward rich or poor alike who were not upstanding.

Melissie was uncannily perceptive. One of my friends, who seemed incredibly unable to cope with circumstances, she treated with warm respect. Others with plenty of this world's goods she practically snubbed. I recall one particular family who visited me during Melissie's "incumbency" and received extraordinary treatment. Melissie made herself as nearly servile to them as was compatible with her dignity. Instinctively she sensed in those people, with no background of servants, the tendency to be on a fellowship level with her. Subtly and kindly she put them in their place. She was exact about the proprieties as she had experienced them.

Melissie looked like the mammy type, but to none was she ever Mammy. She was a fine, upstanding woman who gave to cooking the same dignity and faithfulness she had given once to teaching. Even to the most cunning and adorable children who visited me she was never indulgent. Instead, she maintained something of the ramrod sternness of the schoolroom of her day. As servant and teacher, she was unbending about propriety.

She taught me much. I was able to help her with her hoard of words. She collected them as some women did pitchers. There was respect, even awe, in her attitude toward words.

Constantly she jotted down the unfamiliar ones she heard or came across in her reading, thus continuing her education as she entered her mid-seventies.

When friends accepted invitations to visit us, Melissie went about menu-planning enthusiastically. She took the friends on trust, assuming they were upstanding. Every meal had to be outlined on paper to her hand, from the first supper to the final breakfast. Was it, I sometimes wondered, that with her slave ancestry always in her subconsciousness she never could quite take reading and following written directions for granted, that she had to flaunt her facility a little to herself as to her employer?

"We used to serve little orange cups during my incumbency in Norfolk," she would suggest when I paused in writing down the menu she was planning. "Filled with seasoned sweet potatoes and topped with a marshmallow, they are compatible with either ham or chicken."

On one occasion I listed hors d'oeuvres, asking for suggestions from her. Momentarily I had forgotten that hors d'oeuvres might not be "compatible" with fare in the boarding-house where she had cooked so long. The incumbency there had seemed to equip her in so many ways.

"Spell it," Melissie bade me. She reached in her pocket-book for pencil and paper to jot down the unfamiliar word. She was not going to risk making a malapropism. It pained her that malapropisms and bad grammar were often used among her associates. Sometimes when other cooks spoke of going to church to "wash-up" (for worship) and of cleansing their "sisters" (for systems) with "yarb" tea, Melissie was wont to wince, then to elevate her head a little and let it pass. But for herself she had words spelled out—except one. She continued to call the tributes, written by friends and acquaintances for the burial rites of her people, "condolers" instead of condolences.

Many a "condoler" have I written to be read in her church —as many for white people who called on me to compose their tributes for colored friends and employees deceased as for the colored themselves.

One morning a particular expression bothered Melissie.

"Is there such a word as 'blou-say?' " she queried.

"Blousay?" I repeated.

"I heard a woman use it last night. At your supper table," she added, as though placing the responsibility. "I wondered if she meant somebody was 'blowsy.' "

"Maybe she meant to say 'blasé,' " I suggested.

"How you spell it?" Melissie jotted down another word and went to get my dictionary. Soon afterwards I heard her murmuring the definition. "Having one's taste dulled by over-indulgence—unable to enjoy things that appeal to most people—"

One day later on when she had indulged in too much food that was not compatible with high blood pressure, she said with a twinkle, "I reckon I'm just blasé."

She used my dictionary only a little less than she did my Bible. Her ecstasy over words was not unrelated to that over the precious promises in the Book. She was as content with words as a child is with goodies.

Whenever she called on me to compose condolers for her I was careful to use words that pleased her.

28

Human Interest

INTEREST IN the composition of life around me extended beyond observations recorded in "My Days." I also wrote news items and feature stories for newspapers. There was no direction in this writing beyond the collection of odd facts and human interest.

One item, boxed on the front page of the *Norfolk Virginian-Pilot*, was in the man-bites-dog sequence. It concerned an opossum that feigned death only long enough to make a frontal attack upon the nose of a local hunter. As a result, "playing 'possum" became a meaningful phrase around town. Another was about Sarah and George Davis, sharecroppers on the Russell Harris farm, who gathered about the table each day with sons named Matthew, Mark, Luke, John, Paul, Silas, Lazarus, Simon and Peter.

When Sarah Davis died there was a human interest item about her wake. Two mourners left the "sitting-up" unwontedly early, and soon afterwards the dead woman's chickens were heard squawking. Investigation by Matthew, Mark, Luke, John et alii revealed that the two were escaping with a bag full of chickens. Apprehended and unable to give bond, the two mourners were placed in the county jail.

The escapade of one of Herbert's sharecroppers made the newspaper. After selling his peanuts, Elijah Providence went ritzy, bought a secondhand Cadillac in Norfolk, operated it without license through several Virginia cities, only to fall into the hands of the village policeman at home.

An unusual request made at the local post office window provided a news item. "The most staggering order of all came through the service window of the local post office this morning," I wrote. "Hitherto, according to postal authorities here, many patrons have asked for credit in purchasing stamps, have tried to wangle reduced postal charges on packages, have even offered eggs in exchange for stamps. All that has been in a day's routine. But Thursday while Mrs. Morgan was busy dispatching mail, this inquiry breezed through the window: 'Is there any beer for sale here?' The postmistress, who had been a past president of the W.C.T.U., sternly responded in the negative."

Human foibles and virtues were recorded in another medium. Original drama became a lively interest. I helped to organize towns throughout our county as units of the Northampton Players, whose sole purpose was the production of one-act folk plays in an annual drama festival. Membership groups were from Conway, Jackson, Rich Square, Seaboard, Severn and Woodland. Teachers, businesswomen and businessmen, county officials, farmers and housewives rode ten and twenty miles to rehearsals.

An adult playwriting class that met in my living room provided the plays for awhile. Those who joined the class became interested in local lore and legends, in the drama of the everyday and in the moving potentials of ordinary people living along little roads of sand and ruts.

A little more understanding and warmth were added to our perception of people because of the unpretentious plays the class turned out. Social injustice among the sharecroppers was the theme of one. The vanity of men, as represented by a father and son, was another. An old couple after deciding to part became so incensed at their family's acquiescence that they eloped and lived happy together ever afterward. A bootlegger from our Fountain Creek triumphed when he made the revenue man drink up the evidence. This one, which we called "The Evidence," was bought by Samuel French. All of the original plays were produced locally and some of them at the drama festival in Chapel Hill.

An original play with a racial theme projected the tragic consequences that involved a girl from Northampton's Portuguese settlement after she had secured a teaching job in a white school in Wilson County. Ephraim's light, which burned steadily for decades after a slave was burned at the stake near Seaboard, was used as the basis of a play. Another used Beaufort County lore which featured the dramatic opening of a featherbed during a thunderstorm. A local milliner satirized for the stage the foibles of women in their selection of hats. The preacher's wife enlivened the playmaking with the introduction of a poltergeist which threw rocks and could not be caught in the act. Religious plays and pageants were written and presented generally on Sunday nights in place of church services. The Methodist minister portrayed the Rich Young Ruler. The Baptist minister wrote symbolically about gold in the hills, enlivening his play with bits of broad comedy.

Human interest abounded in the playwriting experiment. The beginner playwrights often drifted into gossip. Family skeletons rattled threateningly. There was a great deal of unmotivated action and dialogue. Characters bustled around on the stage covering miles of territory without getting anywhere. Characters walked through pages of manuscript without saying anything, only saying nothing colorfully. Amid discussion of conflict between protagonist and antagonist, talk inevitably turned to gardens and chickens and cooks. Scenarios split time with Rhode Island Reds, expository devices with salad combinations, and kings who paid the wages of sin with casseroles.

When the class disbanded, I wrote the plays. The idea of Kalline as a dramatis persona had interested me for some time. So I wrote an one-act play about her which won a drama award at the drama festival in Chapel Hill. I enrolled in a correspondence playwriting course under Dr. J. O. Bailey, university English professor at Chapel Hill. Following this, I wrote "His Jewels," "Open House," "Pair of Quilts," "Special Rates," "Three Foolish Virgins," "Judgment Comes to Daniel" and others which also were winners in the state drama festival. These were produced by the Northampton Players, the Norfolk Little Theatre, the Raleigh Little Theatre and the Carolina Playmakers.

Through these experimental plays and human interest stories, I found direction. An old hope of my childhood was realized. I became a novelist. It was like opening the Bible on a wish and finding, "And it came to pass." It was the *Raleigh News and Observer* that helped point out the direction.

· 29 ·

Swatches of Purslane and Portulaca

"Why don't you write a novel?" Jonathan Daniels of the *Raleigh News and Observer* wrote me after reading one of my feature stories in his paper.

Loretto Carroll Bailey, playwright of Chapel Hill, addressed the same question to me after reading my plays. She said my stage directions were as good as the stage talk in my little one-acts, so she thought the medium of the novel might be indicated.

These challenges, no less than circumstances at the time, prompted me to start a novel. There had been a growing sense of the bounty of living that is not defined by land holdings and standing timber. I had known the warmth and fullness of family and community life, had savored values that had nothing to do with money. Because of my bad health and the uncertainty of its outcome, I began to feel an urgency to say something about what life and people could be in terms of what they were and had been, to write little vignettes that would say it for me while there was still time.

The mood was not just nostalgia. It was protest, too, at

the stresses and anxieties over property involving people I knew. I wrote steadily. For my persistent anemia that kept me shut in for awhile, Herbert began to dose me with bootleg toddies. I never knew who our bootlegger was, though I came to recognize his tap on our back door. Writing, I learned, was better medicine for me.

At the time there were lawsuits over Harris boundary lines. After a brother's death in 1938 there were legal tangles and confusion over family property, and Herbert as one of the collateral heirs was involved in the proceedings. There was supposed to be a marriage contract between the deceased brother and his wife, who were childless. The marriage contract, it was claimed, provided that the husband's property should revert to his family in case he died first, just as her property was to revert to hers under the same circumstances.

The marriage contract was not found. There was deep emotional stress along with legal action. The lawsuit was compromised. But all the conflict and tension elevated Herbert's blood pressure dangerously. Aware of such conflicts and emotional stress over property, I felt impelled to make some kind of affirmation about people who without extensive property holdings could know vast bounty.

I made that affirmation in *Purslane*.

Purslane was submitted to The University of North Carolina Press by Dr. J. O. Bailey of the university English department who first read it for me. The director of the Press, W. T. Couch, was "wildly enthusiastic" about *Purslane*, Dr. Bailey reported. It was accepted at once. It was reputedly the first novel ever to be published by a university press.

Conferences, publicity interviews and pictures followed. Often before the cameramen I found myself wanting to retreat to the third row, as in the Academy picture. I was timid and tense.

Mr. Couch, Miss Porter Cowles and others of the Press were kind and helpful to me in my newness as an author. Mrs. Alice Paine was a fine editor. Putnam's of London, whose firm became my first English publisher, also gave me skillful editing.

I immediately started working on a second novel for the Press. From a poem I selected a tentative title, "Morning Is Spent." This later was changed to "Portulaca." Under the transport of new authorship, I made the mistake of using an editor for my hero and of naming him Constant. This honor must have startled my London editor at Putnam's whose name was Constant Huntington.

It is not surprising that I made mistakes. I was totally unprepared for what developed. *Purslane* became something of a sensation. From a New York editor came the suggestion that it should be submitted for a Pulitzer prize. Archibald Henderson, official biographer of George Bernard Shaw, summed it up before the state Literary and Historical Association by saying it was "burning up the woods."

Metropolitan dailies and weeklies alike gave this first novel unstinted praise. Reviews appeared under double-deck headlines throughout the country. Literary magazines, even *Time*, had good words for it. Critics wrote that they were "moved by the power and beauty of it." The *New York Times* reviewer spoke of it as a unique adventure in reading, with the beauty of *The Yearling* in its pages. Gerald Johnson in a front page review in the *New York Herald Tribune* wrote that it had extraordinary beauty, that it was a "startling book, full of hilarity and profoundly true."

Purslane was hailed by Dorothy Canfield Fisher in *Book-of-the-Month Club News* as an "American classic." Parallels were drawn between my writing and that of Thomas Hardy and Mark Twain. One critic said I had charted another Wessex here in America. A New York editor summed it up by calling it a "stunning book."

The book was well received in Great Britain. From Scotland, the *Glasgow Herald* wrote: "All the characters, major and minor alike, are brought alive with a truly creative verve and a great deal of charm." There was this excerpt from the Scotsman: "The lights and shadows of a rustic community—weddings, baptisms, Christmas festivities, the heartbreak of young lovers, the pathos of old age—are all given in leisurely detail which makes pleasant reading."

Frank Swinnerton in the *London Observer* called it a modern "transatlantic *Cranford*." Enid Corrall in the *Daily Sketch* wrote: "Like Mark Twain she [Mrs. Harris] has written about the loves and hates of the people among whom she was born—so that for 393 pages their laughter and their tears are real." The reviewer in the *Times Literary Supplement* said the story was "solid and sure and actual." The *Yorkshire Post* observed that *Pates Siding* (as *Purslane* was called in England) was "a warm strong narrative of youthful tragedy, set against a carefully observed and honestly recorded North Carolina family background." I was further referred to in England as an "American Mary Webb."

I was stunned by the acclaim.

Purslane was a first in three respects. It was the first novel ever to win the Mayflower Cup, annual award given by the Mayflower Society for the most distinguished North Carolina book in the combined fields of fiction, non-fiction, drama, poetry and juvenile books. Subsequently the fields were divided and awards given in each. *Purslane* was the first book by a woman to be awarded the Mayflower Cup. It was the first novel to be published by a university press.

There were inquiries and pressures regarding the next book. Agents communicated with me about handling my rights and royalties. Booksellers arranged autograph parties. Clubs invited me to review my book. Groups honored me at dinners, luncheons and banquets. Radio executives came to Seaboard to talk about serializing *Purslane* for radio drama.

Editors continued to inquire about my plans for the next book. They were meticulous about the proprieties, eager not to trespass upon commitments with the Chapel Hill publishers. Since university presses were not in the business of fiction, though, I was advised to choose a trade publisher. Special delivery mail, letters, telegrams and messengers made suggestions about the choice.

In response to a messenger from a highly regarded publisher in New York, Mr. Couch wrote on April 29, 1939: "Tell them that we already have Mrs. Harris tied up for three additional books. I cannot keep publishers from communicating

with Mrs. Harris. My guess is, however, that she will stick
with us as long as we can work together satisfactorily. In fact,
I would be willing to bet that no matter what they might offer,
she would not easily leave us."

Mr. Couch would not lose his bet. Although there were
no contract commitments, I meant to stay with the Press.

Yet the idea of commercial publication continued to be
deftly and graciously conveyed to me by such editors as Frances
Phillips of William Morrow, Lambert Davis of Harcourt-
Brace, John L. B. Williams of Appleton-Century (who sug-
gested that *Purslane* be submitted for the Pulitzer prize),
Paul Brooks of Houghton-Mifflin, Thomas R. Coward of
Coward-McCann, and John McK. Woodburn of Doubleday-
Doran. Similarly pleasant inquiries came from Maria Leiper
for Simon and Schuster, William Soskin of Stackpole Sons,
Harper's, the president of Stokes Company and others. Cor-
respondence from fourteen major publishers remained in my
files.

I was overwhelmed by all the attention. Did other writers
receive such invitations after a first book, I wondered, and what
did they do about it? I was so untutored in the writing business,
so transported by all that was happening to me that I felt like
the old woman in the nursery rhyme and found myself thinking, Lauk-a-mercy, can this be I?

It was a pleasant interval, in spite of my uncertainty about
the right course for me to take. I enjoyed hearing from New
York and Boston and London. Book people invited me to lunch
in New York and to fly out to California for dinner, as though
that were a casual thing for me. They wrote of plans to come
South, with Seaboard in their itinerary. The sound of im-
mediacy in their plans prompted us to store up scuppernong
wine to serve as Southern hospitality. Editors sent me books
that their firms had published, until I had to add book shelves
to hold them all. Along with my thanks, I sent them swatches
of purslane from our garden.

I was sure of purslane. It was symbol of people enjoying
their bounty along little roads of sand and ruts, of people
vital and enduring and worthy to endure. It was becoming

symbol of a partnership. Herbert and I were becoming Harris and Harris. One day Herbert told Walmus, the handyman, not to dig up the purslane in our garden. Walmus looked amazed, as though sure Mr. Hub-but had lost his senses. "What?" he demanded. "Leave pussley there in the middle of the butter-bean rows?" Mr. Hub-but ordered it left.

He saw the sense of swatches to New York. He saw the sense of royalties. Hitherto my scribbling had seemed a needless waste of energy and time. Now I was endorsing royalty checks to his credit with something of a flourish. He hurried me on my second novel.

Editors made pleasant comments about the swatches enclosed in letters to them. "Purslane is different from our Northern parsley," one wrote. I wanted to tell him it was different from our Southern parsley, too, but who was I to set New York editors straight on genus?

John McK. Woodburn of Doubleday-Doran referred to the swatches of purslane as "little cadavers," since they were dead on arrival. "I like a title that you can pin to a letter; more manageable, say, than *All This, and Heaven Too*," he wrote. "My difficulty is that I don't know which is purslane and which portulaca, since both were little cadavers when they arrived. Portulaca doesn't look any more cultivated than purslane when both are dead. I suppose that is as it should be, as in the case of aristocrats and common people."

That was, indeed, the point. Portulaca, the title of my second novel, was of the genus of purslane. It was cultivated and grew in flower borders instead of everywhere as purslane did. John Woodburn of Doubleday-Doran sounded like a perceptive editor.

A volume of my one-act plays had now been published by the University Press. Now that my second novel was finished, I had to decide what to do with it. The decision would end all the editorial correspondence, which had entertained me for months. It composed a volume of good writing.

I sent the manuscript to Mr. Couch. With it I made an appeal for his frank opinion about what step I should take.

"I finished reading your manuscript about 2:00 A.M. Saturday morning. I have read few manuscripts that I would rather publish," Mr. Couch wrote in answer to my appeal. "My guess is that we could do better with the book than any of the commercial publishers. I do not want to push you into doing anything with this manuscript that you do not want to do. My chief fear in conection with your work is that you will be spoiled by a lot of attention—"

How perceptive Mr. Couch was, I reflected. As I read his letter, surely one of the finest and most discerning any author ever had from her publisher, I made up my mind to stay with the Press.

Then John McK. Woodburn of Doubleday-Doran wrote me: "I go around like a praying mantis, hoping that Mr. Couch of Chapel Hill will either be touched in the heart by my wistfulness or decide that *Portulaca* in its import demands more *lebensraum* than a university press can give it. As soon as you hear from Mr. Couch please wire me collect. If it is over the weekend, send the wire to 127 West 12th Street. I'd rather not wait till Monday to know. We are having beautiful weather here. The view from my desk would be even lovelier if I had your manuscript before me. Yours wistfully," he signed himself.

There was another interval of uncertainty.

Then one night Mr. Woodburn rang my doorbell. Knowing it was not a caller so late in the evening, I raised an upstairs window to ask what was wanted.

The author of *Purslane* was wanted, I found out. John Woodburn of New York City wished to talk to Mrs. Harris.

Herbert and I hurried down to open the door. Mr. and Mrs. Woodburn, on their way back from a trip to Georgia, had driven by Chapel Hill to get Mr. Couch's sanction to approach me in person about the new novel. This detour accounted for the lateness of the call. We served them scuppernong wine.

They were charming people. I was still unready, though, to give the Doubleday editor my decision. I looked to Mr. Couch for final direction.

Of that trip Mr. Woodburn wrote: "I still keep thinking of that trip to Seaboard as one of the most pleasant adventures of my life. I'd like to see Seaboard by daylight. I remember it only as dark broken shadows and one light, in your house ... I wrote Mr. Couch regarding our conversation and told him it was my hope your manuscript would eventually land in our hands, that should you feel in position to accept, a check will be on its way to you at once. I do hope you and Mr. Couch and I can come to an arrangement enabling you to send it to me."

Mr. Woodburn and Mr. Couch had another conference in New York. Of it, Mr. Woodburn wrote me: "I saw Mr. Couch yesterday and we discussed *Portulaca*. I told him frankly what I wanted and what I thought was best for you and the book, and he was equally frank with me. We agreed that as things stand the decision should be up to you. I sympathize with you completely in your predicament and realize how difficult it is for you to decide. Mr. Couch is concerned with your best interests and your future to an unusual degree, but I still believe you could do better with us because of our greater facilities for promotion and sales. I am eagerly awaiting your reply."

Mr. Couch finally concluded the matter with a very understanding letter. In it he warned that my home town and others in the South might find *Portulaca* too devastatingly true a picture of small towns, that I might be "finished off" by Seaboard after its publication. "While disappointed," he concluded his letter, "I have to agree that it is probably best for you to send the manuscript to New York ... If you ever have anything you care to submit to us we will be glad to have it. I would especially like to get you tied up for an autobiography ten or twenty years hence. My guess is that if Seaboard does not finish you off in the next year or so you will have an interesting story to tell."

I sent *Portulaca* to Doubleday-Doran.

In some dread I waited to be finished off after its publication. A letter from a North Carolina fan did not help to dispel the dread. "If I know my little towns," George Laycock wrote from Shanghai, "Seaboard will give you hell!"

I began to recall characters and events in *Portulaca* that, for all the author's claims they were composites, might be pinpointed in local fact. For the book did contain incidents that had some factual basis. But there was no literal application to people. The characters lived in Bonwell, not Seaboard. Yet resemblance to living persons might not seem purely coincidental enough to local readers.

It would have helped to get a reaction from Herbert. But if I had my way he was not going to read any further novels of mine. He had dutifully pored over *Purslane*. I had been touched by the way he stuck to it. He was an avid newspaper reader, a sharp observer of printed facts and of business and political trends. But novels were not his line. As I had watched him patiently turn the pages of *Purslane* I had been impelled more than once to say, "Never mind!" Moved by his persistence, knowing that his eyes were aching from the continuous reading, I finally closed the book one day and said, "Never mind. I'll tell you the rest of the story."

He reopened it. "I'm nearly through now. I'll read the balance," he said. When he had finished he told me how *Purslane* ended. "She mended the hole in his pocket after he died, did she?" Then like a boy who aims to prove he deserves an "A" on his book report he added, "What did you let him die for?"

Since he would not be reading the new book, Herbert would make no direct identifications. But others might. The religion of blood and of property had their devotees in many communities. They might find themselves on page 275 of *Portulaca*.

Nancy, the heroine, related the religion of blood to lawsuits over property. Property, held in relentless trust for a family that did not believe in heirs, had stood in the way of Nancy's having a son. Would the novel seem impersonal enough?

The Pen Club of Bonwell might conceivably be identified as my play-writing class in Seaboard. On page 219 there was this:

> The talk swerved from story motivation to pickles
> and nail polish and caskets. Seven of the members
> brought stories to the next meeting. Nancy found
> Grace's story improbable and melodramatic. Steenie

had buried hers in a muck of profanity. Lila had rattled too many family skeletons. All the stories were vaguely resented, because each member of the Pen Club identified herself or some of her family with the various situations outlined. Essie climaxed the resentment with her account of a wife's breaking into her husband's assignation with the woman she had thought her best friend. Ellen challenged her source.

Nancy, sensing the disturbed cadences, suggested that all the materials used in the afternoon's assignment were representative, not actual; that there were hundreds of situations so similar that it was easy for people to read themselves into stories, to identify themselves with people in books where no similarity was intended.

I doubted that Nancy's apologia would keep me from being "finished off."

After publication date I lay low. My cook did the errands downtown. I dodged neighbors. The back yard and garden became my range. I tensed every time Herbert drove in from his family's home on the farm. Then one day Bettie, spying me at the back, called across her garden fence, "I've ordered your book. I hear I'm Ellen."

Shortly afterwards at funeral services in a country churchyard, a friend whispered to me, "I've read your book." There was that tense interval of waiting. An author is unsure about the proper response indicated after such announcements. "Thank you" is scarcely right since the reaction of the reader may be little cause for gratitude. "You did?" the author might say, but that is inconclusive since a nod or a single affirmative leaves the matter dangling. "Oh?" is likewise inconclusive. "Hope you liked it," is one way of forcing the issue if the author feels venturesome.

That day at the churchyard I merely waited in awkward silence for the reaction. I was not feeling venturesome. Then this friend who had read my book was suddenly called away to help arrange flowers on the grave. I felt she might be getting ready, figuratively, to arrange flowers on mine.

Later she said to me, "I loved your book. I don't know when I've laughed so much." Then she pinpointed which of our mutual friends I had hit, but good!

Bettie loved it too. She was pleased at being Ellen. She pinpointed several in Seaboard whom I had hit. Other friends and neighbors expressed themselves likewise. I certainly had hit people they enjoyed seeing hit. Herbert came from town one afternoon laughing about the men's reaction to my squirrel muddle incident in *Portulaca*. The men at the Esso place had hilariously kidded the new bridegroom about asking the crowd at the muddle to sing another verse. That guy had really been hit, but good!

I was aware of no unfavorable repercussions at home. Nor did *Portulaca* seem to offend other small towns in North Carolina. Fan mail did not indicate the book was unpalatable to Southern readers. There was an exception to justify Mr. Couch's warning. An anonymous letter came from Bon Air, Virginia, lambasting me under the mistaken impression that I was a Yankee out to do the South wrong. The revelation of small-town ways and small-town people offended the anonymous letter writer. Why didn't I stay up North, I was challenged in angry feminine penmanship, and settle some of the problems and evils up there?

My town seemed tolerant beyond Mr. Couch's belief. It apparently understood a writer's use of the composite and of satire and caricature. It was generous beyond the home-town author's own faith. Seaboard might seem all broken shadows and one light to a Yankee editor, but amid the shadows many bright lights glowed.

Yet, even now after twenty years, *Portulaca* still seems to have certain explosive potential, though the charge has been detonated by time. I am bound to conclude that the town generally could not have read the book.

One by-product of writing books was totally unexpected so far as it was related to me. I was surprised to learn that authors are supposed to be speakers. I was not a speaker, and it was not easy to become one. Yet after the flood of invitations to speak to college and club groups about my work, I tried to do what was expected.

Each speaking engagement has a particular savor among memories. Introductions have often been better than my speeches. This was notably true in Winston-Salem when Frank Borden Hanes presented me to the Friends of the Library of Salem College. The poetic imagery of his introduction made my speech seem very prosaic. Likewise, introductions by Thad Stem and Sam Ragan and Ovid Pierce have been so superior that I have remembered them longer than my talks they prefaced.

Once when I spoke at Woman's College in Greensboro, William Olive's family came to hear me. Alice Jo, a very little tot then, noticed that my audience laughed at certain incidents I related during my speech. She helped out. She began laughing so loudly and continuously that she completely stole the show, and my speech no longer mattered.

I felt no more challenged in cities like Charlotte and Norfolk and Atlanta than in Pendleton and Pinetops and Garner. A great-niece, Sandra Upchurch, was a Busy Bee in Garner High School. She and her little friends had been reading in the newspaper about my appearances in Raleigh and other cities, and in very adult and dignified fashion they approached me about an address for their club. I did my best for the Busy Bees.

It was a satisfying experience to talk to the Negro clubs of Northampton. They wanted to know more about my book people, and since I had written about many of them in composite I was pleased to elaborate on the sources and impressions. Colored friends have been loyal fans. Only Ethel, who was with me through the *Purslane* experience, was noncommital after she had read the novel. "Well," she said at last after she had been pressed for her reaction, "it might be all right for married folks to read!" She was single and fifty-odd. But she had been shocked. Miss Kelly had pinpointed details of a bridal night a little too precisely for her.

Speaking engagements had to be canceled frequently because of Herbert's ill health. Since I had given up trying to drive after my first wreck, Seaboard friends transported me to engagements, Elizabeth Harris and Josephine Parker most often. As time went on, speaking became less an ordeal and more an opportunity. It has been strict discipline from first to last. I have made myself accept invitations to speak.

During a visit to Coker College in South Carolina, I talked on "The Unifying Influence of Community Drama." My illustration was our community original play that involved the opening of a featherbed during a thunder storm. I stated that the featherbed was a truly unifying force. At that point I was interrupted by laughter. When I realized why they laughed, I hastened to explain that the particular featherbed I referred to was a symbol of our unity of mood in Seaboard. For it was the prized possession of the woman who lent it to us only because the play was the thing among us. Dr. French Haynes reassured me by quoting another speaker's slip. "Girls," this speaker had declared to college students, "you never have really lived unless you have gone to bed with Robert Louis Stevenson by candlelight."

Three efforts at speechmaking stand out as the most difficult. One was my first public appearance before the state Literary and Historical Association the year I received the Mayflower Cup at its annual meeting. The topic assigned me was, "After a First Novel." My voice almost failed when I began trying to talk. Some man in the back row called out, "Louder!" It was what I needed. I finished my speech audibly.

Another difficult assignment was my speech before the South Atlantic Modern Language Association in Atlanta. The learned professors' papers on scholarly subjects made me feel that anything I could say about the "Literary Uses of Folklore" was unnecessary and unimportant. I knew I was out of my depth among the scholars. On the way back home I rode with Dr. and Mrs. Bailey and two other English professors of The University of North Carolina. Their talk was on a high plane. I listened. During a lull in the discussion of Faulkner's work I suddenly realized we were crossing over into the Good Old

North State. About to touch home base again, I ventured to say brashly, "I like detective stories."

"He writes them," Dr. Bailey said, indicating Dr. Holman.

Soon after coming home I hastened to read *Another Man's Poison* and *Up This Crooked Way*, and I enjoyed Dr. Holman's mysteries as I was impressed by his scholarship.

My most difficult attempt was the return to a speaking schedule after an enforced lapse of time and a great emotional strain. But the Raleigh Woman's Club that day with incredible kindness and understanding gave me the needed impetus to go on.

I found myself as out of my depth during cocktail hours as among scholars in Modern Language Associations. A non-drinker, I held glasses awkwardly at first. After the Mayflower award was presented me, I was guest at a party in the home of Mr. and Mrs. Jonathan Daniels. My Mayflower Cup, which has a capacity of one pint, was filled with Scotch or Bourbon. I did not know which, since bootleg liquor for low blood pressure was the extent of my acquaintance with strong drink. A few guests sipped politely from the Cup, then passed it back to me. I was stuck with the remaining Bourbon or Scotch. There were no potted plants handy to empty it in, so I kept sipping. It grew warm in the Cup. I grew warm. As I triumphantly neared the last drops, I began sidling up to people and declaring warmly, "I like you!" One of these strangers I startled with my enthusiastic declarations was Margarette Smethurst of the *Raleigh News and Observer*, who subsequently became one of my most valued friends.

There were parties at home. The Seaboard Woman's Club gave a banquet in my honor. Swatches of purslane were painted on the place cards. An original poem was read in tribute. Silver and flowers were lavished on me. Later an autographing party was arranged. Seaboard came through for the home-town author.

· 30 ·

Fan Mail

FAN MAIL amazed me. It was startling in volume and content. Each letter seemed to reflect and fix in time a mood, an idiosyncrasy, a generous impulse, an affirmation of one kind or other. The total represented kindness and warmth, as well as foibles, of strangers and acquaintances. It showed the human instinct to fellowship in happiness as in the distresses of life. I answered the fan mail.

I felt a stir of pride when across the window of the Seaboard post office there were handed me letters bearing the return address and executive seals of the White House, the governor's office, the Mexican embassy and college presidents, one of whom I had taught.

Among them was Governor Clyde Hoey's letter. "I wish to add my word of congratulations," the Governor wrote, "upon the notable success attained by you and upon the high honor which has come to you through the North Carolina Literary and Historical Association. I am happy that your book was chosen for the award [Mayflower Cup] and wish to felicitate you upon meriting and winning this high distinction." There were also the letters of North Carolina's beloved Josephus Daniels who addressed me as "comrade." They prompted no fears that a Congressional investigating committee would ever ferret out any communistic leanings in Comrade Daniels or in the Seaboard addressee.

Foreign postmarks were impressive, too. There was poignancy in the appeal of those university people in Holland who, after Hitler had overrun their land so disastrously, were not ashamed to beg for books. I sent them my current novel. It was pleasant to hear from Bernard Darwin, grandson of the great scientist Charles Darwin, and other British fans who wrote that *Pates Siding* was one of their favorite books. Some of the London correspondence, it was told me, was sunk by German submarines.

There was an inquiry from a New Zealand author. "I noticed the announcement of your book, *Sweet Beulah Land,* that recently came into my hands by way of London, thus bringing to my notice a coincidence of which I might otherwise have been unaware. The coincidence is that in 1942 I published a book of stories under the title *Sweet Beulah Land,*" Roderick Finlayson wrote me on June 27, 1944. "I see that your book deals with rural life. So does mine—with rural life in the Auckland district of New Zealand. The title is a surprisingly unusual one for two authors to choose about the same time, don't you think? But perhaps the allusion isn't so unusual in the States. Most people here didn't know what I meant by such a title. One librarian thought that it referred to a region in Africa. Almost the only people who understood the reference were two U.S. marines who passed this way."

Roderick Finlayson then suggested that we exchange books. I was moved by the contrast in the physical appearance of his *Sweet Beulah Land* and mine and by the explanation of it. "On my publishers' behalf I would like to ask you not to judge the typographical faults of the book too harshly. It was printed," he wrote, "in spite of maddening difficulties, when the Japs, if not exactly knocking at our doors, at least were expected in at any moment—without knocking."

Mr. Finlayson and I were interested to find that both of us had ironical connotations in the use of our titles. "I hope you will have felt beneath the irony that in spite of everything there's faith in the land," he stated in one of his letters. We exchanged information about our genealogy and family and locale, about American writers and our own current work. I have often wondered what became of "Tidal Creek," which he was tentatively calling the book he was writing.

After *Portulaca*, George Laycock wrote a fan letter from a hospital in Shanghai:

It was disgraceful! It was unhealthy! What? The way I laughed and laughed, way down in my fever-stricken insides! I laughed so hard that I had to anchor the gurgles of my liquid diet with three pillows. I laughed until they had to give me three luminal tablets to get me to sleep, and the doctor forbade my finishing the book until I got better.

Here's the scene—an adopted North Carolinian (born in Virginia and still suffering from it!) who has lived in Charlotte, Durham, Chapel Hill and Albemarle, who has traveled into every nook and corner of the State from Manteo to Murphy and from Spruce Pine to Shallotte. I was ill with a sharp attack of flu, and the night before had fainted in the bathroom and gotten a deep gash in my head as I fell. A box came from Dale and Walter Spearman, and in it was THE BOOK which I had previously seen reviewed in one of the New York Sunday book sections. Here I was in my penthouse on top of a maternity hospital, with five floors of wailing newborns beneath me, with Mamas tired of laboring and Mamas heading for labor.

With fever over 103 I started the book. Couldn't exactly figure out the first chapter—thought it was my fever. Then I fell into the book. Bonwell in *Portulaca* might have been Albemarle. Every dog-goned one of those characters I know, have talked to and have listened to. The more I read the more I liked it and the more I laughed. The weird city of Shanghai that lay in a pool of glittering lights below me might have been a million miles away; I had gone back to a little North Carolina town, gone back so surely that I could smell the clean pine scent after a rain and the leaves burning on a fall afternoon. And suddenly I was nostalgic for cornpone and succotash and fried ham. I wanted the slangy talk across the booths in the local drug store, the politics-chewing in front of the filling station, a picnic out at the pond with a lot of senseless chatter and the camaraderie that typifies a crowd of Southerners together. Your book took me back and how!

Seaboard has probably given you hell, if I know my small towns. I hope it hasn't been too bad and that you will go on writing. This is just to tell you that I enjoyed it from beginning to end, and I really believe it's the medicine that has put me on my feet again. May I just plain thank you for writing it?

One day after the publication of my story, "Bantie Woman," in the *Saturday Evening Post*, I had a strange inquiry from a reader, also an author, in Georgia. She had just read "Bantie Woman" and the brief sketch of its author in "Keeping Posted." She had been startled to read the name of my novel, *Purslane*, for she had recently received a communication from Beyond and had been instructed to verify and confirm the authenticity of the message by the word, "purslayne."

After giving the pertinent facts about the loved one she had lost a year before, she wanted to know if I by any chance knew or knew of him. Why had I used the title, *Purslane?* Where had I got it? Did I have any guess as to why it came to her or what connection it had with the Beyond? In calling on me to help establish a veridical connection, she said she was acting on the impression of my human sympathy and understanding derived from "Bantie Woman."

Beyond sending her a copy of *Purslane* to read for clues, I was unable to help her establish any veridical connection with Beyond. Alas, she wrote later after searching the pages, the frequencies had apparently been mixed. "Have you read Stewart Edward White's *Unobstructed Universe?*" she asked.

"In such a universe it might be that a spontaneous and untrained psychic such as I seem to be might mix the frequencies, like the first crude radios, and so get 'purslayne' instead of a similar word which may have been intended." A nickname used in the family, one closely paralleling the title of my novel, already was giving her hope of proof of the veridical nature of the communication from Beyond.

"What could be more important," she concluded, "than to establish the fact that death does not kill us? You know O'Neill's play, 'Lazarus Laughs,' with its refrain, 'There is no death?' Nero, watching Lazarus burning at the stake, says he could not rule men at all if they were not afraid of death. Neither could Hitler."

During World War II there was fan mail from servicemen all over the world. *Portulaca* was among the books purchased in numbers by the United States Navy. Sailors read the book and wrote the author. Many of them were strangers. Some were boys I had known or taught who wrote from strange new worlds their appreciation of my book people and of scenes so familiar and dear to them.

From the South Pacific there were these words from a lieutenant in USNR: "*Sweet Beulah Land* survived the twelve thousand miles and reached me several days ago. Oh, how I love it! How I enjoyed every line of it. And most of all, how close it made me feel to the North Carolina you and I love so much. I'm personally grateful to you for writing it, even if it did make me terribly homesick." Others made similar admissions. They closed homesick letters with a gallant "Ha!" from the far Pacific. "So you don't have sugar. We have plenty. Why, I could take a sugar bath each night," one declared. "Just to be home—! Say, I'd trade chow with you. Ha!"

A technical sergeant in a bomber group wrote from England: "Your *Sweet Beulah Land* is getting dog-eared now, so many GIs are reading it. Your description of autumn in Carolina filled me with acute nostalgia. Your book and Thomas Wolfe's *You Can't Go Home Again* are the two I shall carry in my duffel bag wherever I go."

In another letter there was this: "You certainly have the

gift for making homey people take on sparkle and interest. I know every one of your characters. They are the salt of the earth. Your novel is making the rounds at this camp. It will be taken with me wherever the storms of war blow this GI."

"Au revoir and tous les mieux," they closed letters from France. Sometimes the complimentary close proved valedictory. One volunteer wrote me from France about his blue-eyed sweetheart in Asheville. As his former English teacher, I had tried to break him from dangling participles and splitting infinitives in otherwise flawless themes. I was so touched by his confidences from the battlefront about the girl he had left behind that I never knew whether he had split any infinitives or not. Not long after his letter he was blown to bits by a hand grenade.

It was the sincere, unstudied outpouring of good wishes and congratulations from people like those in *Purslane* and *Portulaca* that gave deepest satisfactions. At the beginning of my novel-writing not many relatives wrote. There were rumors of disapproval among some who felt they had been used as book characters.

I soon learned that no matter how earnestly an author declares the people in her book are fictional and do not represent any living persons except in composite or illumination, acquaintances are going to read themselves into the story. It is inconceivable to those who have known an author in the fortuities of daily living that she can create people and situations. And so she is often credited with a degree of omniscience, with knowledge of things she could not possibly know about.

Some relatives who identified themselves with my book people were not pleased. Sometimes there was good-natured banter in the identification. One family had hilarious fun acting out a scene from one of the books in which they believed they were characters. Among them was the great editor, Santford Martin, of the *Winston-Salem Journal*.

A cousin in Raleigh, formerly of Poole's Siding, congratulated herself that she was not in *Purslane*. "You are in it, too," her sister retorted. "You used to play 'Nearer My God To Thee' with variations, just like the girls in that book did!"

A postal employee from Wake County wanted to know how I ever found out about the itch epidemic he had been a victim of during Academy days. A woman corrected me about the place she and her childhood sweetheart had held their trysts. Other errors in fact were pointed out. Situations and happenings mentioned in my books had apparently involved many people. I was often asked, how had I heard?

The aunts of my Poole's Siding days had, for the most part, died before my novels were published. I had the gentle commendation of those who remained. Members of my immediate family have been constant fans. They have kept a clipping file on me, just as though I were Somebody and not mere kinfolks.

Nannie Lou Barbour of Clayton paid a fine tribute to her writing cousin. In her presence one of our cousins expressed the wish that there were greater appreciation of country life, that some writer would glorify the country and country people. Very quietly Nannie Lou said, "Bernice has done that." It was not unrelated to the tribute of Harry R. Warfel, of the University of Florida at the time. He wrote in his anthology: "Bernice Kelly Harris possibly of all other writers best reflects the spiritual elevation in common humanity."

The identification of characters and events went on in Northampton as in Wake County. An oyster supper at which a missionary society served three oysters in skim milk for twenty-five cents a bowl was pinpointed as a Seaboard happening, whereas I had never heard of it when it was written into *Portulaca,* any more than I had heard of itch epidemics in *Purslane.* Whatever appeared in my books, it seemed, had happened in Wake or Northampton. Likewise, Maine and Vermont readers identified people and events in my book with those of their region. I found that Kalline, for example, had traveled North and South in her trail of homes, that Cousin Sell had sat in sunny nooks and easy chairs all over the United States.

More questions were directed to me after the fifth novel than after any other. In this novel I wrote about colored people as human beings, not as copy. I deleted all reference to color and race, not with any wish to mystify or deceive readers, but rather to point up the essential oneness in the human experience, in happiness and tragedy and in love and hate. There were clues. In the early part of the book the slave ancestors of the principal characters were mentioned. At the end, the doctor who attended Jeems in his last illness called him Uncle and his wife, Aunty. This was supposed to reveal the color of Janey and Jeems.

For the most part the clues were overlooked. Editors and critics praised the "heart-warming story" and found it "moving and powerful." Diarmuid Russell, my agent in New York, commiserated with me. "It is a shame," he wrote, "and quite incredible that all the reviewers to date seem to have missed the point. Here is a book about Negroes as people, just as if they were Laplanders or Southern Baptists. See what happens. Even the supposedly enlightened members simply don't recognize it."

The point was not altogether missed, even before there was clarification from Doubleday. A woman from West Lafayette, Indiana, who planned to review *Janey Jeems* for a group at Purdue wrote to inquire if the book people were colored. "I sensed here and there through the book that they were colored, though it was only a sort of under-feeling," she said, adding that she loved the sort of accomplishment and living Janey typified, whatever her race. Similar inquiries came to my publishers. "Please tell us, was Janey Jeems white or colored?" a Mrs. Clower from Morganton, North Carolina, wrote Doubleday and Company. She and her friends had found *Janey Jeems* a "vastly interesting and authentic picture of, they had thought, mountain white folks" until they learned through advertisements that it was about colored people.

A reviewer in New York had, indeed, placed the locale of *Janey Jeems* in the Blue Ridge Mountains of North Carolina. This reviewer had spent an afternoon observing mountain folk and wondering what their manner of life was, their aspirations. "Now I know," the reviewer declared, "for it has all been revealed through this novel."

A New England woman wrote: "My mind was so attuned to your lovely, vital handling of our white country folk in your other books that I took it for granted this [*Janey Jeems*] was on the same lines and entirely missed the reference to slave ancestry. Now that I know it, I can see a thousand characteristics [of colored people] and I admire your skill the more and your love for human beings. I have a real appreciation of the normal life and simple humanity of our colored people and am sick of the absurd approach which most fiction makes."

Dr. J. O. Bailey stated that he knew Janey and Jeems were colored on the first page. The young daughter of Mrs. Charles Doak of Raleigh said after finishing the novel: "Mother, there's something in this book I want to see if you discover as you read it." Mrs. Doak made the discovery for herself that Janey was colored. Ovid Pierce, whose beautiful novel, *The Plantation*, gives such an authentic picture of colored people, was aware. Doubtless there was an awareness among many others whose reading experience I did not know about.

One reviewer on the *New York Herald Tribune* staff did not miss the point of the book. "Mrs. Harris has apparently written a unique novel," he said. "*Janey Jeems* is certainly the first book I've seen which treats a Negro family without crusading tactics, without condescension and without minstrel-show humor. It is written with such warmth and understanding that one might finish the book and have overlooked the few clues to Janey's color, for her color is simply a physical characteristic, not a cross to be borne, not an excuse to shirk social responsibilities. This is not an agitating novel. But it is one of the finest tributes to the Negro race ever written. That a novel so free of racial prejudice could emanate from the South will likely prove a surprise to many readers."

At first it had been disturbing to me that my characters and locale had been assigned to the Blue Ridge Mountains, particularly when I had written them into the cotton and peanut country in the Elizabeth City area. Then I realized that I had made my point after all. Janey and Jeems were human beings, whose universality made locale and color essentially unimportant. Fan mail helped me to reach this conclusion.

Yankee Editor and the Home Town

MY BOOKS were quietly successful. In comparison with best sellers of the period, the royalties were unimpressive. But I was impressed. And Herbert was.

At first he had opposed my writing. It was not necessary, he said. If it was to keep me company that I wrote—well, wasn't he there? If it was in the hope of making a little extra money—well, we had what we had, didn't we?

Because of the early opposition, I had made a point of writing only when alone in the house. I could understand how pointless the scribbling seemed to a businessman when it did not mean any coupons to clip or dividends to collect. After the *Saturday Evening Post* bought my little story, "Bantie Woman," Herbert's attitude changed. He was amazed at how much was paid for so little. Impulsively he declared he'd hold the flashlight for me to write by if necessary!

Another story, "Yellow Color Suit," was bought by *Colliers*. Doubleday was getting out the novels. *Sweet Beulah Land* had followed *Portulaca*. Then *Sage Quarter* began to take shape. John Woodburn had gone from Doubleday to

Harcourt-Brace, and Clara Claasen had become my editor. The
mood of the new novel was set by a song which an old colored
woman sang to John Woodburn during his weekend visit to
Seaboard, soon after he had changed editorial desks. We drove
down a country road to see old Aunt Tank, the most colorful
character in our area, and she sang with flourishes for the
Yankee gentleman:

> The peach trees is all in bloom,
> The peach trees is all in bloom,
> The peach trees is all in bloom,
>
> So come, my love, and go with me.
> Go with me to the wedding, oh
> Go with me to the wedding, oh
> Go with me to the wedding, oh
>
> Come, my love, and go with me.
> Here, my love, is your wedding ring,
> Here, my love, is your wedding ring,
> Here, my love, is your wedding ring,
> So come, my love, and go with me.

The ballad, not in print so far as our combined research
indicated, fascinated John Woodburn. It was fitting, he observed, that the mood of *Sage Quarter* was peach trees all in
bloom. It was springtime and white hammocks, which the little
Ardley girl in the novel craved as I had in my own childhood.
It was thistlebird's per-chic-oree, lambs bleating in the meadow,
pink fog of blossoms upon upturned furrows, June apples
reddening above a white hammock that was never realized
except in dreams.

That Easter weekend was in the mood of the novel. We
spent it in pleasant talk. We enjoyed Northampton ham and
the best dishes Mattie had in her repertory of delicious meals.
We had a party so that village friends could meet the New
York editor, and throughout the evening the Civil War was
barely mentioned, only Miss Clara did mention that it should
never have been called "civil" after what the Yankees did to the
South. On Sunday we attended church services. John Wood-

burn held the hymnal with me and sang a kind of tenor to my alto.

Of his visit to our little town the New York editor wrote:

> I can't tell you how pleasant, how serene and refreshing my visit with you and Herbert was. I shall never have such food again unless I come to Seaboard, and it will be very hard indeed for me to find nicer people. I want to thank you and Herbert for two and a half of the most golden days I have ever had. Please remember me to all the nice people whom I met and to the village of Seaboard in general. Put an extra dime in the collection plate for Brother Trueblood the next Sunday you partake of his spiritual fare. And put a peanut beside you on the pew to mark my place.
>
> Tell Aunt Tank that I wish she and I had been contemporaries. I would like to have taken her dancing about sixty years ago . . . Some day when I am old and gray perhaps I shall take a place on the Richmond Pike and try to persuade Mattie to leave you and cook for me, and grow fat and lazy on Northampton ham.

In subsequent letters he inquired when I was coming to New York. "When are you ever coming to New York?" he wrote. "Fifth Avenue and Madison and Broadway are murmurous with slurring Southern accents these days. Every summer from June to September the Mason-Dixon matrons put on their orange rouge and come to occupy the city in retaliation, I suppose, for some things that happened eighty years ago. I once saw three of them standing near the entrance to Central Station staring inscrutably at Sherman's statue, saying nothing in a soft Southern accent."

What a capacity the New York editor had to adapt himself to village patterns and moods. Sometimes he seemed adaptable enough to have been one of my own creations, a man of Bonwell in *Portulaca* or of Elmhurst in *Sweet Beulah Land*, or a man of perceptiveness and whimsy and warmth in a novel yet to be written.

In the last letter I had from him he wrote: "Aren't you ever coming to New York?"

Seven years later I went to New York. But John Woodburn was not there.

It was in the *Saturday Review* that I read John Woodburn was dead.

· 32 ·

Distillation

THE SOURCE of my writing has been impressions of people and their inter-relationships. From the little roads of sand and ruts, from village streets and towns, these have been distilled into narrative with whatever creative power has been given me.

Intimations of differences in neighbors and kin around Poole's Siding began in my childhood. People through the decades have validated a belief in their essential goodness, warped and inverted though it often is. It is gratifying to know that a critic found "the spiritual elevation in common humanity" characterizing my treatment of them.

The distillation has included many people. The most comprehensive was the result of an assignment. Soon after my first novel was submitted, W. T. Couch, regional director of the Federal Writers' Project in addition to being director of the University Press, asked me to write for the Project. One of the objectives, in keeping with the spirit of the national administration, was to gather firsthand information about the underprivileged as well as about other groups in our society. Writers were paid a small salary to interview people in various social brackets. I had already been doing something like this for the little personal journal, "My Days." So I agreed to extend the experience and work for Mr. Couch.

My assignment was farm people and those whose work or profession was related to them. Firsthand information and opinion on the current farming situation were collected from an agriculture extension supervisor and from cotton ginners, from a judge of Recorder's Court, from ministers and school teachers, from a general practitioner and a county health doctor, from landlords big and small, from the village insurance agent and the time merchant, from justices of the peace and even from the local undertaker. These, placed side-by-side with the stories of sharecroppers and other farm laborers, were often illuminating.

The urgencies have changed form since the interviews. The status of the people who voiced their exigencies then has been modified by mechanization and industrialization or by an authoritative finality. The human problems and needs have not been resolved by the progress made or by a government's increasing consciousness of the welfare of all the people. For all the improvement, technology has not yet solved the problem of unemployment and substandard housing or of surpluses and starvation. Vital elements, these still do not compose the human story, or novelists might be sociologists instead of creative writers.

On May 5, 1961, Alan Shepherd looked down from space upon the earth and exclaimed, "What a beautiful view!" A close-up view such as I took in the farming area in 1939 would reveal much that is far from beautiful on the earth now as then. It would doubtless reveal beauty among penury and want and despair now as it did in that decade. For love and decency and humor, though not as spectacular as hate and lust and greed, are still essentially the human story.

The human story recorded then is illustrative. In their own vernacular the people related their stories, and afterwards they were distilled into my fiction.

A wretchedly penniless sharecropper lamented not having any Santa Claus cheer for her children at Christmas.

"Clayra Virginia rushed in from school on Friday," she began her story, "saying that Santa Claus come to their schoolroom that day and promised to bring all the little girls and boys whatever they was mind to ask for. She asked Santa for a big doll and tricycle. I told Clayra Virginia you had to pay Santa for him to come to see you.

" 'No, you don't, Mammy,' she said. 'He told us this evening all we had to do was ask for what we wanted.' "

The mother reached to the mantel for a miniature plaster of Paris statue of Santa Claus with an empty bag. "One of the younguns got this little Santa off the Christmas tree one year at school. Clayra Virginia wanted it took off the mantelpiece and hid out of sight, because one of the schoolchildren told her if the sure-'nough Santa Claus came and saw another one here he'd go back to the North Pole and not leave nothing.

" 'Mammy,' Clayra Virginia said to me before she went to sleep, 'don't forget to hide that Santa on the mantel.'

"Next morning when she woke up, she looked all around the room for a doll and tricycle. Then she looked at the mantel.

"The little Santa with the empty bag was there. I'll tell you the truth, I did hide it. I kept it hid just about all night. Before daylight I tipped in to see if anything had been left during the night. Course I knowed nothing had. Course I did. I wasn't simple enough at my age to believe in Santa Claus. But yet and still, yet and still—" Her voice trailed off.

With a start as though she had been dreaming about a Santa Claus from the North Pole, she straightened herself and finished her story. "When Clayra Virginia saw the Santa on the mantel, she turned on me, crying and railing at me for my forgetfulness."

I was startled that the mother took her child's reproaches without telling her the truth. I expressed surprise.

"I tell you the God's truth," she said. "I took it because I didn't want Clayra Virginia not to believe in Santa Claus."

If she had hidden the statue, the real Santa would have left a doll and tricycle. In her warped idea of faith there was a lovely validity. I later based a story on it which I called "Santa on the Mantel."

Colorful personalities, human interest, historical sidelights from slavery days and folklore enlivened the account of urgent social needs and farm problems and illumined people. One of the urgencies, as evident as the social, was the need of the lonely and forgotten to tell all to a sympathetic listener, the personal *all* as well as the economic. In this respect a writer on the Project sometimes became involuntary father-confessor.

This was true in the case of one woman on the *Tobacco Road* level. "I will tell you the God's truth," she greeted me at the door, "we ain't got nothing. Not nothing! Even our turnip patch failed us this year. We had one hoe-cake of corn-bread for our Christmas dinner."

She then began to tell me all—the injustices of landlords, her family's wretched existence, the failures and penury, the illegitimacy of her first child, her sins and shortcomings, her operations at Roanoke Rapids Hospital.

She followed me to the door at the end of the interview and with a kind of desperate brightness in her voice whispered, "Last fall the doctors over at the Rapids took out all my female organs." It was as though she was impelled to brag about something. The final revelation seemed strangely to purge her despair, for she smiled and exclaimed: "But you just wait till the turkle crawls again, and I'll be out a-trying! I'll scrape 'nure out of the road after the horses, and I'll fertilize our turnip patch till it's green as p'ison. I ain't clean down. Me and the turkle will crawl again!"

This general urge for a sympathetic listener made it possible for me to conduct the interviews with little difficulty. Another help was that Herbert, who took me on the missions, knew these people. He had dealt with them at the cotton gin, and they unfailingly without any exceptions trusted and liked him. Otherwise there might have been resentment or withdrawal at the inquiries that often had to be very personal. Even more, any mention of the government as the instigator of these interviews made open sesame for me. The government at that time was the Great White Father for so many.

It was not open sesame among the Portuguese in upper Northampton. These people were possibly descendants of Portuguese traders who had come up the Roanoke River in earlier times. It was alleged that they had intermixed with Indians or Negroes, though many had the blue eyes and straight hair of white ancestors. The colony almost militantly asserted its identity as Portuguese. Census-takers had learned, allegedly at gunpoint, not to ask these people if they were white.

The county provided a school for them, with a white teacher. The churches sent white pastors to conduct services for them in their school building until they were able to build their own chapel. There they worship today, a little colony apart, not accepted by one race and themselves rejecting the other.

The story of a Portuguese girl from this colony who had gone to teach school in Wilson County and who had "passed" successfully for awhile had been intriguing, as told to us by P. J. Long, our county superintendent. Some wayward suspicions of the school community had finally prompted investigation. The Portuguese girl had lost her job in the white school. In my English class a little one-act tragedy had been written with warmth and understanding by Sarah Hart about this girl from upper Northampton.

It was my thought now that interviews might help the situation among these people. Their manner of life was indicated by the drab little houses along their roads. It seemed that most of the buildings leaned toward the west, as though tired from the heat and toil of the day like their owners.

There was the errant hope that somewhere among the Portuguese I might uncover the sequel to the story of the Portuguese teacher and others like it. But there was no cooperation. We were met with cold stares or unfriendliness or suspicion. Guarded answers were made to questions. Most of them were monosyllables. We managed to get invited into the living room of one family, but immediately the exits and

entrances became disconcerting to us. It was as though messengers were being dispatched to outside, as though some
underground were being alerted. Then a silent man came in
with a fierce-looking German police dog and took his seat,
holding the dog in leash. Herbert disclaimed fright, but he
took the initiative in our departure. Not even mention of the
government's wish to better conditions among farming people
availed. Later I wondered if some Indian strain in the Portuguese distrusted the Great White Father in Washington.

Herbert was sure he had a more likely theory. We had
doubtless stumbled upon a bootlegger's headquarters.

Elsewhere personal stories unfolded. Wretchedness was
shockingly evident. Pathos underlay facts. Tragedy stalked
the little roads. Hopelessness waited for the release of death.
Yet there was jollity sometimes even amid the starkness.
Human dignity struggled for expression. A sort of mass
philosophy was articulated over and over.

There was more money in working at the mill in Roanoke
Rapids, as many had done intermittently, but there was better
living on the farm—and both ways a man just broke even.
That was contentment, breaking even at the end of the year and
hoping next year to be ahead at settlement time. The objective
always glimmering before these people was to find a good place
to live, so as not to be constantly "tore up and a-moving." As
for folks of the present time, they were no worse than they
used to be: we just knew more about them, that was the size
of it.

There was the hope for decent burial, even beyond decent
living. In the most wretched circumstances, white and colored
alike prayed the Lord to keep death away till they had some
decent clothes to be buried in, till they were far enough ahead
so they wouldn't have to be put away by the county.

The landlord of a small farm, with his own land problems
too, summed it up on March 11, 1939. "The prospect for the
farmer looks very gloomy today. But we've pulled out of a
lot of bad times in the past, and maybe it will be better than
we think. There were panic years in 1889 and 1893, when

cotton farmers thought they were ruint. But cotton has been as high as forty cents a pound since then. By 1960—but a lot of us won't have to worry about cotton by that time." And, indeed, Mr. Spencer has not had to worry about cotton or anything else since 1943.

I found during this interval, and since, that the human spirit is amazingly resilient and triumphant. There was Miss Sis, whose aim was "not to make a mess of living or of dying." At seventy-five she started attending an adult illiteracy class to learn to read. If a ride to the class was not available she set out on foot the four miles to Seaboard. When she gauged her blood pressure to be higher than usual, she filled her bonnet crown with cool green leaves along the way in order to keep the pressure down so she could read her assignment for the illiteracy class. And with what militancy she read the gentle Shepherd Psalm the afternoon I was there! With what creative militancy she lived. And when time was out for her here, she did not make a mess of dying. She sat in her chair and waited for death, as for company.

With what painstaking care Mrs. Carter read her assignment for the illiteracy class the afternoon I was visitor. "Home is the shelter I build for my wife and my children against all evil. Home is a woman watching from a window for my coming. I pray God that Home may be the memory of kindness left to my children. Home is the hope that my sons shall carry on all I have left unfinished."

There were no sons at the Carters' house. And what would there be left to carry on? They might well pray that Home would be the memory of kindness for their daughters. For all seemed wretchedness otherwise—an old shell of house the wind blew through, heart trouble and hypertension and arthritis for the dwellers within, no money to pay the time merchant or the doctor or the storekeeper for shoes and warm clothes. Topping the misery was fear that Mrs. Carter would have to go back to the insane asylum where she had recently spent five months—a fear that shadowed their activities, forced him to come in constantly to check on her, kept her watching from her window for his coming.

They were thankful for the magazines I had brought. They could not read, but it was company for them to look at the pictures.

"She's about ruint her eyes trying to see out of ten-cent store glasses," Mr. Carter said. He picked up an issue of *Time* and began turning the pages. "My eyes is all right, my arms is just too short." He held the magazine as far as his arms would reach. "Who's this?" he asked pointing to a picture.

"President Roosevelt," I told him.

He studied the picture of President and Mrs. Roosevelt in a car with Mayor LaGuardia. "Fat old scound'el, ain't he?" His tone was full of affection. "Roosevelt's tried to help the forgotten man, he sure has." His eyes were on the Mayor all the time.

"Looks nice to see husband and wife setting side by side," Mrs. Carter said reflectively, looking at the picture. "Me and him has been married thirty years. I fell in love the first time I ever saw him. It was at a pea-popping. I couldn't take my eyes off of him, looked like."

"I thought well of her too," Mr. Carter said.

"He was ugly when I married him," she teased. "See how I've improved him since I got him? La', the girls he did have! He was always kicking me, and I'd cry my eyes out. I've shed enough tears over him to wash my dress."

"She got me though—good got me."

"I've got a valentine he give me before we was married, one of the prettiest you ever saw. I'll show you." She reached into a little tin trunk and held up the valentine.

"Aw—!" he said looking ruefully at the valentine, then glancing in my direction. "It's nothing—just two folded sheets of tablet paper, cut up into lace with the scissors. It's yellow now—"

"Yes," she nodded. "I've had it thirty years. And I wouldn't part with it, for no amount of money."

"Aw!" The weight of his wretchedness lifted suddenly as he looked at her.

"Home is a woman watching from a window for my coming," I said to myself as I left the miserable shack.

The Carters appeared in *Sweet Beulah Land.*

Around the countryside there were people with insoluble problems. There were defections and ill will, greed and envy. There was despair. There was triumph too.

The most colorful of all the persons interviewed was a little brown elf by the name of Tank Daughtry. Diminutive, sparrow-like, wiry and active, this seventy-four-year-old woman lived alone in her unpainted three-room cabin. Two braids of thin gray hair were wound tight with strings across the top of her head. From her ears dangled gold earrings. A silver signet ring flashed on her finger. Large safety pins were strung along the front of her dress like medals. Her tiny feet were encased in narrow brown high-top shoes, pointed at the toes as an elf's should be.

Though old, she was ageless. It would not have been out of character for her to fly like Peter Pan or ride a broom like the witch some neighbors believed her to be. She may have practiced magic, as some said, but her witchery seemed kindly, at least to the casual observer. She was a magical hostess. The stories she told were entrancing. She dramatized them, acting the parts so vividly that the dramatis personae were projected in person there in the quaint cluttered setting of her cabin.

She danced and sang for her guests. It was likely she used folk songs passed down orally from one generation to another, with no printed musical arrangement whatever.

"When I got to going with John Jenkins," Tank began one of her little dramatizations, "my father kept his eye on me so tight I had a time slipping off and meeting him. I was very young, and my folks didn't think anybody was good enough for me nohow. Me and John set a day to run away and get married. I was to meet him in Margarettsville, but by the time I made it there my father was right behind me. He stuck to me so tight there was no chance to run farther that day.

"He brought me back home and put me to spinning. Long

as the loom was running he'd know where I was, he thought. I spun and sung and sung and spun.

"Zoom, zoom—

" 'The peach trees is all in bloom.'

"Zoom, zoom—

" 'The peach trees is all in bloom.'

"Zoom, zoom—

" 'Come, my love, and go with me.'

" 'I don't know what in the world makes anybody think I care about John Jenkins,' I'd say between the zoom-zooming of the loom and my peach tree song, loud enough for my father to hear it.

" 'Come with me to the wedding, O—'

"Zoom, zoom—

" 'Come with me to the wedding, O—'

"Zoom, zoom—

" 'Come, my love, and go with me.'

" 'Nobody needn't think I want John Jenkins,' I'd say for my father to hear. 'I've heard him and Jane Martin is going to be married. Hope they will. Don't make no difference to me who he has.' And all the time my heart was just burning up with love for John Jenkins.

" 'Here, my love, is your wedding ring.'

"Zoom, zoom—

" 'Here, my love, is your wedding ring.'

"Zoom, zoom—

" 'Sooner he has Jane Martin, the better it'll suit me.'

"I finally convinced my father. 'You can quit spinning and go to bed now,' he told me.

" 'All right, Papa.'

"Now, I knowed Papa was going to spy on me awhile when I went to my room, and I knowed I was going to marry John Jenkins that night. Sure 'nough, I saw Papa easing round the corner of the house watching the window, eeldropping on me. I made 'tend like I was going to undress, and I says to my sister, 'I don't know how come Papa thinks I aim to marry John Jenkins. What does he think I want with him?'

" 'Don't go to sleep, John Jenkins,' I'd whisper to myself. 'I'm coming to you.'

" 'That old John Jenkins! I ain't a-studying him. Oh, I'm so slee-ee-eepy. Let me get 'tween them sheets. You won't hear nothing from me till day.'

"That convinced my father. We heard him ease back into his room. I give him time to go to bed. Then I grabbed my accordion under one arm, stole out'n the house and run as hard as I could to John Jenkins!"

Tank danced in the happy rhythm of an old memory. Suddenly she grew tense and still as she improvised weird minor notes for another song.

> I'll build me an eyrie
> In the mountains so high,
> Where the wild birds will see me
> As they pass by—

The words and minor notes suited the little brown elf. Then as though responding to a rhythm beyond any commonplace meter, she began dancing and singing,

> Farewell, goodbye, my love,
> I'll bid you this 'dieu,
> I am ruint forever
> By love of you.
> My mind was to marry
> And never to part,
> The fust time I saw you
> You wounded my heart.
> So farewell, I bid you this 'dieu,
> I am ruint forever
> By love of you.

The song of the Woods was more commonplace. Sharecropper Wood was breaking even. He had $4.90 left over at settlement time. There was little prospect of getting ahead in 1940. His wife was tired and hurting and no longer hopeful. Their high school son wanted to be a pilot or a Carolina Playmaker, though the realization seemed far away. They sang together, accompanying themselves on the broken organ and the banjo with three strings. Their song was,

Home, home, home sweet home,
Be it ever so humble there's no place like home.

The song of Mariah Barnes, born in slavery some eighty-eight years before but now as free as Mister Anybody, was "thank God, thank God, thank God." Other ex-slaves realized freedom less exuberantly in their reminiscences.

"I recollect just as good as if 'twas yesterday when the Yankees come through," Mariah Barnes began her story. "Miss Bettie looked across the field and saw them coming. 'Law, Riah, yonder comes Big Bill on Jenny Lind mule and the Yankees right behind him!' Miss Bettie said and gathered up her apron and begun to cry. After a little while she said, 'Riah, them's bad folks. They gwine kill us!'

"The yard was soon covered with Yankees. I thought they was the prettiest sight, with the blue suits and caps and gold stripes. Right off they wanted the keys to unlock the smoke-house, the dairy and the grist mill. They took sheets out of the great house, poured flour in them and give it all to we colored folks. They give us hams of meat and all the something t'eat they could find on the place. Then they lit light'ood torches and set fire to the grist mill. Course I was young and didn't know no better, but I thought that grist mill burning up was the prettiest thing I'd ever seen. I heard one of the slaves saying it meant freedom, thank God, thank God, thank God.

"The slaves were all mighty proud to be free. Some of the marsters had been good and some mean. Some of them to our knowing would strip the slaves and whip their backs till the blood streamed out, then throw a bucket of salt water over the raw backs. Some wasn't allowed to meet at night to pray and shout, which was all the good times they had. As for us, we slipped off after dark to one of the cabins and held prayer meetings anyway. We turned a wash pot over near the door, up off the floor a little, so it'd catch all the sound. Then the slaves shouted and prayed loud as Mister Anybody. Sometimes when one would get full of grace and raise the shout too high, the other slaves would throw him down on the bed and cover up his head so he wouldn't be heard outside in case the padderollers was proguing round.

"Gen'l Person's folks treated me good. When I was a little thing old mistis used to put me down at the foot of her bed like a hot water bottle to keep her feet warm. I was treated as good as the white children on our plantation. But all the same when freedom come, I chimed in with the other slaves and said, 'Thank God, thank God, thank God!'

"We soon found out freedom didn't fill no stomachs, not for long. It's been a scuffle from then to now. But when I sets down to my little cake of flour bread and my cup of hot water and thinks about the folks that is eating pork chops and beef and drinking store-bought coffee, I thinks to myself I am just as free as they is, and I still says, 'Thank God, thank God, thank God.' "

Berl Barnes seemed less thankful than nostalgic in his reminiscence. He remembered well the day his master explained their new status to the slaves on his place. "We all gathered in the yard and waited till old marster come out," he reminisced. "He walked up to us and said, 'Well, boys, you all is free as I am. If you work for me any longer, I've got to hire you. You're free to make a bargain with whoever you would like to work for now. And don't let nobody pay you with Confederate money. It ain't no good now.' I recollect they give the children Confederate money to play with.

"When we slaves was turned loose we was all give a peck of meal and four pounds of middling meat from marster's smokehouse. Then we was allowed to cut down enough of old marster's pines to put us up little log houses in the clearing of the woods. After freedom all we got for a day's work was nine pence. Them was hard times, sure 'nough. It was the first time I had ever been hungry, after I was free."

The slaves thanked God for freedom, but their children and grandchildren have been climbing steadily to attain it. The daughter of one slave reflects in her effort something of the hard ascent. Sallie Jordan is a widow. She lived just back of our garden for twenty-three years. She slaved day in and day out for her ten children. Once in contemplative mood she said, "I've sharecropped, day-labored, ditched, dug stumps, railed fences, worked all day in the field and then washed and ironed at night. If all the work I ever did was piled up in one field, it would make a mountain too high to climb."

Sallie's father was one of General Matt Ransom's slaves. For years after she moved away from the river plantation, life was extremely hard. With the five dollars a week that she realized from washing and ironing and housecleaning, she somehow managed to feed and clothe her children. Her own clothes she accumulated from white neighbors in exchange for odd jobs she did for them. She named her daughters for these neighbors. (Bernice Kelly Jordan and Bernice Kelly Harris sometimes in later years got their mail mixed.)

"I never heard white folks complain because we lived among them," Sallie began her story. "We've all been neighbors together, helping one another out and sharing whatever there's been to share. If I had greens in my garden and my white friends didn't, I'd send them a mess. And they'd do the same. We were good to one another as we knowed how.

"Douglas, my oldest son, helped pay for his pencils and paper with the money he got for doing little odd jobs for white folks. Before and after school he was always trying to help out, knowing how many I had to buy school supplies for and feed and clothe. He had a feeling for me different from most children. Whenever folks would give him cake or little fancy cookies, he wouldn't eat a bite till he had brought it home and divided with me. He had a regular job once—toting in wood and sweeping porches and bringing mail from the post office— and the lady he worked for always fixed him a lunch to take along to school with him.

"But she began to notice that Douglas always turned back towards home after she had given him his lunch, instead of keeping on to school. She asked me about it. It happened that winter I was down in the bed with rheumatism for days at the time and not able to stir up much to eat for any of us. So Douglas always toted that bagful of vittles back to me and went on to school without any for himself. From a little one, he would divide. He wanted me to have the cake and him keep the bread. When he quit the seventh grade and went up to a CCC camp near Asheville, he made a point of sending me $18 or $20 out of his wages along. That kept up, wherever he worked afterwards.

"Nig was my oldest girl. She was always mighty smart around the house as well as in her books. She had cooking jobs in white folks' houses when she was just a missy girl. Several women wanted to hire her as regular cook for their families, but Nig wanted to go on to school and try to make something of herself. So I wouldn't push her out to work, bad as I needed the money. I boarded her two winters in Garysburg, for there wasn't a high school for the colored in Seaboard then. She paid one dollar a week for room rent and carried enough vittles from home to last from Monday to Friday, excusing maybe a loaf of bread or a can of salmons, which she could buy in Garysburg. I don't know how I paid that dollar a week to keep her in school, but somehow I did, and the two years went by and Nig finished high school."

Later Nig worked in New York and married a preacher there.

"There were times," Sallie continued her story, "when I didn't leave home from Christmas to Christmas, years I couldn't even get over to the river to see my daddy, much as I thought of him, and him only twenty miles away. I simply didn't have clothes fitting to wear out, or a way to get nowhere but walk. I stayed home and tried to send my children out to school and church looking neat and clean. It took a lot to get shoes on ten children's feet and give them two meals a day. There weren't many doctor bills. We have been healthy, or we'd have had to suffer it out anyhow. I use the old home remedies and patent medicine when one of us gets sick. Bettie Blue had pneumonia this past gone winter, and I had to have the doctor once. Mostly I've nursed and doctored my own children. I'm glad to say I've never had to lay one out.

"I never could stand the thought of having any of us put away by the county. So I carry burial insurance for all of us, which amounts to $1.10 a month. Wood is to pay for, coal oil, school books and using things, but that insurance money's got to come. The children get so anxious to pretty up things around here that last spring I bought a little green paint to satisfy them. So they stretched that paint far enough to cover the swing and yard chairs.

"After all them years of staying home, I finally did fix myself up enough to go see May get her seventh grade diploma. Till then I'd never seen a child of mine on the stage. I owe a heap of it to President Roosevelt. When he come in, things got better in this country for poor folks. I got some flour and grapefruit and prunes over at the welfare, and that helped a lot. Then the CCC was a blessing too, bad as I hated to see Douglas leave home. I don't get help from the government now, but I sha'n't ever forget that I did when I needed it so bad. Life don't even look the same any more. Hard as I still have to work, it's all in better heart now. I get out to the P.T.A. and to most all the free programs at school. When Bettie Blue and Dorothy and Bernice Kelly are on the stage, they're bound I shall go and see them act.

"I've brought many a baby into this world, my own and other folks's. I've helped lay folks out and sit up with the dead. I've had white and colored tell me their troubles. I've had plenty myself. I've give way to temper sometimes, let my mad get the best of me. But I've never done nothing I was real ashamed of, nothing my daddy couldn't know—or General Ransom. I don't know what's ahead, but I do know the Lord has blessed me, and I'm thankful for it."

What was ahead for Mrs. Sallie Jordan is now on record. It is a story of accomplishment. She bought a little white cottage in Ghent, the eastern section of town. She sent three daughters through college. Betty, after attending St. Augustine's in Raleigh and New York University, has become a guidance counselor in Durham. Dorothy was graduated at Winston-Salem Teachers College and is now teaching in Coates Elementary School in Seaboard. Bernice Kelly, after finishing at North Carolina College in Durham, became a teacher of commercial education in Stuttgart, Germany. Carl was graduated at New York University and is now a Certified Public Accountant.

David, Calvin and Carl served in the United States Navy; Samuel in the Army. May is a waitress in Brooklyn. The children are scattered now—in New York, in Norfolk, in Durham, in Burlington and overseas. One daughter continues to live with Sallie and teach school. Through them, her usefulness has been extended.

Sallie herself still works every day. She is cook in the Reid Harris home and charwoman for the Baptist Church. In between her regular hours she takes on odd jobs of practical nursing and housecleaning. In christenings or weddings or wakes, white friends want Sallie close by.

On Mother's Day, 1961, her church made Mrs. Sallie Jordan Mother of the Year. She might well have had a sense of looking down from a high mountain.

The persons interviewed during the Writers' Project are representative of people in every community. They are there, to find. Few are like Eddie Davis, a classic example of the triumph of the human spirit.

Eddie Davis was mending a basket. In and out, in and out he tirelessly wove new splints among the old, dark from use and age, until the mended basket became attractively checkerboard.

Eddie was deformed. His spine did not support the frail, misshaped one-sided body. Instead of sitting to his work, he had to lie to it, his stomach across a chair and his weight on one elbow, as he assisted his hands with his teeth. From the blue denim garment, which was like an infant's long dress, his feet lay bare in the sunshine.

The stark feet were not important. The malformed head set on hunched shoulders, the man's features and the infant body, the queer garment that covered his deformity were not important. For Eddie Davis was not of this deformity. He laughed and sang and smoothed off his whiteoak splints, exhibited his handiwork with pride, and explained to his visitor how he made baskets and ferneries and lamps.

"I'm mighty lucky," he said, "for I've got my health and plenty work to do most of the time." He reached among his samples for a flower stand. "This is tedious to make, but not as tedious as the ferneries. I made one for Mrs. Bowers over at Jackson, and it took me three days to finish just a few inches of work. The flower stands I can't sell no cheaper than $1.50 each and come out. Mrs. Bowers give me $15 for a floor lamp I made for her out of my reed work." He reached for other samples of his work. "These trays is made out of reeds, and these little flower holders out of sticks. For a hamper basket like this I charge one dollar. It takes about three days to make it. For a little one made on this order I get fifty cents, though the little ones is more tedious to make than the big ones. Course I get right smart tired pulling on the drawing knife, but I ain't satisfied without something on hand to do.

"About two years ago the county agent brought a woman from Durham here, and she wrote a piece about me for Mr. Goerch's paper, with my picture in it. Mr. Goerch raised money to buy me a radio, and the home agent brought it to me. I have sure enjoyed it. I like string music and hymns the best, though Supper Time Frolic is plenty good. Nothing on the radio beats Governor Hoey. I listen to him teaching the Sunday school lesson every time I can get him. I some kind of wanted to go hear Governor Hoey when he was in Jackson a few weeks ago, but my brothers were tired that night and didn't feel like taking me.

"I've seen one governor, Governor McLean, the time he come to Conway. I never saw a picture show or a circus or the ocean. But I saw a mess of water the Sunday my folks took me over to Edenton. That's the farthest I've ever been. Most of my going is round here in the neighborhood—to church, to the store and to ball games. They put me in this little red wagon—" Eddie pointed to the vehicle, which was like those little boys play with—"then they pull me up the highway to the ball ground or the store of Mr. Harvey Long. Mr. Long's daughter told me the other day that sometimes when I'm up there at the store I can go in their house and see the piano. I never saw a piano, but I believe I could make music on one. I could play with one hand on our organ, if 'twasn't for the peddling.

"We've had our organ twelve years. It's a good one, though it didn't cost us but $12. We got it secondhand from the church in Jackson, when they changed to piano music. I learnt Fennie, my sister, to play organ music by note. It was hard, though, for she had done started playing by ear. I'd rather learn somebody that don't know a note than one that plays by ear. Old Uncle John Peebles, a colored man that lives close by, learnt me my notes and how to sing different parts.

"I can sing a mean bass. Soprano and tenor, too, but not good since I had flu." Eddie turned to his mother. "Ma, bring me some hymn books. I'm going to sing notes to a song and see if Mrs. Harris knows what it is."

He opened the songbook his mother brought and started singing notes.

> Do do do re do do do
> Mi fa sol fa mi do re.
> Do do do re do do do
> Mi fa sol fa mi do re.

Eddie was pleased that I identified "Jesus, Lover of My Soul."

"I sing at church when I go, which is most Sundays we have preaching. I'm a member of Galatia Baptist Church. They put me in a chair to baptize me, and I got along all right with it. I pay around a dollar a year for pastor's salary and more when I can. After that piece in Mr. Goerch's paper, I got a New Testament from a lady in Greenville. She wrote in the front, 'For Eddie, from Mrs. Wilson, Greenville, 1936.' It's such nice big print I can see good to read it. A day don't hardly go by but what I don't read some in my Testament.

"I try to keep a little savings account in the bank, not much, but a little to take care of me when I'm old. I'm pushing on toward forty now. One time I put $100 in the bank and another time $50, saved out of my ferneries and baskets and flower stand money. I helped buy our automobile and pay for the gas to run it. My brothers is good about taking me. I crawl around here in the house and yard. Ma helps me when I get in a tight place."

His mother stooped to pick a piece of shavings out of Eddie's hair. As he opened his purse to place inside the money for my order of baskets, I noticed a roll of dollar bills.

"I'm lucky," Eddie said. "My health's right good. I can eat anything. And there's work to do most of the time. When worktime's over—well, then I can sing a mean bass!"

Lucy Ivory, illuminated in my fifth novel as Janey Jeems, was a genteel and lovable Negro.

"The first time I ever saw Richard Ivory I loved him," Lucy said at the beginning of our interview. "But them days the girls hid their love like a secret and kept the boys guessing. Honey loved me the first time he laid eyes on me, but I kept him courting me five years. I was jubious about getting married, 'cause I didn't know what was to it. Anyhow, at nineteen I married Richard, and from then on I never lived in nobody else's house.

"He had bought a little place on credit, and I aimed to help pay the debts off. 'I didn't marry you to set down on you,' I told Honey soon as we was married. 'Let's put our heads together and study up how to make a living and get something ahead.'

"While he was doing public work off from home to help pay for this place, I worked in the field and the brick hole. I stood in mud knee-deep making bricks, dipping my molds in the ground clay, and then laying them on the table to be burnt. When I wasn't at the brick hole, I used to grub all day and into the night clearing up land for us to farm on. Honey would come home from public work and see what all I had done and say to me, 'Pig, it won't do for you to work like this.' But I wanted Honey to come home and stay, bless his heart.

"When he quit public work and started farming here, I kept helping in the field, and he helped at the house. Wash days he drawed all the water and put the clothes in soak for me, then I washed them out nights after I quit helping him in the field. But I didn't mind no work. I had who God 'lotted for me to love, and I meant to help him. Not that there wasn't little frets between us sometimes. Like the Christmas Eve I rode with him to take some meat and flour bread to a motherless family down the road.

"The man of the house was bed-drunk and had run the children off to the woods, we s'posed, just like he done his wife when she was living. So Honey told me to set in the buggy while he went into the swamp to hunt the little children and take them to their grandmother's.

"Honey was gone so long I got uneasy. I was afraid to call him, lest the drunk man might hear and come out of the house. I tied the horse to a tree and ventured a little way into the woods to listen and call Honey low enough not to rouse the drunk man. Folks said there was painters in that woods and other wild critters. So I was feared to venture far. Night was beginning to fall. So finally I concluded the only thing for me to do was hurry home and get help to find Honey.

"At a tremble, I unhitched the horse and drove home, crying all the way lest Honey had fell in deep water or been attacked by a painter out of the trees.

"Just after I had hitched the horse at our gate, I spied Honey coming out of the woods back of our house, moving along slow with his head down like he was studying. I run round to the back to meet him. Something stopped me. I hushed what I started to say and waited. He looked up.

" 'Supper ready, Pig?' he asked.

"I knowed then he had forgot about me waiting down the road near the drunk man's house. 'Where's the little children?' I asked sharply, soured at his unremembrance of me.

" 'At their grandmother's. I took a short cut through the woods—'

"Then I saw in his face that he remembered his un-remembrance. You know what that fool man done? He scolded me for doing exactly what he told me to. Oh, he r'ared and pitched. He was at a tremble over me. I might have been accosted by drunk men or hurt by painters or wild cats or bears out in the woods. A fool woman, I felt warmed inside by his ranting.

"Soon as we got enough ahead, Honey put up that little store yonder in the corner of our yard, and the neighborhood started toting stuff out of there with no pay except a promise. I finally told him to quit giving credit, or we'd let all we had get away from us.

" 'Pig,' he'd say them times, 'maybe some day we be hungry. Then somebody'll help us.'

"Honey prospered, spite of debts folks owed and grudges that was held 'cause he got ahead. He bought up two more little farms besides our home place. All he got was square and honest. And he left me fixed so I can live easy without having to scuffle in my old age. I love his bones in the grave."

Later, unremembrance became a point of personal identification with Lucy Ivory, the prototype of Janey Jeems.

Herbert and I drove that summer afternoon to one of the Harris farms where they were dusting cotton. In growing anxiety over his hypertension, I made a point of riding with him now whenever he went out of town. I took along my work so that while he walked through the fields I could write in the car.

It was a time of appalling boll weevil infestation, when the country air at night was bitter and the hum of dusting machines made a strange liveliness in the fields.

Herbert directed me to stay in the car, just as I was about to have Jeems bid Janey do, except that he left her in the buggy. Then he went to check the field operations and participate in general supervision of the dusting. This was Moccasin Swamp, he warned me, and snakes were everywhere.

I sat musing awhile on the sense of continuity that Herbert seemed to feel on family land like this. Michael Harris, his grandfather, had come to Northampton from England a long time ago and had settled here. His grave was in the Harris burying ground not very far from where I was sitting. The land sense was strong in his heirs.

I had been trying to project the sense of land in *Janey*

Jeems. The desire of Janey and Jeems was not to be for land per se, but rather for the continuity it symbolized. It was to become for them in the novel almost a religion of land, of title deed to pass on from heir to heir.

But the emphasis was to be on people rather than on property sense or family patterns of land fixation. Title deeds were their means of passing on the composite beauty and mystery and aspiration of humanity.

The strong devotion between Janey and Jeems was to be projected. Intermittently there were to be ups and downs between Honey and Pig. But wise little Janey was to have her own secret understanding of Honey's male vanities and inconsistencies and of the way to deal with them. She was to be wistful over his unremembrance of her at times and to feel oddly cherished when he ranted at her most.

I reached into the pocket of the car for pencil and paper. Except for the hum of dusting machines beyond the little branch it was all stillness. The dust was rising in a thin fog which drifted down to the trees and was losing its whiteness in the underbrush. The woods and thickets were flooded with sunlight. Some of it sifted through the leaves and made fanciful patterns on the hood of the car.

Now and then there was the whir of wings. Birds chirped from a lofty limb somewhere in the green immensity. Twigs snapped in the underbrush as some woods creature moved toward its obscure objective or slithered among dead leaves. There was the sense of watchful creatures near, of the vitality of homing instincts as the afternoon waned. It was cool where I was, with the dampness of stream and embalmed shade. But I knew the fields above the stream would be hot, so I left my notes and went to see about Herbert.

Opening the car door I stepped carefully to the ground, poised to retreat from any slithering noises. I became aware at once of a tense wariness around, a sly withdrawal of the woods creatures into their fastnesses. With more assurance then I moved along what I thought was the path toward the cotton field. I was not yet quite out of the dimension of fiction. Janey Jeems moved with me.

The stream bed widened, then angled sharply toward the swamp. In exploring mood, I walked further than I realized. I found myself hoping there might be another Niagara Falls along this stream, such as I had loved at Rocky Branch in my childhood, such as Tiny in *Sage Quarter* had known at the waterbrook, such as Nannie Lou in *Purslane* and Little Bit in *Sweet Beulah Land* had enjoyed. A stream immutable for children of fact and fiction.

All at once I realized I was encompassed by timber. I took the wrong path, then tried another which was wrong too. The light sifted only dimly through the masses of greenery around and overhead. The still density of the woods became oppressive.

Suddenly there was the smell of burning pinestraw. There were wisps of smoke over the trees.

If Herbert and the tenants had already seen the smoke, I knew he would be waiting with frantic impatience at the car or hunting for me in the woods round about. He would be worried to death about me and in panic over the fire. Momentarily I expected to hear him calling me or sounding the car horn.

Finally I found my way back to where the stream narrowed. Panting, I dashed toward the little thicket where the car was parked. In the lonesome timberland the car seemed like home.

The car was not there.

I stared at the tire tracks. The car had certainly been parked there. It was gone now. There was no hum of dusting machines from the cotton field either.

I traced the tire tracks to the road. There I saw a thin pall of smoke above the horizon. It was clear now that the Harris woods was on fire.

Herbert would have seen the smoke before I did, I decided, and would have rushed off in his car to summon help. Turning back to pick me up, he would doubtless be distractedly looking for me right now.

I took a short cut through the woods to head him off. Distress over my disappearance and panic over the fire were sure to elevate his blood pressure. Censuring myself for the idle explorings, I hurried through the woods in the direction of the smoke.

I came to a clearing. At the opposite end of it a thicket was burning. At first glance it seemed that men were setting fire to the underbrush rather than putting it out.

There was Herbert. He was frenziedly directing the fire-fighting, without regard for personal safety or hypertension. The colored tenants were scattered at intervals along the thicket, each man raking and burning underbrush in the assigned area.

Moving nearer, I saw the sense of what they were doing. In effect they were fighting fire with fire. By clearing the scrub thicket of pinestraw and dead leaves and shrubs, they had made a tentative fire lane alongside the trees. Having improvised a kind of windrow beyond the cleared space, they had fired the underbrush so that the two blazes were meeting.

Against the lurid flames Herbert looked immense and dedicated, like an Old Testament prophet.

The danger was over now. I called Herbert. He looked around and stared at me in utter surprise.

I knew then that he had forgotten about me.

He covered up his forgetfulness with expletives about women who wouldn't stay where they were told to, who might have been killed by snakes in Moccasin Swamp.

Like Janey Jeems I was a little sour at his unremembrance of me. Like her, too, I felt oddly cherished when he ranted most.

Persons "living and dead" are distilled into fiction. They are sometimes illumined by an identification less "purely coincidental" than is indicated in prefaces to novels.

· 33 ·

Home Town

SEABOARD IS not Bonwell. It is not Sweet Beulah Land or Sage Quarter or Seven Hearths. It is not Gopher Prairie. There is distillation from all of them in the small town.

Small towns cannot be generalized or poured from one mold any more than human beings can. Each has its own individuality. Along with its general faults, it has its particular virtues. Seaboard can be particularized as an incredibly generous little town. It forgives much and includes in its community of fellowship the much-forgiven.

Its unique generosity is to the unfortunate. In sudden misfortune or continuous want, the town rallies to organize relief. It does not pause to reason or rationalize about the exigency or wisdom of response. With spontaneity and warmth it hurries to meet the various needs as they appear. Fires, illness, hunger and indigence in general prompt generous money contributions for the victims, along with collection of clothes, pantry supplies and furnishings. If all the help Seaboard has given the distressed were heaped together in one place, it would make a small mountain.

Its entity is reflected in little vignettes.

There is its kindness to dumb creatures. Dogs roam everywhere, relaxed and sure. The town knows Teddy and Fritz and Chang and Daisy and Spot, and a watchful sense of responsibility for their well-being is shared. Their liberty develops into license, but the nuisances consequent to it are absorbed. Dresses are sometimes torn from clotheslines, and garbage is scattered over clean yards by Fido and Ginger and Deacon and Martini. But disturbances among neighbors because of it are minimum.

A stray cat used the roof of a residence on Main Street for her individual maternity ward. Brought down to earth, the mother cat took her kittens right back to the roof where they could not be easily disposed of. The residents decided a cat with that much sense deserved asylum, so they took her in. Residents on Church and on Washington Streets reasoned likewise when mother cats used their refrigerator and station wagon respectively for maternity wards.

Seaboard is not labeled "bird sanctuary." But it is sanctuary. A stray cat symbolizes its instinctive kindness to living things.

One Saturday afternoon I was busy putting pretty kitten seals on Christmas gifts for children. I had just stamped a pink kitten on Bryan's pink elephant when I heard a cat's cry at my door.

My childhood indifference to cats had not changed greatly, in spite of cat-lovers among friends and neighbors. Mellowed now by the pink Christmas kittens, I went downstairs to open my door to the cry there. A little smoky gray kitten rushed to me and cried and purred around my ankles as though he had found his lost home. He did not look like an uncared-for stray cat. His fur was glossy and clean. His eyes were clear blue with an oddly wise glint in them. He kept crying. He was saying he was hungry and wanted food.

I had advanced in cat lore enough to realize that cats can talk. Some years before when I did not have this knowledge, two cats made me feel rather ridiculous. One April night about two o'clock I had been startled out of sleep by strident talking beyond my windows. It was a child's voice. The child seemed to be in distress of some kind. The Marvin Gays' apartment is just across from my upstairs window, so I concluded something was wrong over there.

"Oh, my poor sister," a child was crying. "Oh, my poor sister!"

Poor little Linda Lee, I thought. Or was it Sandra?

I reached for the telephone receiver and held it an instant as I fastened my eyes on the Gay apartment. I was searching for signs of activity there, for lights, for Dr. Parker's car out front or Dr. Vick's. The house was dark. There was no activity that I could detect. No doctor's car was outside in the moonlit street.

I was now aware of two children's voices. One was still crying desperately, "Oh, my poor sister. Oh, my poor sister!" The other's cry was plaintively wordless, like Linda Lee's when she used to hold up her baby arms to me. Poor little sisters, I thought, had something happened to their mother and daddy, to Addie Lee and Marvin both?

Instantly I reached for the light so that I could see to dial their number. In that second there was a deep masculine voice from the opposite window. "Shut up down there!" Marvin exclaimed, indicating clearly the "poor sisters."

I was relieved and a little abashed too. I ducked from the moonlit window while Marvin broke up the rendezvous below.

Well, it was spring, I thought. For all my years I had not known cats were so articulate in their love-making. Uncle Paschal's sassy cat had been Victorian.

This little smoky gray cat at my ankles now was articulate. He was saying he was hungry.

I hurried to take bread out to the garden. The kitten was not going to get any false ideas of security at my kitchen door.

The kitten purred and cried around my ankles, almost tripping me as I tediously made my way to the garden. I dropped the unbroken bread slices upon the dead grass. The kitten relaxed his hold on me, sniffed the bread. Was the little thing too weak with hunger to manage the slices whole? Immediately I crumbled them into bite sizes, as for a child. He gulped down a few bites ravenously. Or was it an act? For as soon as I moved over to the pecan tree he was around my ankles, rejecting the bite sizes of bread on the grass. Purring and crying, he knocked the pecans out of my hands as fast as I picked them up.

I had difficulty getting back into the house, so persistently did the kitten cling to my ankles. When I saw the runs in my stockings where he had clung, I shoved him off and quickly shut the door.

That was that, I thought. I hurried back upstairs to my Christmas wrapping. The cry of the kitten kept intruding. I held out against it awhile.

At two o'clock I went downstairs. The kitten was curled on my back steps very much at home, crying to get inside.

I saw I had a problem. The cat had to be placed somewhere. There was no SPCA nearby to appeal to. I couldn't keep pets since I was away from home too often.

But who could sleep, with a little stray cat crying around windows and doors?

I called the Gays, slyly aware of their softness toward all living creatures. Had they, by chance, lost a cat?

No missing cats, they reported. They dashed over to see the stray kitten. Neighbors joined them. It was love at first sight. The kitten curled around Linda Lee's neck and purred contentedly as though he had found his lost home.

The little thing had been cherished somewhere and was as hungry for love as for bread, neighbors decided, and they organized to help locate his owner. We alternated at the telephone. A report came through that little David Moose had lost a cat. I dialed the Baptist parsonage. The Rev. J. L. Walter Moose is the kind of minister one calls on to help solve a spiritual problem or a writing sequence or a destination for little stray cats at Christmas. A Phi Beta Kappa, with degrees from Wake Forest College and Duke University, he has a profound understanding of the virtues and the foibles in human beings and the wisdom and sense of humor to deal with both. The same applied to all living creatures, we were sure, so our problem was about to be solved.

Sylvia, the minister's daughter, answered the telephone. They had not lost a cat, she said. They couldn't have a cat, since her daddy was allergic to cat fur. It was suggested that we call the Methodist parsonage, since the Mitchell children had lost their little Smoky recently.

I reported to the waiting committee downstairs. I found Linda Lee and Betsey Bradley feeding warm milk and fish scraps to the little stranger. As he gobbled the food, he seemed to glance at my dry bread on the orchard grass, then look up at me with a kind of snicker in his clear blue eyes, as though reminding me I was no wiser about cats' appetites than their love-making.

While neighbors called around town, I telephoned the Methodist minister. We had a pleasant chat about cats. His little boys had lost a smoky gray kitten like the one I described, so Mrs. Mitchell was coming around immediately in the hope of reclaiming Smoky. The town had grown accustomed to kindness and wisdom and good humor from the Methodist parsonage, so we felt good about Smoky's happy reunion there.

Linda Lee began to beg to keep the cat if it turned out not to belong to the Mitchell children. Smoky was niched securely around her neck.

Mrs. Mitchell thought it was Smoky. She took the kitten home for sure identification but brought him back. He lacked an identifiable white star under his neck. It was the third Smoky that had been returned to them, only none had been the right one. She joined the committee to contact others about adopting the little stray cat.

I questioned Addie Lee about adopting Smoky. It was impossible, she said, for them to have any more pets in their upstairs apartment.

Would Marvin kill the cat, then? I asked with faked guilelessness. Surely that would be the merciful thing to do.

Oh, no, Addie Lee said. Marvin was as soft-hearted toward animals as the rest of them were. Some other plan would have to be made for this little cat. Marvin might take care of him at the store, a warm comfortable home for him in case nothing else could be worked out. She began to make calls about placing the little stray cat.

We called many places. Families in town were already too

well supplied with cats, it seemed, but they offered to call friends who might take in the little stray kitten. One neighbor reported she had a colony of stray cats, the latest of which she had given the French name, Merci. But she was not in the mood of thank-you for any more cats immediately.

For the present Smoky had a home. Linda Lee had wrapped him up in her bed where he was going to sleep until a place was found for him elsewhere.

A busy afternoon had been devoted to one stray kitten. Ministers' families had given time and thought to the problem. Businessmen had become involved. A Sunday school teacher had interrupted her study of the Bethlehem story to help. Women had stopped gift-wrapping to co-operate. Engrossed housewives had concentrated on the exigency of Smoky. Telephones had been in constant use about the cat problem. A cross section of town was stirred by one little stray cat at Christmas.

All the cats I had ever kicked around merged into this little Smoky. I felt encompassed, haunted by them. Needing respite that Saturday night I turned on TV for some music to clear the air of kittens. A Welk trio was in progress. The men were singing, "Pussy cat, pussy cat, pussy cat."

Mrs. Mitchell gave the new Smoky a home at the Methodist parsonage. His adventures at the preacher's house have become a town legend.

The legend touches the edge of things. Seaboard's kindness extends beyond little stray kittens. It is comprehensive and warm and spontaneous.

The town's response to the exigency of one stray family symbolizes its creative kindness to needy humanity.

The Prets were stray people who seemed to have come out of nowhere in their rattletrap car, bringing nothing with them. With only rags on their backs, they dropped down on the community in worse plight than stray kittens, than Okies or the Joads. They had seven children, and another was expected soon.

A town landowner settled them on his farm to sharecrop, and Seaboard with heart and will undertook to rehabilitate them. Loads of food and clothes and furnishings were taken to them. In a rare spirit of sharing, the poor and the well-to-do alike contributed supplies of bed linens, mattresses, pillows, chairs, tables, dishes and cooking wear. The Prets' pantry was filled. Dresses and suits from town closets and stores were given, and new cloth was made into garments for them. They were fitted in shoes.

There was no concerted drive or pressure for help. Word of the sorry plight of the strangers got around, and supplies poured in. They included everything from dollars to layettes. It all added up to a festival of bounty.

When Mrs. Pret fell on the soapy floor she was scrubbing and broke her arm, the town saw to medicines and doctor's care for her.

After the baby was born he became in a special way the town's baby, with as much affection as infant wear and baby food showered on him.

Provision for church as well as school attendance was made for the Pret children. Their transformation as they took their places in church pews alongside town children was amazing. They had more changes of clothes than town youth.

Then the baby died. The town mourned. It had expected to help that little boy grow in favor with God and man. He was the creature in the creative kindness, the symbolic Galatea. The town provided a little white coffin, a white wreath and a lot in its cemetery.

After two years the Prets moved on. They traveled light, as they had come. So much had been given them that they adopted the habit of wearing clothes till they were dirty and then throwing them away. Whatever failure followed the town's attempt to transform strays into citizens, it was a good interval. Seaboard measured purpose against accomplishment and knew its own integrity. There had been no self-consciousness in it.

There was no self-consciousness in the spontaneous tournaments which held the interest of old and young in Seaboard. Almost suddenly the town was riding to horse and pony each night, and the vacant lot next to Red Bradley's house was groomed to become a tournament field. Men, women and children gathered around the white fence of the enclosure or sat on adjoining lawns to watch the horses and their riders. The town rode directly or vicariously.

Citizens volunteered contributions for the expenses of lights and upkeep of the field. The town furnished water to sprinkle the riding track during dry intervals. The policeman supervised the sprinkling. There were no intimations of juvenile delinquency during the tournament period.

Television sets all around blared out the story of jousts. "In days of old when knights were bold" was the theme song of one series, and canned tilts moved swiftly and exactly across TV screens. On Washington Street tournaments went on live, if less dramatically than the canned series.

There was a background interest in horse shows, in which Seaboard riders participated and won blue ribbons for their horses. There was the Kempsville horse show at Virginia Beach, during which Seaboard showed seven times and won seven blue ribbons. Some of the horses were off such famous sires or grandsires as Roan Allen, Wilson's Allen, Go Boy, Souvenir. Gay Go Boy G was from Wartrace Stables in Tennessee and had been featured in national horse magazines as winner of blue and red ribbons and championships. Likewise Lady Rhythm and Ruby were Tennessee walking horses and winners in the five-gaited class. The palomino, Silver Bell, had been a steady winner in the pleasure class. Star o' Dixie had shown in Madison Square Garden. Knobby Hill's Fancy, an eight-year-old gelding, was from French Lick Stables, Indiana, and had been tops in the five-gaited class.

The town had a pride in its horses and their pedigrees, and it learned to speak glibly of gaits and geldings. Local owners took their horses off to Tennessee, Winston-Salem and Durham for special training. Children spoke of it as "going off to college."

Little Larigo was the Cinderella of the piece. She was a nobody, not off any name horse. She was just dropped somewhere along a little country road in Northampton. She had no name but "It." When Betsey Bradley, nine years old, acquired her she looked like a hick. One woman thought she was a big shaggy dog. Betsey loved the little pony, without name or training or grace, and induced her daddy to send "It" off to college. "It" was trained and given a name, Little Larigo. Little Larigo, with Betsey driving her to the pony cart, began showing in the Shetland pony class and won six blue ribbons, three red, one reserved championship and one championship. She wore the glass slipper with spirit and grace

The horse interest prompted James Robert, a little Negro boy, to make a pony cart out of some odd boards and wheels. His tournament field was the streets of Seaboard. His animal was a mule. The mule trotted spiritedly. Cars slowed down for the crude mount. Drivers waved from their Buicks and Chryslers at James Robert. The policeman kept traffic moving though he had an eye for the little mule cart.

It was all part of a little town's summer consonance. A pleasant note was that our policeman, prompt and exact in duty, sometimes chaffingly referred to as Two-Gun Drewett, was a birdwatcher.

He was also an actor in local dramatics. One night he pounded on my door and called out in a booming voice, "I'm Lieutenant Neal of the Confederate Army!" Not hearing or understanding the identification, neighbors were aghast. They saw the uniform and policeman's gun, and they wondered if I were being arrested. Later they learned Policeman Drewett had come off duty in a hurry and had worn his artillery to rehearsal at my house. The script called for him to knock on the door, and to make it realistic he went outside and knocked.

The little town has its self-consciousness in other areas. It is aware of its reputation for putting things over. Civic drives and campaigns are so organized that they go unfailingly over the top. A revival at church is put on in something of the same spirit. For practical purposes it becomes a drive.

An evangelist from the deep South is secured. Merchants of all faiths are signed up to close places of business during church services. Clubs postpone scheduled meetings. Regular bridge sessions, both contract and duplicate, are suspended. The country club crowd moves off the courses into pews. The missionary circles arrange hospitality for the ministers and their families. Printed posters announcing services are displayed in store windows and tacked on light poles. Little boys who wontedly add whiskers and wrinkles to the faces of politicians similarly displayed leave the evangelist's unpenciled. Rides are proffered to those on foot. The unchurched are invited to services. The town is shy about labeling people as sinners, but since the object of the crusade is to gather in the sheaves, the pack-the-pews committees function.

At the opening service church members with communal pride fill the front pews. A mass arrangement of crimson gladioli on the altar harmonizes with the upholstery plush of the white pulpit chairs, the carpet and the vivid maroons and scarlets of Biblical robes in memorial windows. The empty choir loft with its mahogany and white pews, brilliantly lighted by prismed chandeliers, awaits the singers in red vestments. Above it the blue waters of the River Jordan, winding in and out of crested hills of green, are pictured in a recess of the baptistry.

It is with pride, too, that members watch their young minister take his place quietly and with dignity. The more exacting who had cringed when a former pastor wore mismatched pants and coat at the sacred desk are seeing with warm satisfaction the present neat and impeccable appearance at their lectern. Many are seeing the reality of the love of God in the walk and talk of the young minister in their pulpit.

The evangelist from the deep South startles and shocks the little town out of its prideful complacency. It is against sin, but vaguely without identifying it too narrowly. The evangelist pinpoints sin. It is drinking and dancing and playing cards and attending Sunday movies and dressing immodestly. It is wearing shorts in public, it is mixed bathing at beaches, it is worshipping mammon.

The evangelist almost at once sizes up the town as worldly and materialistic. And he hammers away at the veneer.

There is little rapport. Pack-the-pews committees have

functioned well, and people come to the sanctuary. The lovely mahogany pews are filled with respectful and attentive listeners. The gloved make a point of holding songbooks with the ungloved. Costume jewelry sobers. Country club sports wear gives way to gray flannel suits. Worshipful mien prevails. The interior is chaste and beautiful. The story of Christ, delineated in warm living colors from the windows, moves and challenges.

But rapport with the lectern falls off. Even those who perceive spiritual meaning in the externals are confused and puzzled by the emphasis from their pulpit. As the evangelist becomes more and more a voice crying in the wilderness against the viperism of his generation, politeness turns to aloofness. He cannot budge members from their mahogany pews even on the mildest of propositions, he cannot budge them however earnestly he preaches the wrath of God, however he exhorts and walks down the aisle to meet them on his invitations.

"Lord," he prays fervently when none will come forward to shake his hand on the propositions, "send storm or sickness or death upon this people that they may be roused from their lethargy and stirred to the righteousness that is in Thee!"

Finally on request rather than proposition he manages to get the officials of the church to the front, he gets the country club boys on their knees.

Humiliated at the spectacle they feel has been made of them, some of the officials absent themselves from church the next night. Then one crushes his finger and has to be rushed to the hospital emergency. Another's child develops a virus infection that is frightening. Another has a sudden elevation of blood pressure. Malaise threatens to become illness. The absentees return.

But a small rift develops. A little core of fundamentalism comes through the veneer of modernism. It crystalizes into the wrath-of-God thinking. The love-of-God is the majority thinking.

The main difference in the little schism is that those who dance and play cards and attend Sunday movies and wear shorts in public and engage in mixed bathing at beaches adhere to the love-of-God school of thought while those who don't, adhere to the wrath-of-God. There are those who see that both sides twist love and wrath according to their predilections, who believe that one is narrow only in the intolerance of the other.

The storm comes. Hurricane Hazel hits both schools of thought. It unifies the town in a communal disaster. The schism is healed.

Less spectacular than Hazel, culture also brought the town together. A revival of interest in community play-making during the fifties and early sixties unified the town amazingly. George Harris directed, the Woman's Club sponsored, and I wrote the plays. The first in this new series was "Yellow Color Suit," dramatized from my story in *Colliers* and expanded in my novel, *Hearthstones*.

It was not a workshop production on the precinct level, as I assumed at the outset it would be, but rather a First Night, a world premiere of "Yellow Color Suit." The town saw to that. Rows of seats for celebrities were ribboned off in the school auditorium, as at weddings. And celebrities from Chapel Hill, Raleigh, Norfolk and Greenville used them. Corsages for guests and flowers for the author were provided. Newspaper reporters and photographers were present. Women in evening gowns ushered, assisted by men who happened to own tuxedos. The mayor was named chief usher. On opening night one woman glanced at his honor's tuxedo and said "I'm glad to see the head waiter's here."

The community was generally serious and wholehearted in its response and support of this cultural project. The president of Farmers Bank and the mayor helped Worthy Matrons and the country club crowd wallpaper stage sets. Wardrobe mistresses studied *The World Book of Styles* and applied new knowledge to patterns and materials for costumes. Members applied themselves to make-up directions. Committees interviewed old ladies in surrounding neighborhoods about how to make Mother Hubbards and nightcaps and paper spills so they would be completely authentic. The props committee scoured the countryside for a spinning wheel of the right vintage, for cotton cards and lambrequins and pillow shams and high-top shoes. A pair of high-tops was finally located at a country store in Diamond Grove and contributed to the production.

Town citizens helped build stage sets after their day at the cotton gin and store and farm. They saw beyond the task at hand. There had been talk among the Lions about the local need for an industry. A Lion exclaimed after one First Night was over, "We needed this!" And there was as much fervor in his voice as if he had landed a shirt factory.

A creative need was met. A community pooled its skills and aptitudes in rare dedication of mood and purpose. There were violations of stage techniques, there were slurred consonants in dialogue. The soldier of World War II pulled out a pack of cigarettes and puffed away on a Salem—the wrong decade for Salems. A sweet old play character in 1942 turned on the stage radio for a girl-and-boy song, and Elvis Presley blasted the audience with a rock-and-roll number—the wrong decade too. The heroine's skirt should have been shorter for the decade she represented. The audience noting the inconsistencies also had its creative part.

There were impressive door receipts. But nobody seemed to be thinking of how much was taken in. The finance committee deposited the proceeds in Farmers Bank, and that was that. The town had together created plays indigenous to the community.

In addition to my full-length originals, one-act plays were again written in a community playwriting class, with five Northampton communities participating in their production. Three generations acted in one play. The oldest actress had played thirty years ago at the state drama festival and had belonged to playwriting classes then and now. Community pastors took part in the plays. One entire family of four acted in the same original. Policeman Drewett, playing the Confederate lieutenant, looked as much at home in the gray as in the blue uniform he usually wore. An undertaker's assistant was a Yankee spy.

The full-length plays were presented in several towns of

northeastern North Carolina, in Goldsboro and in Chapel Hill. At the state drama festival in 1958 the Master Playmaker's Award was presented me, and a citation was read by Dr. Selden of the university drama department. It said in part: "For her distinguished achievement in finding moments of great feeling and excitement in the commonplace lives of her neighbors and for recording these impressions in dramatic form, using the natural rhythms and the colorful vernacular of her region the Carolina Dramatic Association takes pleasure in presenting to Bernice Kelly Harris . . ." The citation was a summation of my thirty years of playmaking activity.

"Yellow Color Suit" went from our First Night to Hollywood, by way of NBC-TV.

Not long afterwards a more general summation was made by Wake Forest College. During graduation exercises in 1959 this college conferred on me the honorary degree of Doctor of Literature. Woman's College to The University of North Carolina conferred the same honorary degree in 1960.

"Your town was all broken shadows and one light—in your house," John Woodburn of Doubleday and Company had written. Our town is broken shadows and a light, the composition of mankind itself. Sometimes there is grayness, and illumination is from technology. But the shadows break, and a primal light illumines, and humanity is of it.

A christening, a funeral and a golden wedding all within a period of four hours gave the home town a rare community sense recently. The same people were in attendance at each. Similar emotions were shared. All families were one family. Each event was all christenings, all funerals, all golden weddings.

Thomas Hardy might have made a story out of it. Or Thad Stem an editorial of rare poetic quality. Or the Preacher might have observed anew, "One generation passeth away, and another generation cometh: but the earth abideth for ever." In Seaboard it was a straight news item.

Amid pink flowers and lighted candles a baby was christened Mary Linda Harris in a memorable service at the Methodist

Church at 11:45. Friends and relatives assembled at the grandparents' home for a lovely coffee hour at noon.

In the same church only a stone's throw away, one of the most esteemed citizens lay in state an hour after the christening. Her shockingly sudden death had made a shadow over the town, a palpable void. It would have been her wish, the word was relayed from her home nearby, that the day's events proceed as planned. Always self-effacing and community-minded, Olive Jenette Vick had had a vital part in civic and church life during her fifty-nine years, in plans for weddings and funerals and christenings . . . A baby had just been christened near the altar where she lay in state under a pall of red roses.

From the town cemetery friends went to the Lions Club building to felicitate the Cleatons, whose children were honoring them on their fiftieth wedding anniversary. Chairs had been provided for the honorees, but in spite of their physical weaknesses they stood. Steadfastly they stood and faced friends and relatives, as they had faced life. They were seeing the yellow carnations and the glowing candles and the golden three-tiered wedding cake no more than they were visualizing the deprivations and sacrifices and simple pleasures of family life and of fellowship with neighbors and kin.

A soloist sang "Precious Memories." The golden wedding couple were remembering the little pillows soothed, the infants' ills anxiously attended together. Even now the mother's left shoulder looked more accustomed to babies than to yellow carnations. They were remembering the shared plans and failures, the miracle of new life and that other miracle of death, the sorrows and joys that had made them mystically one flesh beyond anything the preacher had pronounced fifty years ago.

The same people had attended the three events, shared similar emotions. Each was all christenings, all funerals, all golden weddings. All families were one family.

A little-town Sunday ended. The quietness at dusk had overtones in it.

Last Entry in "My Days"

THE DAY before Christmas Eve, Herbert and I drove to Rogers Farm to get our turkey. Just after we arrived, the fire warden from Margarettsville came with word that Seaboard was burning up. The news had been relayed by the railroad agent, and a call for help had gone out to the fire departments in Weldon and Roanoke Rapids. During that ten-mile ride back home, we were extremely tense and apprehensive. We feared our heating plant, which had been erratic for some time, had blown up and ignited the town.

Silently praying that Melissie got out of the kitchen in time, that our neighbors were not injured in the explosion, I began wondering where Herbert and I would sleep that night. Herbert worried over the pall of smoke which seemed to extend to the Harris timber.

Our street was intact, we discovered upon arrival, the Harris timber was safe. There had been a series of explosions in the fireworks store, with its complete destruction by fire and with three boys hospitalized as a result of their efforts to put out the blaze.

Melissie in her flowered kerchief greeted us, outwardly calm though of course shaken by the explosion that had rocked the town. She and I dressed the turkey, and Herbert hurried to town to hear the details of the fire.

While Melissie tidied the kitchen, I decorated a tray with Christmas fruit, filled candy jars, packed away salted peanuts to enjoy while we listened to Christmas music over the radio. There would be "Silent Night," for all the pressures of the day.

Pap Long, yodeler in one of our original plays at Chapel Hill, brought the Christmas ham, yodeling as he approached the back yard. The ham was prepared for baking. Then I wrote last-minute cards, wrapped uniforms for Melissie and a raincoat for Herbert in readiness for Santa Claus morning. The Hirsches from Atlanta, in town for the holidays, called and gave some interesting sidelights on Georgia politics.

On Christmas Eve, Herbert rested in bed awhile, then drove over to the farm. I iced my last Christmas cake. Lib brought over another poinsettia for us to enjoy while she and Reece were away for the holidays. Bettie ran into the kitchen to get me to type a card to her circle Pollyanna. I dashed off the required greetings. Then Ed Lewis came to leave Herbert's tax slip, the winding up of his tax collecting, he explained, since he was off to Duke Hospital for the critical operation for high blood pressure. If he should die under the operation, he said, he wanted to be cremated and have his ashes scattered from his son's plane over Fountain Creek where he had hunted so many deer and foxes and squirrels. (He survived the Duke experience. Later in his barber shop he ended it all. There was no fanfare about ashes. He was buried in his family plot in the churchyard.)

After this somber note in the Christmas festivity, there was another brief interruption. A paper soliciting help for the widow whose store had been destroyed yesterday was brought to our door and responded to. A book-exchange member stopped by to leave the exchange novel before starting on her Florida vacation. "It's too risqué for me to finish," she said. I knew she had read every word of it.

Back in the kitchen I found little Sandra from next door feeding Deacon, her pretty cocker spaniel. The icing from my cake was the food. Then there came a knock on my door.

Hurrying to the front, I faced a stranger, crippled and rather gaunt. For all the oblique approach, it was at once evident that he was after "points" in a sales contest, so I interrupted his sales spiel to ask what magazines he was selling.

He was a war veteran, he went on to explain, had been in the death march at Corregidor. Only two people in Seaboard seemed to remember Pearl Harbor, for only two had opened the door to him. "They just don't know any better here," he said patiently, "they've forgotten Pearl Harbor in this village." Only 165 "points" stood between him and his wife and baby, whose voices over the telephone from Wyoming the night before had made him cry. At that point I said I'd renew *Colliers* and hastened upstairs for the checkbook. Upon my return I found that the salesman had written an order to suit himself. I let the extra subscriptions stand as filled out in my brief absence. I remembered Pearl Harbor! Before he left I informed him that my village remembered it too, that our sons and daughters had been in the Army, the Navy and the Air Force. I mentioned our Captain Edward Stephenson who had lost his life with the Marines on Iwo Jima, our Lieutenant Baxter Bottoms who had lost his life in France when his plane was shot down, the Webb boy who had been killed overseas.

Back in the kitchen I helped Melissie finish a chocolate cake for her own Christmas dinner. Addie Lee from next door came in to bring some beautiful holly and to take Sandra and Deacon home. I ran back upstairs to get aspirin for Melissie, who had not faltered on the job in spite of a splitting headache and high blood pressure.

An applicant for Seaboard postmaster came to get me to type a letter of recommendation to Mr. Kerr, our congressman.

That done, I spread the best lace cloth on the dining table and started melting the base of white candles to secure them in their silver holders. The makeshift lighter I was using got out of control and spilled fire on the cloth, burning it in spots and sending black ash all over the freshly vacuumed dining room. One tall and ghostly candle fell and broke in half.

Melissie helped sweep and dust again and then went home to get her own bit of Christmas greenery from the woods.

The day was ending now. I was so tired that hands and feet barely responded to the final task. As I swept the front porch, I reflected on the Christmas order of pantry and house. The savor of Christmas festivity was in the air. I visualized beyond the holly wreaths and candles at windows and doors the plump turkeys ready for tomorrow's roasting, the old bacon hams succulent in their cooling broth, the fruit cakes aromatic with spices and sherry, the cocoanut cakes moist and delicious under their white icing, the mixmasters all set to froth up egg and cream into favorite eggnog recipes, the vegetables and salads. The weariness lifted a little as I savored the sense of community well-being.

Suddenly a car swung into our drive. It was Reece's Ford, not our Chrysler. Reece was driving. Herbert was on the front seat.

"He's not feeling at all well," Reece called out to me. "He thinks he's had a stroke."

"No!" I began and seemed unable to check the protest.

I dropped the broom and rushed to the car. Herbert was trying to get out. He could not stand, he had lost use of his left side. Reece brushed me aside, lifted Herbert in his arms, brought him into the living room. I indicated the davenport. Reece laid him there. Shedding my coat, I wadded it into a pillow, then dashed upstairs for the nitroglycerin and ice cap.

Lib arrived. "Call the doctor," Reece directed her.

I put a nitroglycerin tablet under Herbert's tongue as Dr. Parker had instructed me to do. I ran to the refrigerator for ice. "You'll be all right," I assured Herbert while Lib was telephoning the doctor. "Lie perfectly still now, don't move."

He was trying to talk. His tongue was still stiff, his voice muffled. "I knew I was going into the ditch," he said, "but there was nothing I could do about it. I had no use of myself—"

"Just be quiet and relax," I pleaded, standing by the davenport, trying to keep him company in this strange new place he had come to. "Don't try to talk yet."

"You know the first thing I thought? It came to me just like a flash when I fell out of the car and started struggling.

My father died fifteen years ago tonight. I hadn't thought about it before, but it came to me—"

"Just relax," I kept saying.

"Fifteen years ago Christmas Eve night—"

Dr. Parker entered. I told him what I had done. "Give him another nitroglycerin," he directed, "and put a hot water bottle to his feet."

Lib dashed across the street to get her electric pad. Mrs. Bradley came in.

Dr. Parker began to check the blood pressure. All of us stood tense and breathless. I would not watch the instrument for fear Herbert might read the truth in my eyes.

"You know the first thing I thought of when I came to myself?" Herbert was saying to Dr. Parker. "My father died fifteen years ago tonight."

Dr. Parker looked significantly at me. He motioned me aside. Knowing that Herbert was too deaf to hear the words, he spoke frankly. "It won't show up completely until morning, Miss Kelly, but I think it's a cerebral hemorrhage just like President Roosevelt had down at Warm Springs, remember. This is just the beginning. By tomorrow morning one side is likely to be completely lame. There might be coma. As I told you when we took him to Duke—how long has that been?"

"It was nineteen-thirty-eight," I said dully.

"Eight years ago, then. With arteriosclerosis and malignant hypertension such as this, you'll just have to prepare yourself."

I deliberately closed my ears to the rest. There had to be a semblance of composure. Herbert's brown eyes were very sharp and discerning.

"I'd move a bed downstairs," Mrs. Bradley suggested. Her husband, Herbert's partner until both had to retire because of malignant hypertension, was an invalid upstairs at the Bradley home until not long before his death he had to be moved downstairs. Mrs. Bradley's suggestion was out of hard experience.

"Let him lie where he is for awhile," Dr. Parker directed.

"I can use this arm now," Herbert said flexing his fingers, sounding lonely over there on the davenport.

"Go for Melissie," I bade Reece.

Reece hurried off in his Ford.

Dr. Parker left. I seized a bridge pad from the table drawer and wrote shakily: Phenobarbital every four hours, nitroglycerin three times a day, alophen at bedtime. Dr. Parker promised to return as soon as he could find Jethro.

"What was my blood pressure?" Herbert asked.

"Not so high."

"It didn't feel high. I felt pretty good until I lay there in the ditch."

"Let's sit down," I suggested to neighbors. We were hovering too much. I kept filling the ice cap, emptying refrigerator trays, adjusting the heating pad and blankets over Herbert's feet. At intervals I sat by the davenport, hovering as little as possible.

Reece returned with word that Melissie was in the woods after her Christmas tree. Ethel had gone to find her for me.

"Is my car wrecked?" Herbert asked plaintively.

"No," Reece assured him. "The boys at the filling station pulled it out of the ditch without any trouble. It's in your garage, practically unscarred."

Herbert relaxed a little. There was a quiet wait, with only a subdued murmur now and then. Dusk began to fall. I turned out all the lights except one in the kitchen, willing twilight to ease gently down on us. Mrs. Bradley went home for supper.

Through the front windows I spied Melissie's flowered kerchief in the dusk outside. I slipped out to the back door. Melissie was there. Our arms were around each other. I felt stronger already with Melissie in the house. She went upstairs to get the beds in order. Lib and Reece left.

Addie Lee called to offer her services. James Bradley, Herbert's former junior partner at the gin, came in. Herbert told him about his father's death fifteen years ago on Christmas Eve night. James informed me that Dr. Parker was planning to take Herbert to Roanoke Rapids Hospital as soon as Jethro could be located. I knew Herbert did not want that, but since we had to defer to the doctor I rushed upstairs to pack our clothes. I aimed to stay in the hospital with Herbert.

Hurrying downstairs, I heard Mrs. Bradley's voice at the front door. She bade Melissie turn on the light. They were fumbling with the three-way controls, trying to lower the bright light that had been switched on. In the glare I saw the Methodist and Baptist preachers standing near the davenport. Concerned and sympathetic, they had come to offer their services. I knew if Herbert glanced around and saw the preachers standing in force at his head, he would be startled. Even the kindliest hovering seemed to increase his tension. So I dashed to the lamp and switched off the light, apologizing for the darkness. I accepted the proffered services by sending the preachers to the farm to notify Jethro and the sisters of Herbert's illness. He dozed lightly, unaware of the call. In time, how aware we both became of the kindly ministry of our pastors, Mr. Pegg and Mr. Morgan!

Dr. Parker checked in and out. Lib and Reece returned. Herbert lay in the darkness quiet and relaxed. I lifted his head for another tablet. Miss Clara and Elizabeth called to offer their services and to bring fruitcake. Across the street there was a burst of fireworks. Herbert did not hear, but the flash was reflected on the living room wall, and he asked anxiously if there was a fire somewhere around. I dashed out to stop the fireworks, for which the nice college boy on our street apologized. He had just got home from Wake Forest and had not heard of illness at our house.

I returned to the living room. Edith Bradley came in, anxious and visibly distressed. Tonight was very reminiscent of the night her father passed away, she said, offering to stay and sit up all night. Later when the need was greatest, Edith stayed with us many nights.

Left alone, Melissie and I sat waiting. Quiet settled over the place. The houses along our street that only a few hours ago seemed to radiate Christmas cheer were now becoming places where people had died . . . The sudden death of Reece's father, Lib's voice in the night calling neighbors. The plaintive cry from next door that September morning Mr. Kee slipped away while the nurse was washing his face. The long night that friends waited up in Bettie's home while she traveled the lonely road from a Raleigh hospital with Billy's body. The shocking strangeness of the Bradley home the morning after Mr. Bradley left it. The suicide across the street and the devastating disposal of personal possessions consequent to the intestate status of the decedent. The house on the corner where Herman scarcely settled into married life before he died. Places where people had passed away, my street seemed tonight.

Dr. Parker returned with James and Henry Russell, the latter having left a Christmas Eve party to help Herbert upstairs. I switched on the light, explaining at Herbert's startled look that two of the town's strong men had come to carry him upstairs to bed. Henry Russell, lean and slight of build, laughed. I had forgotten about laughter.

Herbert was helped upstairs, upright between the two "strong" men. Dr. Parker, Melissie and I followed. We laid Herbert on his bed, helped him into pajamas. The men left.

Now Melissie and I had the long night to ourselves. She was calm, unruffled. I refilled the ice cap, adjusted the heating pad. Herbert dozed.

It was eleven o'clock. Melissie suggested that I ought to eat some supper.

I had forgotten about food, as about laughter. "I can't," I said.

Melissie brought pears and grapes from the Christmas tray. We ate together in the study adjoining the sick room.

Refusing the extra bed, Melissie made herself comfortable on the study sofa. I went to my vigil by Herbert. Insomnia, a constant accompaniment to my nights, deserted me now that I needed it. I fought sleep in the intervals that I was not slipping downstairs after more ice or emptying trays to freeze more or listening to Herbert breathe. In the big easy chair, with blankets pulled up around me, I devised ways to stay awake. I played the piano on the arm of the chair, as I had played it on window sills when I was a child. I typed imaginary greetings to Pollyannas and manuscripts to Doubleday and letters to my congressman.

At four next morning I removed the ice cap, turned off

the electric pad, checked the patient's cover and then eased down under my blankets for a little nap.

I woke in the cold dawn of Christmas morning. Transiently my thoughts were on the millions of homes where Santa Claus had been during the night, where excited children were waking to that special aura that is over Christmas dawns. I thought of my own little nieces and nephews in various parts of the state, of Sandra and Ann and Betsey who called me Aunt Kelly though I was no kin, of Linda Lee next door who from baby days had called me K. K. I thought of the raincoat secreted in the guest room for Herbert's Santa Claus, of the pretty uniforms in Melissie's Christmas package, of the black uniform I had given Ethel some years ago which she had used for mourning.

Suddenly there was the sound of talking downstairs. It was a woman's voice that I heard in a conversational tone below. It seemed to be a one-sided conversation, for the same voice went on and on. Someone had called very early to inquire, I decided, and Melissie was solicitous, shielding me while I finished my nap. At that point Herbert called, and Christmas Day began.

A strange Christmas Day, centered around sedatives and nitroglycerin and fruit juices. Jethro arrived early to offer his services and to take word back to the sisters. The Baptist pastor checked by to inquire and to leave his address for the holidays in case he should be needed. Mrs. Kee came with a plate of caramel and cocoanut cake, Edith with an assortment of fruit, a florist's messenger with a dozen red roses from the Bradleys. These roses were placed in a silver vase at the foot of Herbert's bed, where he could feast his eyes as he began the starvation diet of fruit juices.

"Move them," he said with a little note of jesting in his voice. "Looks too much like I'm lying in a coffin that way."

His speech was clear this morning.

Dr. Parker came by to check his blood pressure. Ten points down, he reported, but still dangerously high.

"How is it?" Herbert queried.

"Down," I said quickly. Dr. Parker believes in telling the truth when asked for it.

"Don't let it get too low," Herbert cautioned.

Dr. Parker gave me the truth when I saw him to the door. There might be a number of little cerebral accidents such as Herbert had the day before, he said, but the big stroke would come. So I might as well prepare myself. "I'm sorry for you," he added as he left.

There was a long distance call from Lib and Reece wanting to know how Herbert was, offering to come back from their holiday vacation if they could help. Family telephoned from Wake County. Bettie came in at the back so tearful and upset that I had to forget myself and comfort her. The Methodist preacher inquired at the front, followed by other friends and neighbors.

During a lull I asked Melissie who came at dawn. She shook her head, puzzled over the inquiry.

"I declare I heard talking," I said.

"Oh, that was me," she nodded in understanding. "I was asking the good Lord to give us strength to do all we can and then for Him to take hold where we leave off."

There was an eggnog party up the street, with cars going and coming. Whiffs of roasting turkey and savory dressing were over the house as Melissie prepared our lonely dinner. Little Ann Bradley came to bring "Aunt Kelly" a lovely gift. The little Gay girls brought pretty packages for K. K. There was a steady stream of gifts and cheer throughout the day.

For Melissie and me it was constant trips upstairs and down for ice, fruit juices, pills, wood for the heater. For our heating plant had begun to make that rumble-bumble sound that indicated trouble, and we had hastily installed a little tin heater. With uncanny intuition Herbert asked if the furnace was running all right. Since I needed his advice about what to do, I had to admit there was trouble. He sent me to the cellar to clear the carbon formation.

Melissie fearfully watched me break the carbon globe according to Herbert's instructions. She knew I had no mechanical sense. After the heavy furnace door was back in place I turned on the current. There was an interval of rumbling, then the furnace quit. Melissie ran from the cellar.

James came at my call, checked the oil in the tank, touched a little red button at one side of the plant and started it running again. Not for long. It quit with finality. The house grew cool. The nearest service man at that time was in Weldon, twelve miles away. He had installed our heat. We called him. He was not on duty during Christmas. He finally came two days later and reported the transformer had burned out. It was almost impossible to get a transformer now. War shortages were still not over in 1946.

We had no heat, no further reassuring word from Weldon about transformers. Sunday was very cold, with snow clouds banking above the horizon. Another frantic call finally brought the service man over to show us how to start the furnace by hand, so that it would run an hour or two before having to be started again.

Nervously Melissie stood by while I tried to start the heat according to directions. I failed. A spurt of flame flickered, died. Melissie begged me not to fool with electric gadgets I knew too little about, though she stayed by me to be blown up, too, in case my tinkering brought that to pass. I could not let Herbert know what straits we were in, how pipes threatened to freeze during the icy nights, why we wore heavy coats in the house. In desperation I called Reece, back home from the Christmas trip now, and he took over our heating problem. Mornings before going to work in Jackson, he came over to start the furnace. When it cut off after two hours I raced to the cellar to turn off the current. Melissie raced, too, to risk her life with me.

We succeeded in keeping Herbert unaware of the situation, though he often insisted that the thermostat should be set higher. Though he was comfortable under the cover, the house seemed a little cool to him. Dr. Parker wanted the room temperature kept low, I explained, shivering unobtrusively in my heavy wraps. Each evening upon his return from work, Reece checked our furnace and stood by while the house warmed up.

During this heatless interval I was warmed by the kindness of neighbors. Was there a little town in the United States, I often wondered, with so much warmth and consideration in it? The next little town I created would be different from Bonwell in *Portulaca*.

As Herbert's blood pressure dropped our hopes rose. Dr. Parker continued to warn us. With malignant hypertension, the patient might be expected to have massive cerebral hemorrhage or coronary thrombosis. It would be only a matter of time before the big stroke came.

The trips downstairs with the doctor were filled with kindly warnings about what to expect. I began to send Melissie to the door in my place. I had to take care of the patient, in hope.

After three weeks I employed a newly arrived local electrician to install a transformer, and the furnace ran sweetly after that.

Rachel Floyd wrote that she feared I had lost pounds those three trying weeks. I should have gained. Besides our own Christmas supplies, friends and neighbors brought in cakes, pies, candy, fruit, eggs, sausage, scrapple, chicken, eggnog, ham and turkey. We had roast turkey, turkey hash, creamed turkey on waffles, turkey croquettes, turkey sandwiches, turkey soup, turkey salad.

Herbert began to get out a little. Mrs. Bradley told Melissie that I looked worse than he did.

Dr. Parker was right, though. The big stroke came.

· 35 ·

Affirmation

EARLY IN 1947 Herbert was paralyzed. Melissie and I took care of him during his long invalidism.

They were years of stress. Rachel Floyd died with shocking suddenness, and a few months later Elwood had a coronary occlusion. That same year a nephew died unexpectedly of a heart attack, then a brother-in-law. Injured by a fall on the ice, I rode to Duke Hospital in spite of the injury to visit Rachel Floyd. I recovered from an illness following her death in time to visit Elwood in a Fayetteville hospital and then attend his funeral.

Otherwise, life was defined by my invalid's needs.

Then Melissie's health failed, and she went home to die. Once she left her sick bed to see about us, still hopeful that her "incumbency" with me was not over. She died the first week in July, 1950. For her funeral services I wrote a "condoler." I tried to use words that would have pleased her.

Sallie Jordan and Carrie Dowtin, dependable colored women, alternated in the nightly vigil with me. Magdalene became our cook.

Even after the trained nurses came, Herbert called for me if I were only an instant out of his sight. Until his throat was paralyzed, too, and he could not speak. Then somehow he managed my name. It was not distinguishable to the others. But I understood it.

The nurse told me at dawn on July 13, 1950, that he was gone.

I knew there was no going or staying that we were not in together. Forever we had what we had had.

That affirmation faltered before the facts of intestacy. Partnerships and family business complicated legal procedures. My royalties had merged into the estate for equitable distribution. Personal possessions that had been integrally of life and love for a quarter century became items to be evaluated for pro rata shares of collateral heirs. The sofa and bed and table I had recognized for my own that day in the Norfolk furniture store were divisible at a price. Home became real estate.

The legal percentages of farm chattels were more impersonal. Except for the mules. I thought of those fatuously affectionate mules I had observed the afternoon Herbert and I returned from our honeymoon. Were they still trembling as with palsy when separated, as they had done in their young days? Or had mortality overtaken their good mule flesh? Had one been left to tremble alone in wintry pastures?

I felt insecure even in identity. As "widow of the decedent" I was a stranger to myself. The decade ahead looked bleak.

In time, I began to think of the people I had written about. They had made affirmations and had stood on them. Dele in *Purslane* had not been daunted. Resolutely through her own anguish she had willed peace for Calvin as he had sought it in suicide. She had gone about the hard routines demanded of a mother at that hour. In selecting clothes for Calvin she had come across the little sailor suit he had worn in the school picture when he was a child. There was a hole in the pocket. She mended it. Then she handed Uncle Wes the clothes she wanted Calvin buried in. She was in her son's going or staying. In that spirit she faced life ahead.

Old Miss Partheny in *Sweet Beulah Land* through incredible difficulties had lived her affirmation that she was not going to make a mess of living or dying either. Knowing that time was out for her on earth, the indomitable old lady had bathed and dressed herself, then in independence of spirit had sat in her rocking chair waiting for death, as for company.

Janey and Jeems had affirmed as they lived. Their affirmation became white steeples. Nancy in *Portulaca* adjusted to Kirke's idea about property and family, while continuing to validate for him her own ideal. Tiny in *Sage Quarter* and Lallah in *Hearthstones* translated the meaning of life positively. Kalline in *Wild Cherry Tree Road* created an identity for herself at the poorhouse, created it so affirmatively that former neighbors believed she had gone off to the poorhouse and got the big head.

"My Days" was not resumed. It ended on Christmas Eve. Writing for awhile was more discipline than direction. I worked on stories and essays and little dramas, read numerous manuscripts of published and unpublished authors, judged entries in writing contests, became the subject of a biography by Richard Walser. I kept an interest in writing through association with authors who lived near me—Mebane Holoman Burgwyn, Ovid Pierce, the Gilbert Stephensons and the Holley Mack Bells. Margarette Smethurst, Charlotte Green and Bernadette Hoyle often joined our sessions. They included Thad and Dety Stem who were neighbors in spirit in a most sustaining way.

The association was extended to writers throughout North Carolina by way of writers' conferences and groups. The first North Carolina Writers' Conference was held at the suggestion of Inglis Fletcher in the summer of 1950. It was agreed that there would be no formal organization with constitution and by-laws, that membership would be limited to established authors.

Richard Walser became permanent chairman, and he has been assisted by annual chairmen and secretaries. Programs and discussions of writers' problems may not have increased literary productivity among writers, but the sessions of good talk and agreeable fellowship have helped to develop professional solidarity and friendships. Paul Green, only Pulitzer prize winner among the members, justified the assemblies by saying that barbers and sheriffs and plumbers meet annually to talk over their interests, so why not writers?

Certain features, not apposite to programs or problems, are associated with each place of meeting. Cherokee was the wigwam conference, with the Indian idea predominant in the plans. Beside a little mountain stream there was a row of wigwams from which writer squaws and chiefs came out to smoke the peace pipe together after heated discussions on the mountain side. We toured the reservation and took pictures of Indians in front of their cabins. At a crafts shop the tables were turned on the writers. An Indian youth snapped as many pictures of us as we did of his family.

Edenton provided gracious hospitality for the writers, but could do nothing about the unprecedented heat wave that engulfed them, sapping their energies and manners. In spite of it the program went on that night at Bandon Plantation even though a terrific storm had blown fuses and competed with the talking inside the house. The discussions went on in darkness, then candlelight.

The conference at Boone was highlighted by fine addresses and some notable hospitality. James Street made an affirmation at one of the meetings. The subject for discussion was "North Carolina Materials," and panelists gave their ideas. Suggestions were made from the floor. One author contributed Grandfather Mountain as substantial material, in graceful compliment to its grandeur observed from the windows and porches of the Cokers' home. Another offered plank roads as colorful materials for writers. At that point James Street cried out in sharp protest, "Scenery! Plank roads! Don't you know it's people that are your North Carolina materials!"

Hatteras was the mosquito conference, when writers bought out the island's supply of insect repellents without making an impression on the gigantic mosquitoes. It was here that it was decided in an after-session to specify the great men of all time. Writers were asked to select a minimum number of names to be placed in a time capsule which would not be opened for thousands of years. An author rose to the challenge. He offered two names, discussed their fitness. So that night the North

Carolina writers were asked to seal up Moses of Mt. Sinai and Harry Truman of Independence in a time capsule together.

James Street made another affirmation at Hatteras. Though one of the most successful writers, he stated in an after-session of this conference that he was not satisfied with the quality of his work. He declared he was going to write books that would meet the artistic standards he admired in other writers' work. *Goodbye, My Lady*, his current novel, was good, he agreed. But he was going to write better ones.

At Hatteras it seemed we had a special affection for James Street. Always he had enlivened conferences, had listened to problems and suggested solutions, had spoken for us. It was as though he had a special feeling about the Hatteras conference too. On Sunday morning after it was over, we saw him riding slowly by the Coast Guard building in which we had held our meetings, moving along in front of the apartment houses that had been home to writers' families for three days, hesitating before them as though reluctant to leave the scene. As he drove out of sight down the ferry road there was an odd sense of shadow over that Sunday morning. It was his last conference. Some two months later he died suddenly of a heart attack.

Pisgah View Ranch, with its rustic setting, was an ideal retreat for writers. The conference there was highlighted by a visit to Thomas Wolfe's home. The Greensboro meeting became known as the late-late conference, with programs sometimes hours off schedule. Two conferences, professional and graced by courtesies of local writers, were held at Chapel Hill. Morehead City was the fellowship conference, when writers joined with state solicitors, also in conference at the Biltmore that weekend in July, to sing folk ballads and to dance and to test the drunkometer.

The note at the New Bern conference was elegance, with yacht rides and rum cakes and a preview of Tryon's Palace which was not yet opened to the public. One night as though to balance the elegance some of the writers seemed to be taking to, two poets created extemporaneously in the dining room of the Governor Tryon a folk ballad about a North Carolina bootlegger in the news that summer. It was the only time that even a semblance of literature was created on the scene.

The conferences at Blowing Rock and at the Plantation Inn near Raleigh were remembered for good programs and for the hospitality of the chairmen and Raleigh writers. Many of the best sessions have been the unplanned get-together meetings after scheduled programs. The sum of talk and activity, always strictly off the record, might make as interesting a book as the fiction writers create. Some of it would be less probable.

The Roanoke-Chowan Group is a smaller conference than the North Carolina Writers. Geographically restricted, it is composed of writers, musicians, painters and patrons of the arts in northeastern North Carolina. It was organized and shaped by Gilbert T. Stephenson, and seven of us who write are members. The Group sponsors a Poetry Cup which is presented each year for the best volume of poetry by a North Carolina author or by an author whose residence is in the state.

The largest cultural group in the state is the North Carolina Literary and Historical Association, Incorporated. I served as its president in 1961.

The book people have served me.

36

Triumph of Spirit

OLD PEOPLE have their uses in fiction. Editors and literary agents advise writers that the reading public does not want an old man as hero, unless he is pitted against the sea by a Hemingway. The buffeting must be heroic.

When bereft parents are pitted against the necessity of breaking up homes to go live with children, there is buffeting of a kind. It is not majestic like the sea's, but it has its fictional potential. So I wrote about an old man in *Special Rates*. Old Alf was no more bereaved by the death of his wife than by the consequent breaking up of his home. He did not give in to life as it was patterned for him by his children, but with spirit triumphing over circumstances he went back home and set up housekeeping for himself.

There was old Mr. Bill in *Purslane*, neighbor to John and Dele Fuller. There was old man Sempt in *Portulaca*. Both were victors over their buffetings. In *Sweet Beulah Land* old Miss Partheny sometimes had to become a righteous wildcat to maintain her independence and keep her home. There was old Grandfather Ardley who had seen the apples redden so many summers and whose gentle kindliness and philosophy helped family and neighbors deal with their particular kind of buffeting. There was old Nurmama in *Sage Quarter*, potent tyrant amid the vicissitudes of life. There was Kalline in *Wild Cherry Tree Road* who in her old age found a satisfying identity at the poorhouse.

There was Papa in the factual story of the decades. Papa was ninety-seven years old on April 10, 1956. He and his second wife, our Miss Myrtle, lived at the old homestead in Wake County. We children of the first marriage had established homes of our own at various points in the state. Haywood, only child of the second marriage, lived with his family not far from the aged parents.

As Papa and Miss Myrtle became feebler, we tried in various ways to ease the insecure situation involving them. For three years I spent a part of each month with them. The others checked often. We hired farm boys to do chores, farm women to help at the house. They were dismissed when our backs were turned. Our efforts to add to the comfort and security of the old folks were blocked. It was their home. Their independence was security for them. We had to let them have it so.

On Sunday afternoon, May 6, 1956, as Olive's family and I rode into the grove surrounding the old place, we glanced toward the front porch and were surprised to see Papa sitting on the edge of the floor with his feet dangling. Ordinarily he sat in the corner rocker or lay on his porch couch. We noticed he was waving his cane as though to attract attention.

Then we glimpsed something lying on the floor beyond him. Instantly we knew it was Miss Myrtle. We dashed from the car toward the house.

We saw that she was dead.

Through the routines of finalities, softened as always everywhere by incredible kindnesses of neighbors and friends, Papa surprised us. For a good while it had seemed to us that he had resigned from life. He had left realities to be dealt with by others and most often now remained in a contemplative haze, incurious and passive to talk or activity around him. Miss Myrtle had been doing his thinking for him, his seeing, his hearing. She had shouldered his duties and responsibilities, handled his business.

We older children remembered how Papa had once set the pace in living around him, had dominated the conversation and activities, had directed hospitality, had run the farm with vigorous efficiency, had unequivocally handled his pocketbook. Until comparatively recently he had declared himself still in the eighties, refusing to leave the decade. Whatever the record said, he stayed eighty-nine. Then, almost suddenly, he had given in to the nineties and had begun declaring he was nearly a hundred. Lately, it seemed, he had relaxed his hold on life altogether.

He began to emerge from the haze a little. There were intimations of the erstwhile head of the house. He rode with us to the Raleigh funeral home when we went as a family to be with Miss Myrtle for awhile. He satisfied himself that she was being put away nice, hoped she was at rest . . . As he expressed that hope I recalled so vividly his birthday prayer, just over three weeks ago, which at the time had startled us and made us wonder about its portent. Long-time deacon in old Mt. Moriah Church, he had prayed in public when called upon, but we had never heard him voice a prayer at home except in grace at the table. Yet on his recent birthday, as though under some strange impelling, he had followed the customary grace with a fervent prayer for his family and a moving petition that the Lord would take us when we were "played out here to rest in our bright home in heaven."

Though he had managed the trip to the funeral home very well, we urged that he not try to attend services on Tuesday morning at church. "I feel it's my duty to go," he said. He went.

Even on the way home from the cemetery he stated that somebody would have to live with him.

Tactfully we began to project the idea of his breaking up and living with us. We all wanted him in our homes. We tried him out for an evening at Haywood's, only a half mile from the old place. By bedtime Papa was so devastatingly homesick that we were all upset by his misery. He wore himself out hobbling precariously back and forth on the waxed floor, his cane occasionally slipping as he tried to anchor it on the sleek surface. Intermittently he lay on the couch. He plodded unsteadily to peer from the picture window, searching for the moon and not finding it in its right bit of sky.

He wanted his chair, his couch, his bed. "If it wasn't so dark I'd foot it home," he kept saying miserably.

On Sunday, Mary and Olive tried him out at their home in Raleigh. Later there might be Darwin's home near Wilmington and mine in Northampton. At Olive's, Papa's homesickness became so acute that soon after the noon meal he had to be taken home.

Efforts to induce him to change failed. He was welcome in any of our homes, he was assured, we wanted him to live with us. There was one answer. He had to stay at the old place to look after things. He could not leave the farm. He was not going to break up.

We faced it. We had a problem. Force seemed too harsh to apply to a man ninety-seven years old. Age was his ally, his infirmities spoke for him. His roots were like ironweed that grew around the place and could not be pulled up. Grandpa Kelly had established a home here a hundred and fifty years ago. Papa had been on this land nearly a hundred years. On it he had watched Yankee soldiers swarm by, had refused as a very little rebel to crawl under the house to get the Yankees a chicken. On it he had his sustenance while Abraham Lincoln was still alive.

Yet, most of us had grown roots like ironweed in other soil. We had our homes, our work, our friends, our life elsewhere.

What were we going to do?

We sought advice.

"Put your father in a good nursing home," Miss Myrtle's oldest sister advised. Aunt Minnie, only surviving member of Papa's family, thought a nursing home might be the solution. Others in the family favored it. Nursing homes in and around Raleigh were checked.

Mr. Phipps, the faithful community pastor, thought it would kill Papa to uproot him. Dr. Yates, the family physician, thought Papa's general unawareness would facilitate adjustment to a nursing home. Neighbors who knew the situation agreed.

Reason and common sense were on the side of the nursing home, where there were orderlies and nurses to take care of the exigencies that were beyond us. We could not bring ourselves to follow reason and common sense.

Our first plan was to employ a couple to live in the old home and to give Papa the care he would have in a nursing home. Somewhere in the state we felt sure there were middle-aged or elderly couples who wanted a home and the salary involved in the care of a still ambulatory patient. Papa had to be bathed and changed, but for the most part he dressed himself mornings and walked to his meals and to the bathroom.

So Olive ran advertisements in the *Raleigh News and Observer*: "Wanted, a couple desirous of a home and reasonable salary to take care of aged man."

We children decided, while waiting more definite arrangements, to take weekly turns at the old place, to shift crews, as Olive called it. Of course, that could only be done on paper, we agreed among ourselves, as the difficulties rose to daunt us.

But we did it.

The plan became prolonged since the ads did not yield favorable results. There were many responses to the ad, but the qualifications given did not seem applicable to the situation. One couple seemed to feel qualified because they had been taking care of a fish pond. A man wrote that his wife was the best cook in the world, she could cook "anything they are to cook." Papa was on liquids and baby foods. Another wrote to the effect that he and his wife were against sin, as though a man of ninety-seven might need to be held in line. After a satisfactory interview we hired a couple. But the wife had a sudden illness, and this plan fell through. We considered employing a male companion who came for an interview, but he was seventy-five years old and might soon be needing care himself.

So the shifting crews began. Because of circumstances, only three of us children composed the crews, with a grandson, Carey Coats, bringing his family up from Fayetteville to take turns too. Other grandchildren assisted—Rosalie Upchurch, Rosa

Jean Wrenn, the Beasley girls. Mrs. Louisa Buffaloe, Miss Myrtle's youngest sister and secretary of the Granville Presbytery in Raleigh, came out to keep me company at night.

For I was timid about staying alone in the big old farmhouse. Too many windows opened low on porches, too many old-fashioned door latches were insecure, too few neighbors had telephones. There were reports of thievery and bootlegging in the area. Strangers constantly turned into the grove to make inquiries or to try to sell something.

One morning I confronted a strange man in the back hall using the telephone. After stating he wanted to place a call, he had been invited by Papa to go right on into the house as though he had been a neighbor. Another morning a stranger called me out to his truck to see the fish he claimed to be selling. I was wary. For in situations like this people were often knocked in the head and robbed. I measured the distance back to the house in one glance. Nowhere in the nearby fields could I spy any of the tenants. Brownie, the pet dog, was not around to bark an alarm. Butch, the "took-up" dog as the tenants called him, was also out of place. I began backing away from the truck toward the house. No, I did not want any fish today.

Like a shot came the challenge. "Are you a Christian?" the fish man asked.

After my stammered reply, he explained. My refusal to buy fish was destiny for him. The Lord had called him to preach, so he declared, and not one fish had He allowed him to sell all day. So as a result of my negative the fish man was giving in to the Lord.

There was the report of a nude woman roaming Little Creek woods. Officers had recently shot at her as she darted from tree to tree just off Papa's land. There were cars that parked late in the night just beyond our grove. There were lights flashing across the darkness as though in some kind of weird signal.

It was useless to warn Papa to be wary about strangers. He was consolidating his forces against us otherwise, against the threat of change we seemed to represent. He asserted his will. Russell Smith, the faithful colored tenant who had been on the place more than thirty years, frequently had to be called from the field for orderly service. This brought on a crisis each time. Papa with strong expletives asserted himself against the bathing-and-changing routines his children tried to establish. He used language strange on his lips. Once as children we had heard him say "confound" to Mr. Claude's mule, just as John Fuller had to a neighbor's mule in *Purslane*. It had scared us then.

I wondered now if the strange profanity was not less senility than instinctive declaration of manhood, the effort of spirit not to revert to the facts of babyhood. Russell absorbed the strange words and abuse connected with it and with gentle persuasiveness took the orderly duty.

Diets were related to Papa's new independence of spirit. For years he had relished only oatmeal, with an occasional dish of oyster stew. We began to serve him more varied and balanced meals. These he refused. The more I wheedled and reasoned, the more he stood out against me. "You have to eat this," I told him of a custard I had made.

"No, I don't either!" he countered and did not eat it.

He had become Papa again, and no girl-child was going to tell him what he had to eat.

I sensed it was all part of the emergence from apathy and acquiescence. So I began trying to out-smart him, get proteins in him by strategy. Without knowing it, he took many a raw egg in his milk drinks and ice cream sodas during the summer of 1956.

Papa outsmarted me about his pet dog. I was fond of Brownie, but she was a nuisance in the house. I undertook to make her stay outside. As often as I fastened the screen door against her, Papa opened it. When I disciplined her, Papa began to chant, "Poor little puppy, Mama's gone." Wherever I worked that plaint reached me. I gave in.

But I worked on the nuisance Brownie's presence created. I tried to get rid of the flies she let in through the screened doors. I sprinkled fly flakes inside. Since directions on the container warned that these flakes were poisonous to pets, I stealthily kept the doors hooked against dogs. But on a

Saturday afternoon little Jerry slipped Brownie inside the house. She ate some of the flakes and became ill. By nightfall she had lost use of herself. After tumbling headforemost down the front porch steps, she made her way to the big oak the lightning had struck the summer before and there on the dead grass lay down to die.

I did not sleep that Saturday night. Neither did Butch, the father of Brownie's puppies. All night he barked. He grew hoarse, but he kept howling and keeping vigil.

At ten o'clock I went out to the oak. "Come back, little Sheba," I felt like crying. There was no stir of life under the tree.

At twelve I ventured to the front porch, unafraid of thieves or bootleggers or nude women or fish men. I peered through the dim light to where Brownie lay inert, a little brown patch of lifelessness in the moonshine.

I spent the hours after midnight rehearsing the morning procedure that faced me. Before Russell left to sing with his radio quartet Sunday morning, I was going to have to get him to attend to the finalities for Brownie—the removal of the little brown patch of lifelessness near the oak, the composing of the body in a suitable box, the digging of a grave beyond the car house. Most of all I rehearsed telling Papa. How should I say it?

"We have a new little Brownie for you, Papa, a cute little puppy with brown spots. Brownie has been ailing, and last night—"

Or tactfully, like the doctor told Papa that Sunday afternoon on May 6 while Miss Myrtle lay lifeless on the front porch. "I'm sorry to have to tell you—"

Or directly, without preliminary. "Brownie's dead, Papa. But one of her puppies is just like her, so this will be your pet now."

Over and over I tried different approaches. At four o'clock I went to the front porch again. In the dimness of early dawn I saw the little brown patch near the oak, still and somber.

Suddenly I felt something soft against my bare ankles. I looked down quickly. There was Brownie. Her tiny head was tilted wistfully to one side. Her brown eyes were asking for food.

All dogs on the place fared well that day.

If I had been wearing my bifocals, I might have seen even in the early dawn that the patch of lifelessness was the dead grass on which Brownie had lain down.

I found out we had another "took-up" dog. Butch had tolled her to our grove the Saturday night Brownie lay lifeless under the oak. His vigil had been a tryst.

We rediscovered the place. We found ripe grapes and figs in forgotten haunts. The June apple tree of our childhood still bore red apples. Among the ironweed there was love vine which we used to hang up in trees laden with wishes about young love. There was ticklegrass with its lavender mistiness just right for pottery ware in halls. Down the hill there were poplar shrubs like those from which we girls used to gather leaves to make summer hats. There was poison oak among the honeysuckle, distressingly potent I found out by experience.

We discovered a community store named Sorrell and Son.

We found the village preacher right out of Goldsmith. This community pastor stood beside the sorrowful and dismayed. Prompt at every call, Mr. Phipps moved among his people.

Most of all we discovered an old man resuming life he had resigned from. The front porch seemed related to that resumption. We had made the screened back porch a pleasant living room, with a little alcove for meals. Papa could not be prevailed upon to join us there. The front porch was a fixed idea for him. He liked his refreshments there, his medicines, his meals such as he could be persuaded to eat.

From the front porch he was participating in the farming operation. The farm animals were in the barnlot across the highway from the porch. Vicariously he fed and watered them. From the front porch the farmlands that he had so loved to cultivate were in sight, the tenant houses with their teeming families. Papa thought of himself now as general overseer. His duty was to be at his post, in sight of the tenants who tilled the land. For the most part he could not distinguish man from mule, but he was aware of movement and knew when it ceased. He heard the rattling of chains at the lot well, and so from his post he helped water the stock. He saw Russell and Goldus and Sonny and David going and coming from the fields, and he went with them—by way of the front porch.

The moon also seemed to belong to the resumption. Night after night he questioned us about the moon, its time of rising, its phases. We went to the almanacs for pertinent information, laughing a little at our ignorance of moon phases.

"What time does the moon rise?" he continued to ask and we to answer. The moon more than people now living gave him a community of memories. And it was in its right bit of sky.

Papa seemed to see a little better. For some time optometrists had not been able to hold out any hope for his fading eyesight. Details still escaped him, but he was becoming alert to general shapes and forms. He might not have seen shapes of TV persons exactly as we did, but he always cried out, "Whoopee!" at the right time.

As host, perhaps his instinct was to amuse us with his reaction to forms moving across the screen. Forms might be girls, and all screen girls were Mae West to him. And "Whoopee!" went along with her appearance. There had been hilarity among us some twenty years before when Papa and Herbert, both innocents in Hollywood, had started teasing each other about Mae West. The teasing had started after the following incident which I relayed to the family at a Christmas dinner.

The story had to do with Herbert's utter dislike of picture shows. He could not be induced to go to any except those starring Will Rogers. A great fan of the cowboy philosopher, he never missed one of his shows if he heard about it in time. The filling station boys knew about this enthusiasm. One day after hearing Herbert rave over a Rogers picture, they told him if he liked Will Rogers so much he ought to branch out and see Mae West. He raced home and told me to get my coat, for we had to rush to Roanoke Rapids to see Mae West, its last showing today. Startled at first, I soon realized from his version of the filling station talk that he thought Mae West was the name of a Will Rogers picture. The story sparked the merriment at Christmas dinners a long time afterwards.

Papa was host. He had an instinct for continuity of merriment. His "Whoopee!" became reminiscent of a last "Ha!" from the far Pacific.

His hearing seemed to improve, along with his eyesight. For years we had had to raise our voices to make him understand, often repeating and rephrasing our sentences. Now we discovered that he was overhearing conversations not intended for his ears. We were discussing in lowered tones one day the sudden death of Papa's beloved Sunday school teacher. We decided he should not be told of the death. Yet shortly afterwards he asked, "Isn't Jim Lane dead?"

I hesitated an instant and then said, "Yes."

It was uncanny. He had not been told, but he knew. How could he have overheard us? How much of the plans and problems involved in the present situation he had overheard us discuss we could not be sure, but we became careful. We detected a new wariness in his manner too. He grew foxy. He began to outsmart us.

When it came time for us to leave our weekly post, it was our idea to accomplish the shift quietly while Papa was still asleep mornings, so he might wake to the new set-up without having to witness the mechanics of leavetakings. He caught on. He began to beat us up mornings before we could ease out. Just as the front porch established him as overseer, necessary to the farming operation, so did seeing us off make him host, homing him the more securely.

He had begun to hobble up and down the hall to lock doors that already had been attended to and to check on sleeping arrangements. At bedtime, with the aid of his cane, he now began to push his couch to a sheltered corner of the porch before we could get to it.

Remonstrating one night, I assured him that I would attend to this chore each night, it was too much for him. "Yes, but I've got a walking stick, and you haven't!" he retorted and went on with his task.

He became head of the house in divers small ways. TV

audio and video were his to adjust and regulate, though the adjustment blotted out sound and picture for everybody. He had to see that the clock was wound, however diligently the routine had already been attended to, that lights were turned off at bedtime, that the family crews were directed to the right beds.

Senility? It didn't seem so to us. It was human spirit, triumphant in a very old man.

"What time does the moon rise?" he continued to ask as though to draw us into the community of memories.

In September a granddaughter and her family moved in to live with Papa. In their kindly care the old man of ninety-seven faced the winter.

Then the winter ended for him. He died at the old home place on November 28, 1956.

John in *Purslane* died then.

37

Reunion at Astolat

OUR FIRST family reunion after our father's century of living ended in 1956 was held at Rocky Branch.

There was singular unanimity about meeting place. Rocky Branch had always had special meaning for our family. Old Aunt Cherry had told us long ago that we, as babies, had been found in old stumps there. Papa had often taken us to the little branch to wade, to catch minnows, to send leaf boats over the rocky falls we called Niagara. Here there were pine saplings like those that had been our steeds for many a ride to Astolat. On this reunion day it was as though some sense of nativity, some sense of trysting with childhood dreams and of commemorating the strength of the patriarch, who had been with us through last October, was present in all of us.

He had gone in strength of spirit to Rocky Branch when he was past the physical effort. We were remembering the strength that had prompted his effort to be independent when he was left alone in May 1956, his effort to communicate once more with the generations left so far behind, to be Papa again—to direct his gray-haired children to their beds as when they were little, to lock the doors and wind the clock and follow the old patterns of bedtime routines.

We were remembering how we had alternately left our own homes to keep house for the old man after he had refused to break up and live anywhere except the old place. To outside observers this had seemed a unique arrangement for mid-twentieth century, with the patriarchal pattern of sons and sons' sons relaxed to fit the times. Unique to us was the vitality of spirit we found in a very old man, in his retort over an evening routine. We would not forget how he had insisted on pushing his day-couch into a sheltered corner of the porch each evening, though he had been told over and over to leave the chore to us. "Yes, but I've got a walking stick and you haven't!" he had retorted to our remonstrances. It came to be a family challenge.

Today it gave us a sense of touching home base to go back to Rocky Branch. It was continuity as well as brook.

It was a beautiful afternoon, reminiscent of other times when we had assembled in family solidarity for reunions. Only, there was a little shadow over the solidarity now. Provisions of a last will and testament could not be kept entirely out of our awareness. We tried. We were determined not to meet in somber mood. So we began recalling light-hearted family stories that had enlivened occasions like this. Our favorite of all time was the elephant tale which recounted Papa's terror when he had mistaken a neighbor's mule one night for an elephant.

We could still laugh, too, over the school story of Papa's childhood, now tape-recorded in his quavery voice. William Wall, a young schoolmate of Papa's, had been persuaded unwittingly to say this speech one Friday afternoon: "Oh, Lord of love, look down from above on us poor scholars. We hired a fool to teach our school. And paid her forty dollars!" The consequences in that day of stern teachers had been fearful. Even as old men, the former schoolmates always had an interchange about that speech wherever they might meet. "And paid her forty dollars!" Papa would shout across street or store or church grounds. And Mr. Wall would shout back petulantly, "Now you hush that, Bill!" It became a ritual.

Even the great-grandchildren had learned to repeat the story in their Grandfather's manner.

He had a gift for telling stories. Unhurried in recital, careful with his cumulative details, versed in colorful vernacular, Papa could make a rousing climax out of inconsequentials. The way he told the story of a hunter he knew about provoked mirth that caused a kind of chain reaction among listeners who laughed at those who laughed so convulsively at Papa's sequences.

A hunter went out one fall day wearing bargain-sales pants. As he waded into the dew the bargain pants became soaking wet at the bottoms, and they began to stretch. He took out his pocketknife and cut off a portion from the pants legs. As he waded further into the dewy underbrush, the pants continued to stretch. So he had to continue whacking off portions with his knife so that he could walk. Then the sun came out and dried the wetness of pants and underbrush. The pants started shrinking. By the time the hunter reached home, according to Papa's tale, he had on mighty little bit of pants from the bargain counter in Raleigh.

While we made lemonade for our refreshments, the lemonade story of another outing was recalled. Papa had often recounted this with gusto. The community pastor had been guest at one of our picnics. He had been something of a fanatic about germs. To his hale and hearty flock, he had seemed over-meticulous. His children were not allowed to drink from the picnic pail of lemonade. He provided a separate bucket for his family, with sterilized cups to drink from. The picnicker who spied a dog drinking from the preacher's pail never did let him know his family had drunk after the dog.

For all the old family stories and chatter this afternoon we were very conscious of our last reunion with Papa and our stepmother, when the note of valedictory had been so clearly sounded. On the occasion there had been the usual blessing, repeated at table so many years without variation, and after that Papa's sudden and unexpected prayer. The petition was improvised out of established faith rather than out of any fluency of articulation. "When we are played out here, take us to our bright home in heaven," Papa had concluded his moving prayer for his family on that evening.

We were very conscious now, too, of business adjustments to be made, of an estate to be settled. There had been a last will. But some of us who were beneficiaries felt it did not speak for our father. In his competency he would not have forgotten children in the dispensing of such bounty as he had to leave.

So it was ours who benefited by the provisions to speak for right and fairness that were our heritage too. It was ours to validate the justice associated so definitely with the century of living before senility clouded the image. We had to make secure the family ties that could so easily be frayed over inequalities in the situation. The restoration of the image of paternal justice had to make children and grandchildren all heirs of values beyond tracts of land or personal possessions. This would be encomium beyond inscription in stone.

"To advance rather than to seem to" was the motto on our family coat of arms. Advancement had never been defined for us by boundary lines and timber and land holdings.

So there at Rocky Branch we were trying beyond our wont to realize family solidarity. And to keep it. There was consideration in our fellowship today, but it was a little tense and self-conscious as we tried to make the reunion casual.

We were secluded in our valley. Steep hills sloped up from the branch. The slopes were covered with dead leaves fallen from many summers and with shrubs perennially vital and green. Only a little sunshine sifted through the overlapping trees and made leafy patterns on rocks and water.

One family from Fayetteville had provided a grill and tables beside the little stream. Soon the aroma of coffee and broiling meat was over the place. A baseball minor leaguer of a former decade compared world series notes with a young brother who still played league ball in the minors. They bridged the decades with their common interest.

Little Jerry unknowingly spanned the decades, too, with his tale of a puppy trade. A sign at the highway in front of his house advised motorists that puppies were available there.

Brownie was producing more puppies than could be sold or given away to neighbors. Brownie was Papa's loved terrier, and it was hoped that good homes might be found for her puppies. There was no idea of collecting money in the transaction. The peach man stopped by to ask about the sign. He wanted a dog for his little boy, he said, if the price was right. Jerry, six years old and alone at the time, traded a puppy for a bushel of peaches.

Along this same road we had bargained with the peddler who traveled on foot, had traded nickels and dimes for needles and thread and side combs and breastpins. Papa's youngest grandson was now carrying on the bargaining, though the peddler had become the peach man on a motor truck.

We glanced at the water moving toward the overhanging rocks that made Niagara Falls. The water, we knew, wouldn't ever pass here any more. But the stream would be there, as living would be—living represented by this family group this October, by other family groups other Octobers. Both were a stream immutable.

Two little boys, warned by their mothers to stay away from the water, eased their cowboy boots over the edge and waded. Barefoot boys had waded there long ago, and before them moccasined feet had doubtless left their imprint on the clay bottom.

We were part of it all, we reflected. People move on, like the little stream over the jutting rocks, and are gone. The old leisurely pattern of the rural South is being replaced by the hurry and exigencies of urban life. In its march of progress, technology has still not solved the underemployment of human resources or achieved a satisfactory level of living for all. But life continues. The reach toward excellence in those simpler days of peddlers on foot and in the age of peach men on motor trucks alike are in the continuity. The essential content of living is immutable like little Rocky Branch.

We touched home base that October evening and went on back to homes in Alamance and Cumberland and Hoke and Onslow and Northampton and Wake. But we left knowing what we had to do.

Since then we have spoken as a family. We have validated the fairness which characterized a century of living. The unremembrance from old age and affliction has been seen in the perspective of pity and understanding. We signed an agreement to benefit alike, irrespective of last wills and testaments, to share equally in the bounty not defined by boundary lines. The benefit is not impressive as material bounty, but it has its spiritual value.

Not far from the stones marking the resting place of neighbors and kin there is a monument to the old man of our family. The monument not in stone is sons and sons' sons.